META-ANALYSIS

A Comparison of Approaches

META-ANALYSIS

A Comparison of Approaches

Ralf Schulze

 Hogrefe & Huber

About the author

Ralf Schulze is currently scientific assistant at the Psychologische Institut IV, Westfälische Wilhelms-Universität Münster, Germany. His research interests span the fields of statistics, research methods, psychological assessment, individual differences, human cognitive abilities, and social psychology.

Library of Congress Cataloguing-in-Publication Data

is now available via the Library of Congress Marc Database under the

LC Control Number: 2003116468

National Library of Canada Cataloguing in Publication

Schulze, Ralf
    Meta-analysis : a comparison of approaches / Ralf Schulze.

Includes bibliographical references and indexes.
ISBN 0-88937-280-2

1. Meta-analysis. 2. Social sciences–Statistical methods. I. Title

HA29.S44 2004   300'.7'27   C2003-907355-6

Copyright © 2004 by Hogrefe & Huber Publishers

PUBLISHING OFFICES
USA: Hogrefe & Huber Publishers, 875 Massachusetts Avenue, 7th Floor,
                 Cambridge, MA 02139
                 Phone (866) 823-4726, Fax (617) 354-6875, E-mail info@hhpub.com
Europe: Hogrefe & Huber Publishers, Rohnsweg 25, D-37085 Göttingen, Germany,
                 Phone +49 551 49609-0, Fax +49 551 49609-88, E-mail hh@hhpub.com

SALES & DISTRIBUTION
USA: Hogrefe & Huber Publishers, Customer Services Department,
                 30 Amberwood Parkway, Ashland, OH 44805,
                 Phone (800) 228-3749, Fax (419) 281-6883, E-mail custserv@hhpub.com
Europe: Hogrefe & Huber Publishers, Rohnsweg 25, D-37085 Göttingen, Germany,
                 Phone +49 551 49609-0, Fax +49 551 49609-88, E-mail hh@hhpub.com

OTHER OFFICES
Canada: Hogrefe & Huber Publishers, 1543 Bayview Avenue, Toronto,
                 Ontario M4P 2B5
Switzerland: Hogrefe & Huber Publishers, Länggass-Strasse 76, CH-3000 Bern 9

Hogrefe & Huber Publishers
Incorporated and registered in the State of Washington, USA, and in Göttingen, Lower Saxony, Germany

Printed and bound in Germany ISBN 0-88937-280-2
D 6

Preface

Meta-analysis is a method for systematic literature reviews on a certain substantive question of interest. In contrast to the more traditional narrative review it explicitly includes elaborate methods for an evaluation of a corresponding research database. Meta-analysis is one of the more recent additions to the researchers' methods toolbox. It enjoys a growing interest in many research domains beyond subdisciplines of psychology as well as in methodology and statistics. The increasing number of research articles, using and further developing this method, are indicative of its perceived high value for researchers. Yet, there are also controversies still surrounding this method, parts of which are concerned with the implications of meta-analysis for the entire research endeavor, that is, how we should conduct research and how to interpret single study outcomes. Notwithstanding such controversies, meta-analysis has become a standard in the methods canon, at least in psychology but also in other disciplines like medicine as well. Hence, when considering these facts, one might easily think that there must be a consensus on an exactly specified single best way to conduct a meta-analysis, because it appears as such a well-established method in widespread use.

At least for correlation coefficients as effect sizes — on which the present book focuses — this is not the case. There are several specific sets of procedures available, so-called approaches to meta-analysis, and the research consumer of meta-analyses is confronted with their application in various contexts. In such a situation one may presume that differences in procedures are inconsequential for the substantive results, or alternatively wonder whether the application of different procedures may lead to differences in results. The meta-analyst who wants to conduct a review of the literature also faces the situation of many available approaches and has to make an informed choice between them.

This book provides an in-depth analysis and evaluation of extant meta-analytic approaches for correlation coefficients as effect sizes. The approaches are described and compared from a theoretical-statistical viewpoint as well as on the basis of the results of a Monte Carlo study. Under which circumstances the approaches produce comparable results and when they differ substantially is evaluated. The adequacy of the specific procedures for the application to a series of potential true situations in a universe of studies is assessed and a comparative evaluation of the approaches is thus provided.

The book is divided into four parts. In Part I, the basics of meta-analysis are introduced. The development and growth of the method is described from a bird's eye view. The basic steps of meta-analysis are explicated and briefly summarized with respect to their function for a review of the literature. In this first part, the fact is highlighted that several author groups from different research domains in psychology have more or less independently established sets of procedures for meta-analysis. The emergence of these approaches is described to have eventuated partly for historical reasons and also because of the strong interest of the approaches' proponents in certain substantive research problems from the areas of industrial and organizational (I/O) and clinical psychology, respectively. It is shown that most of the basic steps of meta-analysis — from problem formulation to public presentation of results — are in fact common to *all* approaches, but several differences in procedural details at the analysis stage prevail. The analysis step of meta-analysis is the main subject of the second part.

In Part II, statistical methods of meta-analysis are specified. This part of the book begins with a chapter on effect sizes, the data used in meta-analysis. The properties of the most famous families of effect sizes, correlation coefficients r and standardized mean differences d, are described from a theoretical viewpoint. A clear emphasis is, however, placed on the properties of correlations. Beyond such a description, several characteristics of the effect sizes, supposedly of relevance for the comparison of approaches, are analyzed and the conversion of effect sizes from both families is specified.

After the presentation of effect sizes, general frameworks of meta-analysis are presented. The general frameworks are fixed versus random effects models, mixture models, and hierarchical linear models. These frameworks are very helpful to look at the approaches of interest from a very general perspective to recognize their particularities and limitations. Furthermore, the models are introduced to enable a classification of the subsequently outlined specific approaches to meta-analysis of correlations. The most well-known approaches are specified in detail in this part of the book. Moreover, several refinements of the approaches are presented, some of which can be classified as fixed and some as random effects model approaches.

Furthermore, the series of models leads to certain classes of situations for the application of meta-analysis. The framework of mixture models is used to conceptualize the research situation of meta-analysis and the specific situations under investigation in the Monte Carlo study in Part III. The situations of relevance are the homogeneous case with only one constant effect size in a universe of studies and heterogeneous cases. The first heterogeneous case is specified as a uniform two-point distribution of different universe parameters to be estimated, and the second case is a continuous distribution in the universe of studies.

After having presented and examined the approaches in detail, some consequences of choosing between approaches are pointed out from a theoretical viewpoint. It is shown that such a choice is not inconsequential in general, as is often implicitly assumed. The approaches are finally compared and statistical methods are summarized. The classification and comparison of the approaches is done with respect to the following characteristics: fixed versus random effects models, use of effect size measure (correlation coefficient, Fisher-z transformed correlations, corrected versions of correlations, and transformation of r to d), and weighting scheme used. All of these characteristics are proposed to be relevant for the outcomes of meta-analysis and approaches are differentiated along these lines.

In another major part of the book, Part III, the results of an empirical comparison between the approaches by using Monte Carlo methods are presented and differences in results are investigated. The very common assumption of researchers that the choice of an approach is merely a matter of taste and that results from applying different approaches to the same data are not different is once more scrutinized in this part of the book. The refined approaches considered in Part II are also part of the Monte Carlo study so that their quality can be assessed in comparison to more well-known approaches.

The theoretical analyses and results of the Monte Carlo study are summarized and discussed in Part IV. Recommendations for the application of meta-analytic methods to a database of correlations are provided and the implications of using suboptimal methods is discussed.

It is hoped that the presented analyses and results will help to further understanding and evaluation of the methods of meta-analysis. In addition, it is hoped that the present book will be instrumental for the interested meta-analyst and research consumer in making an informed choice and evaluation of the approaches and the corresponding results.

I am much obliged to the following individuals whose support have made this book possible or helped make it better than it otherwise would have been: Dankmar Böhning, Michaela Brocke, Vanessa Danthiir, Heinz Holling, Andreas Jütting, Malte Persike, Bernd Schäfer, and Oliver Wilhelm.

Of all the individuals who were supportive in a scientific sense in writing this book, I am most grateful to my colleague Heiko Großmann. The many day- and nighttime discussions with him will be a lasting pleasant memory. His suggestions were helpful at all times and his criticisms always a challenge. They have changed the way I think not only about the methods of meta-analysis, but also in a wider sense about my work.

Last but not least, I would like to thank my wife Claudia, whose incredible patience with me and enduring will to support my work in all conceivable ways continues to amaze me.

RALF SCHULZE

MARCH 2004, MÜNSTER

Contents

Part I

Introduction

1

The Growth of Meta-Analysis and Implications for Methodological Controversies

The research literature in most fields of science is steadily growing at a seemingly ever increasing rate. Nowadays, it appears to be virtually impossible for a researcher even in a relatively restricted field of study to keep track of all relevant published articles. Hence, there is a strong need for summaries of recent theoretical and empirical results in all scientific areas. Traditionally, there are reviews published in periodicals like the Annual Reviews, for example, where experts of the field are invited to present the current state of a field of study. Besides the function to inform interested researchers about the recent developments and findings such reviews are also relevant for an evaluation of the state of knowledge of a scientific area and even to guide decisions of policymakers to find scientifically well-founded solutions for everyday problems. However, clear-cut summaries of a research field are only easily established with a fairly consistent empirical basis, which is rather an exception than the rule, at least in the social sciences.

As Hunter and Schmidt (1996) have described for the field of psychology, making sense of heterogeneous results can be rather frustrating not only for researchers but also for policymakers. This may have the adverse effect of a negative appraisal of a whole scientific area potentially leading to cuts in funds and bad reputation. This kind of situation characterized the state of affairs in psychology in the early 1970s in the United States, with the negative consequences just described. It was in this climate when researchers became more occupied with the way summaries and reviews were actually carried out. Although the problem of summarizing the state of knowledge was not an entirely new one, the scientific examination of the review process itself was immensely intensified from this time on and ideas on the methods for a synthesis of research began to appear in publications (e.g., Light & Smith, 1971). Yet it was not until Gene Glass coined the term *meta-analysis* (Glass, 1976) that the ways to conduct literature reviews and the synthesis of empirical evidence in a field of study became a research area of its own. From this point of time on increasing research activity was devoted to the development of guidelines and techniques for the conduct of systematic reviews now having its own name meta-analysis. However, meta-analysis was not associated with the invention of a new research problem, as Olkin (1990) has highlighted (see also Hunt, 1997), but with calls for more procedural and statistical rigor in the preparation of literature reviews. It is this rigor that still most prototypically marks the difference between traditional reviews and meta-analysis.

However, this was not the only attribute which appealed to members of the scientific community. The introduction of meta-analysis to the statistical toolbox was not totally detached from substantive problems. The motivation for its development was sparked by the interest to find answers to two very important problems in psychology, namely the comparison of the effectiveness of psychotherapies on the one hand, and the situational specificity of predictive validities of personnel selection procedures in occupational settings on the other. The former problem motivated Glass and co-workers to develop their methods of meta-analysis (see Glass, McGaw, & Smith, 1981). They subsequently published the first meta-analysis in clinical psychology (Smith & Glass, 1977) which provoked great interest[1] as well as harsh criticism of the method (Eysenck, 1978). The latter problem was addressed — coincidentally at the same time — by Schmidt and Hunter, and resulted in the development o6f their methods (Schmidt & Hunter, 1977), followed by applications in the area of personnel selection (for a recent overview, see Schmidt & Hunter, 1998). Thus, meta-analysis forcefully caught the attention by the early 1980s via two routes, methodological rigor and the potential to provide an elegant solution to substantive research problems.

After the inauguration of the term, presentation of procedural details, and publication of the first applications, meta-analysis was quickly adopted in the scientific field, and psychology in particular. This growth of meta-analysis in the past 30 years can be illustrated, for example, by the frequencies of published articles related to meta-analyses.

Figure 1.1 depicts the number of publications up to 2003 that matched the query "meta-analy* or metaanaly* or 'integrative review' " in two of the main databases of psychological research literature: PsycINFO (mainly English literature) and Psyndex (mainly German literature). The "hits" in this literature search represent articles concerning the development and evaluation of the statistical methods as well as applications of meta-analysis in psychology. It is clearly evident that the new field of research is still growing and tends to produce itself an enormous amount of research articles. As a caveat, however, it must be added in this context that the number of articles per year includ-

---

[1] At the time of writing, this article reached a citation count of 749 in the ISI Web of Knowledge.

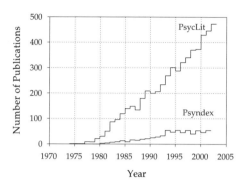

Figure 1.1   Number of publications in the research databases PsycINFO and Psyndex from 1974 to 2003.

ing these search terms may partly reflect expanded journal coverage of the databases. Nevertheless, along with this rising interest in the development and applications of meta-analysis the technique also seems to have been adopted in the canon of research tools in psychology. This is evidenced, for example, by the fact that general introductions to meta-analysis have found their way into general methodological handbooks (Cooper & Lindsay, 1998) as well as treatments of methods in more specific areas like social and personality psychology (e.g., Johnson & Eagly, 2000), organizational psychology (e.g., Holling & Schulze, in press), and clinical psychology (e.g., Durlak, 2003).

In some areas of research in psychology, there is now even a need to summarize applications of meta-analyses to keep track of the main empirical results in a field of study. There are, for example, mainly narrative reviews of meta-analyses for entire subdisciplines of psychology (e.g., Hunter & Hirsh, 1987; Tett, Meyer, & Roese, 1994) as well as more focused and even quantitative reviews (i.e., "meta-analyses of meta-analyses"), for instance on the relationship between personality measures and performance (Barrick & Mount, 2003) and personnel selection (Hermelin & Robertson, 2001). Moreover, the integration of meta-analytical findings can also be used to assess methodological effects in scientific research (e.g., Wilson & Lipsey, 2001). There are even reviews of meta-analyses for psychology as a whole discipline (Lipsey & Wilson, 1993) which are generally favorable in results as far as the effectiveness of psychological treatments is concerned. This fact may also have contributed to the popularity of meta-analysis as a new research tool, because it was associated with the promise of revealing "true" effects of psychological treatments which are otherwise buried in an enormous morass of contradictory study findings.

Interestingly, with respect to the seemingly inconsistent and highly variable results in psychology and related fields already mentioned, the application of meta-analysis also lead to the conclusion that the results in psychology are actually no more variable than results in some quarters in the physical sciences, which often are taken as the standard of so-called hard sciences (Hedges, 1987;

but see also Sohn, 1997, for a contrarian view). This possibly added to the evolving positive attitude towards meta-analysis, at least for those social science researchers somewhat envying their colleagues in the natural sciences for their hard facts.

Moreover, supplementing the expectations of unravelled research controversies by applying meta-analytic methods, meta-analysis was also proposed to even be a useful tool for theory development and testing (Miller & Pollock, 1995; Viswesvaran & Ones, 1995). Hence, in addition to serving an expedient function for the synthesis of extant empirical evidence, meta-analysis may also have the promise to generate new knowledge in a field of study and help in developing and testing new theories. Furthermore, its results may also be used to focus new research efforts and designs on interesting effects emerging from its application (see Czienskowski, 2003).

In addition to these results now rather indicating the successful application of psychological interventions, meta-analysis has also been connected with more far-reaching implications within the realm of epistemological questions of scientific research in the social sciences. The related discussion in methodological quarters of the social sciences centered around the notion of science as an endeavor of the accumulation of knowledge and the way current empirical practices may have to be changed with the methods of meta-analysis at hand, especially the use of significance tests in the social sciences. Whether science in its entirety, and social science in particular, is cumulative in nature is a controversial issue that has its supporters (e.g., Hunter & Schmidt, 1990, 1996; Schmidt, 1992; Schmidt & Hunter, 1995) as well as critics (e.g., Meehl, 1978, 1990; Sohn, 1997). Meta-analysis as a research tool touches upon this issue for it is applied to synthesize current knowledge and its results are supposed to "reveal" or even prove the cumulation of knowledge by "cleaning up and making sense of research literature" (Schmidt, 1992, p. 1179). This conveys the notion of psychology as a research discipline that produces reliable and useful results, a highly welcomed point of view for scientists and the research consumer with a positive attitude towards the social sciences. Furthermore, it has been claimed that meta-analysis is a valid tool to fundamentally change current research practices by *replacing* significance tests, which have been identified as retarding cumulation of scientific knowledge (Rossi, 1997; Schmidt, 1996; Schmidt & Hunter, 1997). Along with this position comes a devaluation of the impact of individual studies and the view to regard them only as data points for a subsequent meta-analysis. Again, there are also critics of meta-analysis that raise serious doubts about the notion of accumulation of knowledge in (social) sciences and support significance testing as a tool in a theory-corroborating scientific approach (e.g., Chow, 1988; Mulaik, Raju, & Harshman, 1997). Although the notion of devaluing individual studies as merely providing data points for a meta-analysis has also been heavily criticized (Harris, 1997; Landy, 2003; Sohn, 1995, 1997). A discussion of these issues can be found, for example, in the volume edited by Harlow, Mulaik, and Steiger (1997) devoted to the significance test controversy in psychology.

However, critics did not only address philosophy of science issues. Applications of meta-analysis were also criticized for various other reasons mostly on substantive grounds (e.g., Eysenck, 1978). Objections were raised, for example, under such headings as "mixing of apples and oranges" to point out potential problems in meta-analyses combining results from studies in which very different characteristics were measured (see also Cortina, 2003), experimental manipulations were different, and so forth. Moreover, the so-called "garbage-in, garbage-out" objection addresses the problem of pooling studies of very different quality, an issue that may, however, be dealt with within the framework of meta-analysis (Wortman, 1994).

In sum, meta-analysis is not only regarded as a new data-analytical tool, but it is also associated with more far-reaching consequences, though the role of meta-analysis in the ongoing significance test controversy in the methodological literature is not yet entirely fixed (Andersson, 1999; Chow, 1996), and the replacement of significance testing by meta-analysis has not taken place to date (Hubbard, Parsa, & Luthy, 1997). This replacement will presumably also not happen in the future since the excessive promises associated with the method are still opposed by challenges of the usefulness of meta-analysis as a method to synthesize the research literature (e.g., Bobko & Stone-Romero, 1998; Chow, 1988). General reviews of meta-analysis as a method also discussing various problems that may be associated with it can be found in detail elsewhere (Beelmann & Bliesener, 1994; Bailar, 1995; Sharpe, 1997).

Finally, it is interesting to note that meta-analysis is now also widely recognized in other sciences like medicine (Dickersin & Berlin, 1992; Normand, 1999; Sutton, Abrams, Jones, Sheldon, & Song, 2000) with positive appraisal in majority (Lau, Ioannidis, & Schmid, 1998; but see also Bailar, 1995; Feinstein, 1995). Controversies like the one described above do not seem to have taken place but other methodological issues are more intensively debated. For example, the value of meta-analysis is challenged on the grounds that it is more of an observational study type and may therefore not lead to reliable causal claims (see e.g., Sauerbrei & Blettner, 2003). This controversy, in turn, is not an issue in psychology where meta-analyses are classified as quasi-experimental (e.g., Farley, Lehmann, & Ryan, 1981). Furthermore, even when considering the same issues researchers in different fields seem to come to different conclusions. For example, whereas in psychology single studies are not given very high value in deciding upon controversial research issues (for reasons, see Gadenne, 1984), single (large) clinical trials are taken as a standard of comparison for the results of meta-analyses. They are even used to judge the validity of claims made on the basis of meta-analytical results. Hence, different research traditions lead researchers to focus on different issues and potential problems of meta-analysis and may fruitfully complement each other in advancing the development of the techniques (for an overview of recent developments in medical and social sciences, see Schulze, Holling, & Böhning, 2003).

2

Basic Steps of Meta-Analysis and the Emergence of Approaches

Up to this point it has not been clearly stated how the stronger procedural and statistical rigor of meta-analysis in comparison to traditional reviews manifests itself. In this chapter, the basic steps of meta-analysis will be outlined. Meta-analysis is conceived as a process comprising several steps of which one — methods of statistically aggregating study results — is the main focus of this book. Before the statistical details will be presented in the next chapter, meta-analysis will be presented from a bird's eye view. The emergence of meta-analytical approaches is outlined subsequently.

2.1 BASIC STEPS OF META-ANALYSIS

It is useful to commence with the introduction of terminology. Most researchers are familiar with methods to analyze original data from an individual study. Such analyses will be called *primary analyses* in the present context. Another form would be *secondary analysis* which designates a reanalysis of existing data to apply different and supposedly better analytical methods and/or to answer new research questions (Glass, 1976). This latter form of data analysis will not be of concern in what follows.

Normally, the data in primary analyses results from measurements of person characteristics (individual units), like abilities, attitudes, and the like. A primary analysis is mostly conducted to describe these characteristics and/or relate them to or explain them by other variables. Thus, in a study on the predictive validity of an intelligence test for job performance, for example, a number of n persons participates in a study and provides a number of n pairs of observations for the two variables.[1] As a result of a primary analysis, the typical outcomes are a correlation coefficient for the two variables and a test statistic to make inferences to a population. In this case, the correlation coefficient is a measure of effect size, because it expresses the strength of the (linear) relationship.

Now consider that after publication of the results of the first study a second one on the same relationship is conducted. In the second study a new sample is drawn with a different number of n individuals, and the correlation is again computed in a primary analysis. Additionally suppose that the effect size in the second study is different from the first one. The question — typical for all literature reviews — arises what a good summary of both studies' results is in the given case. Further assume that the second study could be considered to be a replication of the first one. That is, the same measures were used, the sample was drawn from the same population, and so forth. Under these circumstances it would be reasonable to pool the data of both studies, if available, to arrive at a single effect size based on the total sample of both studies. Unfortunately, this is rarely the case and the task then still is to somehow summarize the effect sizes.

Taking this idea of additional study results on the same research question further, a situation is given that calls for an integrative review of empirical studies. Such a situation is illustrated in the lower and middle part of Figure 2.1 (Level 0). Here, different individual units are sampled in a number of k different studies on a common research question.[2] At this zero level, primary analyses result in empirical reports to be summarized, which include a number of (at least) k effect sizes. Figure 2.1 provides an illustration with correlations $(r_1, \ldots, r_k)$ as effect sizes — the main focus of the present book. Of course, it is not necessary to always collect pairs of observations at Level 0, nor is this process only applicable to correlations as effect sizes.

In a broad sense, meta-analysis is a systematic process of quantitatively combining empirical reports to arrive at a summary and an evaluation of research findings. This "analysis of analysis", as Glass (1976, p. 3) has defined it, can be located in the upper part of Figure 2.1 (Level 1). In analogy to primary analysis, it includes the statistical aggregation of individual units. In contrast to primary analysis, however, the individual units are aggregate measures resulting from Level 0 analyses. The result of a meta-analysis is symbolized only by θ in Figure 2.1. Much more will be said about such a pooled estimate of an effect size in the following chapters. Here, it suffices to say that one of the aims of most meta-analyses is to arrive at such a single summary measure.

Nevertheless, meta-analysis is characterized by many more attributes than simply a step of statistical aggregation. One of the other important attributes of meta-analysis is the more general call for a stronger procedural system-

---

[1]That is, a total of n pairs $(x_1, y_1), \ldots, (x_n, y_n)$ are observed, where x_1 denotes the intelligence score of Person 1 and y_1 his/her job performance score in the example.

[2]Of course, sample sizes need not be the same in such studies, a fact that is not necessarily clear when inspecting Figure 2.1.

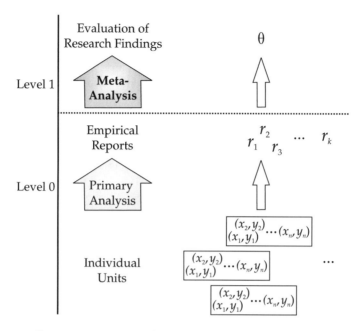

Figure 2.1   Different levels of analysis: Primary analysis and meta-analysis.

atic reviewing of the literature. Correspondingly, several guidelines for meta-analysis have been published. Some focus more on the whole process (e.g., Jackson, 1980), others rather give methodological guidelines (e.g., Cook, Sackett, & Spitzer, 1995). One widely accepted specification of the stages or conduct of a meta-analysis was presented by Cooper (1982; Cooper & Hedges, 1994a), which is formulated in close analogy to the stages of primary analysis:

1. Problem formulation
2. Data collection
3. Data evaluation
4. Analysis and interpretation
5. Public presentation

For each of these stages, attempts were made to clarify the questions to be answered and the methods to arrive at the respective solutions to problems posed. At every stage there is a demand of the meta-analyst for a maximum of explicitness. The whole process of reviewing has to be structured, and it has to be made reconstructible to the research consumer as to how the reviewer arrived at his conclusions. Thus, one of the main criticisms of traditional reviews is addressed by this requirement.

The first stage not only includes the tasks of clearly specifying the research question to be answered by a review and laying the foundations of exclusion and inclusion criteria for the studies to be synthesized, but also covers questions about what statistical model is to be assumed in a meta-analysis. The problems and corresponding solutions for the formulation of the research question to be answered are presented by Hall, Tickle-Degnen, Rosenthal, and Mosteller (1994) in detail and need not be repeated here. What is of much greater concern for the present study are the statistical models available for research synthesis. The available models will be presented and discussed in considerable detail in Chapters 4 and 5. It is important to note that first, statistical matters are not only questions about the proper formulae to use, they are also *conceptual* questions that cannot be answered on the sole basis of empirical results (Hedges, 1994b). Much of the theoretical as well as empirical parts of the present book are devoted to the explication of models and evaluating the performance of statistical procedures associated with different models when their assumptions are met or violated.

The second and third stages of the process concern data retrieval and its evaluation. Tasks and potential problems arising in connection with the former step are presented by White (1994) as well as Reed and Baxter (1994). Data evaluation is the task to judge the quality of the retrieved literature and (optional) assignment of quality scores to the studies under review that can be used in subsequent steps to weight the studies in the process of aggregation (Wortman, 1994). Of course, catalogues of quality criteria are essential at this stage and are available for research in medicine (Chalmers et al., 1981) and psychology (Shadish, Cook, & Campbell, 2002), for example. The idea guiding these two steps is to disclose procedures and criteria for data collection, selection, and weighting in the process of synthesizing. Traditional reviews are often criticized for not being explicit enough at these stages in particular.

Before collected data is actually aggregated, it has to be extracted from the available empirical reports. What is meant by the extraction of data will be detailed in Chapter 3 on effect sizes. The task to be dealt with here is to quantify the results of interest in a measure of effect size common to all studies under investigation. The quantification to be carried out aims at making the results of the studies amenable to statistical aggregation. This represents an essential part of a meta-analysis on the one hand, and another important difference to the narrative review on the other. Hence, meta-analyses are in general also more precise in results as compared to traditional reviews and enable the meta-analyst to make statements about the size of an aggregate effect and its significance. This goes beyond more vague summary statements ordinarily made in narrative reviews. For the last stage of presenting results of a meta-analysis there are also rather precise guidelines. Special forms of reporting meta-analytical results have also been developed. More information on this topic can be found in the works of Halvorsen (1994) as well as Light, Singer, and Willet (1994).

In sum, all these stages of meta-analysis can be characterized as an effort to more precisely structure the whole process of reviewing the literature, explicitly state the goals, and give guidance as to how to tackle with potential problems of each stage. Comparisons with traditional reviews, for example by Cook and Leviton (1980), are therefore strongly in favor of meta-analysis as the method of choice. An empirical comparison between meta-analysis and traditional reviews has been conducted by Beaman (1991) who also concludes that meta-analysis seems to be the preferable method.

What is quite clear from the preceding account is that meta-analysis is not yet another arcane set of statistical formulae a scientist has to deal with but a method to successfully treat the whole complicated process of synthesizing the scientific literature. There surely are a lot of steps in this endeavor that can be classified as qualitative rather than quantitative and these very aspects have mainly been the focus of critics of the method (e.g., Eysenck, 1978). Although the statistical methods of meta-analysis have also been the subject of several controversies (e.g., see Chapter 4) they were not the main target of fundamental critics.

In comparing primary analysis and meta-analysis, several similarities can be noticed. Of course, this is due to the process of meta-analysis being specified in analogy to primary analysis, as outlined above. This makes it quite easy to understand what meta-analysis actually is about and what its basic aims are. Taking a closer look at statistical aspects (Stage 1 and 4), things get more complicated because a higher level of abstraction from the original data is introduced. The statistical foundations of meta-analysis have been presented in various articles in a more concise form (e.g., Hedges, 1983a), introductory books (e.g., Hedges & Olkin, 1985; Hunter & Schmidt, 1990; Lipsey & Wilson, 2001; Rosenthal, 1991) as well as handbooks (Cooper & Hedges, 1994b). What makes an acquisition of the techniques somewhat difficult for the uninitiated is the unfamiliar statistical data to deal with. Ordinarily, a researcher in the behavioral sciences applies data-analytical techniques to the results of an experiment or observational study (Level 0 in Figure 2.1). A number of individual units provide measurements on a set of variables of interest, with measurement instruments chosen to represent the true scores of the persons on the variables as reliably and validly as possible. If a researcher aims at testing certain theoretical propositions, the size of prespecified relationships between the (observed) set of variables is estimated and tested by using data resulting from the measurement process. Estimation and tests in this context are conducted to arrive at statistically well-founded propositions about the relationships of interest in a *population* of *persons*. These outcomes, the estimate and test results, constitute the data basis of meta-analysis. The meta-analyst therefore does not directly deal with measurement of persons but results from studies which can be viewed as aggregated measurements. As a result, the objects of examination are studies and not persons, and the inference the meta-analyst aims at is not from a group of persons to a population of persons but from a group of studies to a *universe* of studies. Analogously to the situation in primary analysis, the empirical reports collected at Stage 2 are conceptualized as a sample of studies from a larger universe of studies. Inference in meta-analysis refers to such a universe, and one of the most difficult questions to be answered in meta-analysis is how this universe can be conceptualized or characterized — though it might be noted that a specification of the population in primary analysis is not an easy to answer question either (Frick, 1998). Variants of universe characterizations will be presented in Chapter 4 in detail, so their discussion is postponed till then.

To summarize, the principles of applying statistical techniques almost remain the same for meta-analysis, but an additional level of abstraction is introduced. The transfer of questions arising in the context of primary analysis to meta-analysis is helpful for understanding the method and raising critical questions in its application.

2.2   ON THE EMERGENCE OF APPROACHES

At least in the field of psychology there are some obvious peculiarities stemming from the history of meta-analysis in this field (for an interesting and comprehensive overview, see Hunt, 1997). In the early 1980s several proponents of meta-analysis presented comprehensive treatments of the subject (e.g. Glass et al., 1981; Hunter, Schmidt, & Jackson, 1982). As mentioned in Chapter 1, these collateral specifications of meta-analysis were concerned with developing methodological solutions for vastly different substantive problems. On the one hand, Glass and colleagues dealt with (quasi-)experimental designs on the comparison of psychotherapies, and Hunter and Schmidt were concerned with the problem of predictive validity in personnel selection. Hence, the former focused on methods to aggregate mean differences and the latter on correlations. Furthermore, there have been specific features in these areas of application that have caused different accentuations. For example, in the area of personnel selection it is customary to apply corrections to the correlation coefficient for range restriction in the sample. This is due to the fact that at least for one of the two variables to be correlated (job performance, for example) only scores of a subsample of the total applicant pool are available. Hence, the treatment by Schmidt and Hunter considers such corrections as being of utmost importance, and a large part of their methodological contributions to meta-analysis is concerned with them, whereas those of others are not.

These two groups of authors are not the only ones who have presented comprehensive treatments of meta-analysis in the psychological literature. Again, additional presentations have a somewhat different focus. Rosenthal (1978) presented methods for the combination of probabilities as study results and was the first to consider the so-called *file-drawer problem* in meta-analysis in depth (Rosenthal, 1979). The file-drawer problem refers to the suspicion that in the behavioral sciences the publication of significant results is favored by editorial policies and journal reviewers' evaluations, thereby causing a biased sample of study results to be available to the meta-analyst. Another major effort — if not the most detailed and statistically elaborate in the behavioral sciences to date — to specify the (statistical) methods of meta-analysis was presented by Hedges and Olkin (for a comprehensive overview, see Hedges & Olkin, 1985). Here, the main focus was not a substantive problem, but a precise statistical formulation of the models in meta-analysis and the presentation of corresponding proofs for the situations given in meta-analyses.

In sum, different groups of authors with different substantive and technical focus have dealt with the methods of meta-analysis — many of them simultaneously — to arrive at a pre-packaged comprehensive treatment of the topic. Such packages, associated with different author names, focus, and procedures, will be called approaches in the following. The publications corresponding to the approaches soon became standard references in certain subdisciplines in psychology. For example, the work of Hunter et al. (1982) became a quasi-standard in the field of industrial and organizational (I/O) psychology, whereas the work of Glass et al. (1981) was the main reference for meta-analytic research in educational psychology. It quickly became accustomed to researchers from different areas to rely on these different approaches. They also became deeply entrenched in research habits in certain subdisciplines. Thus, many researchers either thought that the application of the approach most pertinent in their field of study was the only (correct) option (e.g., Huffcutt, 2002), or the choice of an approach would be inconsequential for the results, or even that differences between the approaches in recommendations, treated effect sizes, and formulae were perhaps simply another mystery of statistical methods in the social sciences.

Several different approaches are identified in the psychological literature. As might be suspected, classifications of proposed techniques into approaches do not always fully agree. For example, a trio of meta-analytical approaches is identified by Andersson (1999) as well as Johnson, Mullen, and Salas (1995), but other categorizations have also been made (Bangert-Drowns, 1986). What is important in the present context is that different approaches still coexist in the psychological literature and their differences are at least partly due to historical reasons, specifics of the substantive research question, and only rarely on diverging mathematical-statistical derivations.

It is interesting to note that in a field like medicine, where scientists adopted the methods of meta-analysis considerably later and with more reservations as compared to psychology, such differences in approaches hardly exist. When inspecting overviews in medical research (e.g., Sutton et al., 2000), nothing comparable to the situation in psychology can be recognized, and the focus is more on statistical models rather than substantive questions.

To summarize, developments of the methods of meta-analysis are different in diverse fields, they were influenced by historical and substantive aspects, and specific approaches are almost tied to different subdisciplines in psychology. Finally, it should be added however, that the differences between approaches concentrate on their procedural recommendations. That is, study retrieval methods (Stage 1), data evaluation (Stage 3), and public presentation format (Stage 5) are highly similar. The differences can be located at Stage 1 in the formulation of the statistical model and Stage 4, the analysis procedures. The following presentation therefore focuses on these aspects in comparing the approaches. A detailed theoretical comparison is given in Chapter 5, and the comparative quality of results is assessed in a Monte-Carlo study to be presented in Chapters 7 and 8.

Part II

Statistical Methods of Meta-Analysis

3

Effect Sizes

In the following sections the type of data used for meta-analysis, the so-called effect sizes, and their statistical characteristics are introduced. The focus here will be laid on measures of effect sizes that are typical research outcomes in the social and behavioral sciences, especially in the field of psychology. Other measures will only be treated in passing. The statistical models to be applied to this form of data will then be presented in detail followed by sections on specific statistical approaches to meta-analysis that can count as the most common applied in research up to date.

The study of a series of research articles in any field of psychology still leaves the impression that the main goal of applying statistical methods is predominantly testing of null hypotheses (Vacha-Haase, Nilsson, Reetz, Lance, & Thompson, 2000). This seems surprising given the high information value ordinarily attached to effect sizes (but see Chow, 1988), and policies articulated by large psychological organizations — like the American Psychological Association — are clearly in favor of reporting effect sizes in research articles (American Psychological Association, 2001; Wilkinson & Task Force on Statistical Inference, 1999). However, a recent study on the editorial policies of the reporting practices has revealed that these policies still have not been fully adopted by editors of major research journals in psychology (Vacha-Haase et al., 2000). Hence, encouragement to report effect sizes is not translated into action. Yet there are also reasons to believe that simple calls for the reporting of effect sizes in publications may not be sufficient to eliminate bias of published results (Lane & Dunlap, 1978).

The lack of reporting effect sizes poses a problem for the meta-analyst because the data to be analyzed are often not readily available from study reports. As a result, effect sizes have to be extracted from research reports when sufficient information is available. There is a host of publications which illustrate that this aim may not always easily be achieved (see, e.g., Olejnik & Algina,

2000; Rosnow & Rosenthal, 1996; Seifert, 1991). Furthermore, design characteristics also have to be taken into account when extracting an effect size, otherwise wrong measures may result (Dunlap, Cortina, Vaslow, & Burke, 1996;
Morris & DeShon, 1997). In a reanalysis of 140 studies on psychosocial treatments or prevention studies in psychology Ray and Shadish (1996) have shown
that different techniques to extract effect size information, proposed in the literature, lead to different magnitudes of effect sizes. Moreover, Matt (1989) has
shown that judgmental factors in extracting effect sizes also play an important
role for the establishment of a database for meta-analysis. In sum, there remain several problems in extracting the relevant information for effect sizes in
some areas of research. The techniques for aggregation of effect sizes, to be
introduced, presume that there is a database of effect sizes already available
and problems of the form just described are not of relevance.

The next section provides an overview of certain families of effect size measures that are most common in psychology. The focus here will be laid on
the correlation coefficient as an effect size. A second common measure, the
standardized mean difference, will also be considered. These two effect size
measures are by far not the only available to researchers, but they are those
of highest importance for the present purpose of evaluating meta-analytical
approaches in psychology.

The effect sizes of interest in the present context belong to two families, the
r and the d family (Rosenthal, 1994). In short, they are comprised of correlation
coefficients on the one hand and standardized mean differences on the other.
They can both be characterized by one of the main features of effect sizes, the
provision of a standardized measure for an effect of interest. First, focus will
be on the correlation coefficient.

3.1   CORRELATION COEFFICIENTS AS EFFECT SIZES

The sample correlation coefficient r, usually designated as the Pearson product
moment correlation, is based on n pairs (x_o, y_o), $o = 1, \ldots, n$, of observations
and is given by

$$r = \frac{\sum\limits_{o=1}^{n} (x_o - \overline{x})(y_o - \overline{y})}{\sqrt{\sum\limits_{o=1}^{n} (x_o - \overline{x})^2} \sqrt{\sum\limits_{o=1}^{n} (y_o - \overline{y})^2}}.$$

The corresponding pair of random variables for (x_o, y_o) is (X, Y). Here, and
in what follows, it should be noted that the correlation coefficient can also be
considered as a random variable based on the variates X and Y. This will occa-
sionally be highlighted in the following by the symbol R, although the symbol
r will predominantly be used. It will be clear from the context when r should
be understood as a random variable and when it should only be considered as
a sample statistic.

The corresponding population correlation coefficient ρ is given by

$$\rho = \frac{E\left((X - E[X])\,(Y - E[Y])\right)}{\sigma_X \sigma_Y}.$$

As is easily seen from these equations, the correlation coefficient can also be regarded as the covariance of standardized variables. Hence, it is extremely useful for measurement at the interval scale level because it is invariant with respect to — not necessarily the same — positive linear transformations of the variables. This is exactly what is most frequently intended by the computation of effect sizes in psychology, to express an effect free from the influence of specific standard deviations of measurement instruments. What is commonly viewed in the behavioral sciences as an advantage of effect sizes, namely to represent the size of an effect irrespective of the scale it is measured on, has also raised questions about the meaning of the resulting scale-free measures (Feinstein, 1995).

The question arises how the variate r may be distributed. Fortunately, it is well-known that r is approximately normally distributed with *large* samples. However, convergence of the distribution is very slow and it is said to be unwise to assume it for $n < 500$ (Stuart, Ord, & Arnold, 1999, p. 481), a case most frequently encountered in practice. The distribution of r is a very complicated statistical topic that cannot be fully dealt with here (for overviews, see Johnson, Kotz, & Balakrishnan, 1995; Stuart & Ord, 1994). The focus of the following presentation will therefore be on aspects of importance to meta-analysis. That is, first, the distribution of r when the pair (X, Y) follows a bivariate normal distribution, and second, point estimation of ρ.

The exact probability density function (PDF) of the distribution of R for r in the interval $[-1, 1]$ is given in the seminal paper by Hotelling (1953, p. 200) as[1]

$$p_R(r) = \frac{\mathrm{df}}{\pi\sqrt{2}}(1 - r^2)^{\frac{\mathrm{df}}{2}-1}(1 - r\rho)^{-\,\mathrm{df}\,-\frac{1}{2}}(1 - \rho^2)^{\frac{\mathrm{df}+1}{2}}$$
$$\times \,\mathrm{B}(\mathrm{df}+1, \tfrac{1}{2})\, {}_2F_1(\tfrac{1}{2}, \tfrac{1}{2}; \mathrm{df}+\tfrac{3}{2}; \tfrac{1}{2}(r\rho + 1)) \tag{3.1}$$

where B denotes the complete Beta function, $\mathrm{df} = n - 2$, and ${}_2F_1$ is the Gaussian hypergeometric function:

$${}_2F_1(a_1, a_2; a_3; a_4) = \sum_{v=0}^{\infty} \frac{\Gamma(a_1 + v)\Gamma(a_2 + v)\Gamma(a_3)}{\Gamma(a_1)\Gamma(a_2)\Gamma(a_3 + v)} \frac{a_4^v}{v!}.$$

In this formula, Γ represents the Euler Γ function. There are also some different forms of the density to be found in the literature based on different derivations

---

[1]Note that the exact form given by Hotelling differs somewhat from the form given here which better fits in the notation already introduced. The equivalence between both forms is seen by noting that n is in Hotelling's paper the symbol for the degrees of freedom and by noticing the following equivalencies: $\mathrm{B}(a, b) = \frac{\Gamma(a)\Gamma(b)}{\Gamma(a+b)}$, $\Gamma(0.5) = \sqrt{\pi}$, and $\Gamma(a + 1) = a\Gamma(a)$.

(see Johnson, Kotz, & Balakrishnan, 1995), but the presentation here will focus on the one provided in Equation 3.1.

Obviously, using this distribution for tests of correlation coefficients is not feasible when $\rho \neq 0$. Only for $\rho = 0$ is r distributed as t with $n - 2$ degrees of freedom, and hence tractable. However, interest in the present context also lies on the nonnull distribution of r. For testing purposes, various approximations to the distribution of the correlation coefficient have been proposed. A series of these approximations will be presented as well as evaluated. Results are reported in Subsection 7.5.1 of Chapter 7, so that a discussion of most of these approximations is postponed. Nevertheless, one of these approximations will be introduced at this point because of its high relevance for the approaches of meta-analysis to be presented in Chapter 5.

The most popular approximation was given by Fisher (1921)[2] who also derived the distribution in the bivariate normal case (Fisher, 1915). He suggested the following transformation to be applied to the correlation coefficient

$$z = \tanh^{-1} r = \frac{1}{2} \ln \frac{1+r}{1-r}. \tag{3.2}$$

In analogy to the case of the correlation coefficient, z can be considered as a random variable Z, but it will be denoted by a lowercase z in most of what follows. The corresponding transformation for the population correlation ρ is

$$\zeta = \tanh^{-1} \rho = \frac{1}{2} \ln \frac{1+\rho}{1-\rho}.$$

As an inverse transformation

$$r = \tanh z = \frac{\exp(2z) - 1}{\exp(2z) + 1} \tag{3.3}$$

is specified for the correlation coefficient, and, again, a corresponding transformation for the population correlation given by

$$\rho = \tanh \zeta = \frac{\exp(2\zeta) - 1}{\exp(2\zeta) + 1}.$$

What happens to the correlation coefficients when the Fisher-z transformation is applied? In Figure 3.1, the transformation provided by Fisher is illustrated. As can be seen, the transformation stretches the values in the boundary regions. Furthermore, the possible values of z are not bounded by -1 and 1, as is the case for the correlation coefficient. Instead, they span the whole interval $[-\infty, +\infty]$.

What are the main virtues of applying the Fisher-z transformation to correlation coefficients? First, the transformed correlation coefficient (z) is approximately normally distributed. That is, the result from stretching the values is to

---

[2]See also Konishi (1978, 1981) for a more concise derivation.

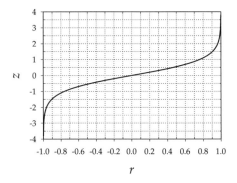

Figure 3.1   The r to Fisher-z transformation.

achieve an approximate normal distribution. In contrast to the distribution of r, the distribution of z converges to normality very much faster.

A second benefit of applying the transformation is stabilization of the variance. This can be seen from Equation 3.4 which gives the approximate variance of Z

$$\sigma_Z^2 \approx \frac{1}{n-3}. \tag{3.4}$$

The variance of z is stable in the sense that it does *not* depend on the parameter ζ but only on the sample size n. As will be seen, this highly desirable feature stands in contrast to the variance of r, which does depend on the population parameter.

The approximate variance of z can easily be computed in practical applications and used for tests as well as for the construction of approximate confidence intervals for ζ, a third beneficial aspect of the transformation. Construction of confidence intervals is easy because it is possible to draw on the normal distribution to find the interval limits. Having found the confidence limits for ζ, it is also possible to transform them to limits for ρ, a procedure that will be outlined in the context of presenting the various statistical approaches to meta-analysis in Chapter 5. The possibility to conduct a statistical test as well as to construct confidence intervals is the main reason why this approximation is so popular in practice.

In sum, by applying the transformation to the correlation coefficient it can be said that one changes spaces. That is, the examination of the linear relationship between two variables starts in the space of r with random variable R and population parameter ρ. The transformation leads to an examination in the space of z with random variable Z and population parameter ζ. The whole purpose of applying the transformation is to make inferences about the population parameter ρ by exploiting desirable properties in the space of z, and thereby avoiding to deal with the complicated PDF.

Apart from examining the distribution of r and its approximation, the question arises whether the Pearson product moment correlation constitutes an unbiased estimator of the effect. That is, whether the equality $E(r) = \rho$ holds for all ρ. This is not the case, and r is therefore a biased estimator of ρ. Hotelling (1953) provided the moments of r about ρ of which the first moment ($\Xi_1 = E(r - \rho)$) is given as

$$\Xi_1 = \left(1 - \rho^2\right) \left(-\frac{\rho}{2(n-1)} + \frac{\rho - 9\rho^3}{8(n-1)^2} + \frac{\rho + 42\rho^3 - 75\rho^5}{16(n-1)^3} + \cdots\right)$$

(Hotelling, 1953, p. 212). The bias is usually approximated by truncation of the series, resulting in

$$\Xi_1 = -\frac{\rho(1 - \rho^2)}{2(n-1)}.$$

This is the well known formula for the *negative* bias of r as an estimator of positive ρ. To compensate for this bias in r one could apply the following correction

$$r^* = r + \frac{r(1 - r^2)}{2(n-1)},$$

which is almost identical to an approximation to the unique minimum variance unbiased (UMVU) estimator by Olkin and Pratt (1958) to be presented below (page 26).

Hotelling (1953) also provided the moments of z about ζ, of which, again, only the first moment is given here

$$\kappa_1 = \frac{\rho}{2(n-1)} + \frac{5\rho + 9\rho^3}{8(n-1)^2} + \frac{11\rho + 2\rho^3 + 3\rho^5}{16(n-1)^3} + \cdots$$

As is obvious, a *positive* bias of Fisher-z for positive ρ is present here. A question that was discussed in the literature of meta-analysis with correlations as effect sizes is which of the biases is smaller in absolute value. Whereas Hunter and Schmidt (1990) claimed to have shown a smaller absolute bias of r in comparison to z, Corey, Dunlap, and Burke (1998) reported results of a Monte Carlo study in which they found the opposite result. Using the formulae given by Hotelling and truncating the series, the biases of the two estimators can be evaluated. For a direct comparison, the biases resulting from the formula for κ_1 were transformed into the space of r by the inverse Fisher-z transformation given in Equation 3.3 and plugging in κ_1 for z. In Figure 3.2 the resulting biases are illustrated.

The bias of both r and z for ρ is shown across different values for ρ as well as sample sizes n in the left panel of Figure 3.2. As can be seen, the bias of both estimators vanishes at $\rho = 0$. The light surface in this graph depicts the the biases of r and the shaded surface those of z. With higher values of ρ the bias continuously increases for z, whereas the bias of r attains its maximum at $\rho \approx .583$ for positive ρ and at $\rho \approx -.583$ for negative ρ. The right panel provides absolute differences in biases with positive values indicating higher biases for z. All values of the difference surface indicate higher bias for z, except for $\rho = 0$, thus z has a larger approximate bias in comparison to r.

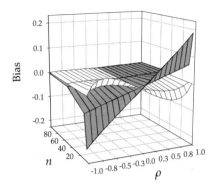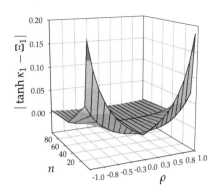

Figure 3.2 Bias of r and z in comparison. The left panel shows the bias for r (light surface) and z (shaded surface). The right panel shows the absolute difference surface for the biases.

In the methodological literature on meta-analysis based on correlational data, the use of Fisher-z versus r as estimators of ρ has attracted considerable attention, especially in the validity generalization literature (e.g., Corey et al., 1998; Law, 1995; Schmidt, Hunter, & Raju, 1988; Silver & Dunlap, 1987), and the bias of these statistics has been quite a controversial issue (see Hunter & Schmidt, 1990; James, Demaree, & Mulaik, 1986). As shown here, it is expected that Fisher-z will exhibit a larger bias from a theoretical point of view. In the Monte Carlo study to be presented in Chapter 7 and 8, it will be examined whether these expectations hold under the conditions of the simulation procedure.

Hotelling proposed several improvements of the Fisher-z transformation. First, he suggested the substraction of $r/(2n-3)$ from z when ρ is unknown to correct for its positive bias (Hotelling, 1953, p. 219). This correction was evaluated in a Monte Carlo study by Paul (1988), who concluded that for the estimation of $\rho < .50$ the modification of Hotelling performed best amongst the estimators he considered, and for $\rho > .50$ Fisher-z performed best. Alexander, Hanges, and Alliger (1985), in contrast, found no substantial differences between these estimators in their Monte Carlo study.

A further improvement was proposed by Hotelling (1953, p. 224) as

$$z^{**} = z - \frac{3z+r}{4(n-1)} - \frac{23z + 33r - 5r^3}{96(n-1)^2},$$

however the quality of this modification has not been sufficiently evaluated to date.

In contrast to these procedures, some authors in the methodological literature of meta-analysis, for example, Erez, Bloom, and Wells (1996, p. 288), and

Overton (1998, p. 358) used the correction

$$r^\# = r - \frac{r(1 - r^2)}{2n}$$

to compensate for the positive bias in z. This correction was followed by an application of the Fisher-z transformation in both authors' work. Although this procedure obviously lowers the positive bias of z, it is of unclear origin and lacks a clear rationale from a statistical viewpoint. Because at least Erez et al. (1996) attributed the correction to Hotelling (1953), it may be speculated that (a variant of) Ξ_1 was used to correct the bias in z. How this flaw in procedure affects their results is however unclear.

As an important contribution to the statistical literature of estimators of ρ, the UMVU estimator was presented as

$$G = r \times {}_2F_1 \left(\tfrac{1}{2}, \tfrac{1}{2}; \tfrac{n-2}{2}; 1 - r^2 \right) \tag{3.5}$$

by Olkin and Pratt (1958, p. 202). The following formula gives an approximation of G

$$G = r \left(1 + \frac{1 - r^2}{2(n - 1 - 3)} \right)$$

(Olkin & Pratt, 1958, p. 203). G has the same range and asymptotic distribution as r, but larger variance and smaller mean-squared error in general (Hedges & Olkin, 1985, p. 226). Surprisingly, although this estimator has very desirable properties from a statistical viewpoint, it is not widely used in the literature. This may be due to unawareness or due to statements in the literature that not much can be gained from an application of the correction of r (Hedges, 1989). It is expected from the statistical properties of this estimator that its usage will lead to a minimum bias among the estimators in the Monte Carlo study to be presented.

In addition to the bias of an estimator, its variance is also of great importance for meta-analysis. The variance of r is usually approximated in practice as

$$\sigma_R^2 \approx \frac{\left(1 - \rho^2 \right)^2}{n - 1} \tag{3.6}$$

which is Ξ_2, the second moment about ρ presented by Hotelling (1953, p. 212) truncated after the first term in the series. In practice, this approximation is used by plugging in r for ρ in order to estimate the variance. This may, however, not be a good approximation. The reason for this is not only truncation, but most importantly the very slow convergence of the distribution of r to the normal distribution. As will be noticed, ρ (or in practical applications r) itself is involved in the variance approximation. In Figure 3.3 the dependency of σ_R^2 on ρ is illustrated. As can easily be seen in this figure, the variance is at max-

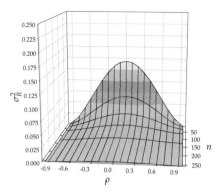

Figure 3.3   Variance of r across different values of ρ and n.

imum when $\rho = 0$, across all values of n. The variance changes maximally at $\rho \approx .577$ for positive values[3] of ρ.

The variance of G, in contrast, can be estimated by

$$\hat{\sigma}_G^2 = G^2 - 1 + \frac{(n-3)(1-r^2)_2F_1\left(1,1;\frac{n}{2};1-r^2\right)}{n-2} \tag{3.7}$$

(Hedges, 1988, p. 198; see also Hedges, 1989, p. 477). Again, the variance of the estimator is dependent on the parameter, though not as apparent as in the previous case. Figure 3.4 illustrates the relationship.

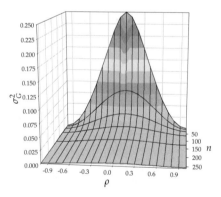

Figure 3.4   Variance of G across different values of ρ and n.

By way of comparison of Figures 3.3 and 3.4 it becomes clear that although the relationships are similar in form they are actually quite different with a stronger change in variance for G. The largest change in variance occurs at $\rho = .347$.

---

[3]This value results from taking the partial derivative of the variance and finding its minimum.

Up to this point, only the Pearson correlation coefficient has been examined, but there are several other correlation coefficients in the r family available (see Rosenthal, 1994; Rosenthal, Rosnow, & Rubin, 2000). The properties of other indices, like the point-biserial, biserial or rank correlation coefficient, for example, are not of concern here as only the correlation coefficient for the bivariate normal case is under scrutiny. For the distribution theory and examinations of the robustness of the coefficients reported in this book the reader is referred to Johnson, Kotz, and Balakrishnan (1995).

3.2 STANDARDIZED MEAN DIFFERENCES AS EFFECT SIZES

As previously mentioned, a second common effect size measure in the psychological literature is the standardized mean difference. It is mostly used in a situation when two groups of participants are examined and differences of means are of interest. More succinctly,

$$X_{o_1} \sim \mathcal{N}(\mu_1, \sigma^2) \qquad o_1 = 1, \ldots, n_1,$$

and

$$Y_{o_2} \sim \mathcal{N}(\mu_2, \sigma^2) \qquad o_2 = 1, \ldots, n_2.$$

That is, both random variables are assumed to be normally distributed with common standard deviation σ but not necessarily with the same number of observations n. For this case, the effect size — also known as Cohen's d (Cohen, 1988) — is defined as

$$\delta = \frac{\mu_1 - \mu_2}{\sigma}.$$

The estimators proposed in this family are different with respect to the choice of the standard deviation (S). They are all computed by the generic form

$$\frac{\overline{X} - \overline{Y}}{S}$$

and therefore represent a standardized measure of the effect. There are three popular coefficients that are presented here. The first will be denoted by d and results from inserting the pooled estimate of the standard deviation in the denominator of Equation 3.8. The pooled estimate S_{pool} is given by

$$S_{\text{pool}} = \sqrt{\frac{(n_1 - 1)S_1^2 + (n_2 - 1)S_2^2}{n_1 + n_2 - 2}},$$

where S_1 and S_2 are the sample standard deviations for X and Y, respectively. Therefore,

$$d = \frac{\overline{X} - \overline{Y}}{S_{\text{pool}}}. \tag{3.8}$$

Another estimator was proposed by Glass (1976; see also Glass et al., 1981) and will be denoted by d'. It is given by inserting S_{con} in the denominator of Equation 3.8, where S_{con} represents the standard deviation of a control group. The control group is ordinarily chosen as the reference group in a two-group experimental setting.

Both d and d' have a distribution related to the noncentral t distribution (see Hedges, 1981; Hedges & Olkin, 1985). Let

$$\tilde{n} = \frac{n_1 n_2}{n_1 + n_2},$$

then $\sqrt{\tilde{n}}d$ and $\sqrt{\tilde{n}}d'$ follow a noncentral t distribution with noncentrality parameter $\tau = \sqrt{\tilde{n}}\delta$. Bias as well as variance of d are smaller than those of d' (Hedges & Olkin, 1985). The focus will therefore be on d.

The expected value of d is given by Hedges (1981) as

$$E(d) = \frac{\delta}{f(m)},$$

where $m = n_1 + n_2 - 2$ and

$$f(m) = \frac{\Gamma\left(\frac{m}{2}\right)}{\sqrt{\frac{m}{2}}\Gamma\left(\frac{m-1}{2}\right)}.$$

Hedges (1981) also derived an unbiased estimator d'' of δ by drawing on this result. It is given as an approximation in the following equation

$$d'' = d \times \left(1 - \frac{3}{4(n_1 + n_2) - 9}\right).$$

This is also the UMVU estimator when $n_1 = n_2$ (Hedges, 1981). Further properties of this estimator are not given here as the focus is on the more common estimator d.

The asymptotic distribution of d is normal with expected value δ. The asymptotic variance of the random variable d is given by

$$\sigma_D^2 = \frac{n_1 + n_2}{n_1 n_2} + \frac{\delta^2}{2(n_1 + n_2)} \tag{3.9}$$

(Hedges & Olkin, 1985, p. 86, Equation 15). Customarily, the variance is estimated by plugging in d for δ in practical applications. For an equal number of persons in both groups, this variance estimate based on Equation 3.9 reduces to

$$\hat{\sigma}_D^2 = \frac{4 + d^2}{n}, \tag{3.10}$$

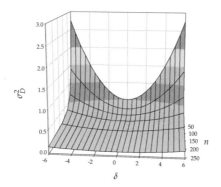

Figure 3.5   Variance of d across different values of δ and n.

where $n_1 + n_2 = n$. As can easily be seen from these equations, the variance (estimate) depends on the population parameter (or d) itself as was the case for the correlation coefficient. To provide an impression of this dependency, consider Figure 3.5.

As can be seen, the relationship between δ and the variance of the estimator is quite strong for large absolute values of δ and different in shape in comparison to the relationships previously examined for correlation coefficients. Since these variances play a central role in meta-analyses using d as an effect size, this may have unwanted effects on the results.

The details on the r and d families of effect sizes necessary for the present purposes are outlined at this point. Discussion will now turn to the question of the relation between r and d measures.

3.3   CONVERSION OF EFFECT SIZES

The conversion of effect sizes is one of the central features of meta-analysis. Effect sizes have always to be converted when the database does not provide coefficients from the same family. For example, it may be the case that one half of available studies reports the results from experiments and therefore d values[4], whereas the other half has observed the bivariate linear relationship between variables of interest and reports r values. The question arises in such cases how different effect size measures may be analyzed in a single meta-analysis.

Conversions of effect sizes are intended to homogenize the database to one single effect size (family). A host of conversion formulae for the various specific effect sizes has been presented to date, that will not be repeated here (see, e.g., Olejnik & Algina, 2000; Rosenthal, 1994). Instead, only the following formulae for the conversion of the Pearson correlation coefficient and the stan-

---

[4]Depending on the design, other indices than the d as introduced here may be appropriate.

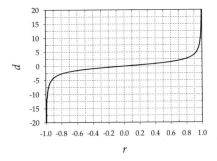

Figure 3.6   The r to d transformation.

dardized effects size measure d will be presented. They are given in various resources for the case of equal group sizes (i.e., $n_1 = n_2$) as

$$r = \sqrt{\frac{d^2}{d^2 + 4}} \tag{3.11}$$

and

$$d = \frac{2r}{\sqrt{(1 - r^2)}} \tag{3.12}$$

(e.g., Cohen, 1988; Hedges & Olkin, 1985; Lipsey & Wilson, 2001; Rosenthal, 1991). The conversion with Equation 3.12 is illustrated in Figure 3.6.

In Figure 3.6 it can be seen that the conversion of r to d has a similar shape in comparison to the Fisher-z transformation presented in Figure 3.1 but is much steeper in the tails. This suggests a normalizing transformation of the correlation coefficient as was the case for the Fisher-z transformation but may not result in an equally good normal approximation. Conversely, a transformation of d to r leads to relatively large differences in the space of r for values near zero being relatively close to each other, but large differences far from zero translate into small differences in absolute values of r.

Aaron, Kromrey, and Ferron (1998) provided a derivation of the conversion for equal n that slightly differs from Equation 3.11

$$r = \sqrt{\frac{d^2}{d^2 + 4 - \frac{8}{n}}},$$

where $n = n_1 + n_2$. For the case of unequal n they proposed

$$r = \sqrt{\frac{d^2}{d^2 + \frac{(n_1 + n_2)^2 - 2(n_1 + n_2)}{n_1 n_2}}}.$$

The authors also showed that discrepancies exist between their corrected formulae and results from Equation 3.11. The reported differences were considered as negligible for the balanced case when $n > 50$.

However, it is not clear from Aaron et al.'s (1998) presentation whether their corrected formulae provide more accurate procedures for *estimating* the correlation coefficient by way of d. As is the case for the standard formula in Equation 3.11, their derivation also draws on the *null* distribution of both effect sizes that is approximately t with $n - 2$ degrees of freedom. Assuming both effect sizes to have an equal distribution seems to be *only* justified in this case. Yet, for the nonnull case (i.e., $\rho \neq 0$ and $\delta \neq 0$), neither the distribution of r nor the distribution of d is exactly (noncentral) t. As a consequence, there is no statistical derivation available for the conversion of r to d or vice versa for the nonnull case. Hence, when there is a lack of a standard for comparison, there is no way to theoretically evaluate the quality of the conversion formulae.

One possibility for evaluation, that is pursued in the following Monte Carlo study, is to apply the conversion proposed in Equation 3.11 to simulated data and study the behavior of converted statistics. This will enable the examination of the implicit assumption, by the widespread application of Equation 3.11, that the conversion itself does not have any influence on the results in meta-analysis.

4

General Frameworks of Meta-Analysis

As an example, suppose a group of researchers has succeeded in collecting all empirical studies judged as relevant in a field they are interested in. Recognizing the shortcomings of narratively summing up the collected evidence and confronted with a large amount of empirical evidence, they are interested in statistical methods to quantitatively aggregate the effect sizes extracted from the study reports. Before the researchers turn to specific computational procedures of conducting a meta-analysis, to be described in Chapter 5, they might first consider the following questions:

1. Are there good reasons, theoretically or based on previous evidence, to assume that only *one* universe effect size is underlying all studies? That is, do all studies estimate exactly the same effect?

2. What kind of inference is intended? Should generalization from the results pertain to all potential studies in a field of interest, or should interpretations be restricted to the kind of studies in the collected sample?

3. If studies are not all assumed to estimate the same effect size,

   - are there any theoretically assumed predictors which correspond to observed characteristics of the collected studies to explicitly model potential effect size differences and/or
   - are there potential differences in universe effect sizes that are due to unobserved (latent) variables?

In essence, by answering these questions, the researchers are making a decision between models to be applied to the observed effect size data. Such decisions and arguments to substantiate them have not always been made explicit in published meta-analyses. Often, the choice of a model has been made implicitly by the choice of an approach to meta-analysis. For example, the researchers may turn to one of several textbooks on meta-analysis and apply the computational procedures outlined in there before considering and answering all the questions outlined above. Unfortunately, not all available textbook resources are explicit with reference to the statistical models implied by the procedures described therein (e.g., Wolf, 1986; but see in contrast, Hedges & Olkin, 1985). Approaches are intimately tied to statistical models, so that the choice of an approach is also the choice of a model. The present section is intended to clarify the basic characteristics of models in meta-analysis. This will provide the framework to classify the specific approaches presented in the subsequent section.

It is important to recognize that *definite* answers to the questions presented above cannot be given on the sole basis of any form of data analysis. The choice of a model has to be made at a conceptual level (Hedges, 1994b; Hedges & Vevea, 1998). This becomes most evident, for example, by considering the second question: What kind of inference is intended? This question can only be answered as a result of careful consideration of the object of inference. On the other hand, there are data-analytical procedures providing some indication of the tenability of a model by way of testing some of its assumptions. In the following sections, such procedures will be presented and their performance under different models will be evaluated on the basis of results of a Monte Carlo study to be presented in Chapter 8.

With respect to the choice of a model, meta-analysis is not at all different from other familiar statistical techniques. Estimation of the parameters of a model is always done by assuming a certain model beforehand, implicitly or explicitly. Structural equation modeling, which has become a very popular statistical technique in practice in recent years, is a prototypical example where one has to choose a model before estimation can be done. However, not all data-analytical techniques force the user to specify or choose between models. Meta-analysis as practised in the field of psychology seems to have become one of these types of data-analytical tools, where decisions of a user are more focused on the choice between sets of computational procedures rather than models.

The question at this point is what kind of models there are available in meta-analysis and which meta-analytical approach corresponds to what kind of model. The following sections are intended to answer these questions. The presentation will thereby be kept more general in comparison to the subsequent presentation of specific approaches (see also Shadish & Haddock, 1994). Although presentation will be focused on the correlation coefficient as an effect size there is no need to restrict the treatment of the subject at this point. Keeping the general perspective in mind, it will be much easier to recognize the similarities and differences of the meta-analytical approaches, and their statistical procedures in particular, to be presented in Chapter 5.

4.1   FIXED EFFECTS MODEL

The fixed-effects model (FE) can still be regarded as the most frequently assumed model in practice. An often stated basic assumption of the FE model is represented in the first question to the researcher in the above list: Are there good reasons to assume a universe effect size that is common to all studies? If the answer to this question is "yes", then the researcher assumes that all observed effect sizes are estimates of a single parameter. The fixed effects model is appropriate for this case.

Let θ denote the universe effect size measure of interest and suppose there are k independent observed effect sizes. This may be the case when an experiment is replicated 10 times ($k = 10$) and each experiment is conducted by a different researcher, in a different place, and so forth, so that all results can be considered as independent. The differences between studies (researcher, place, measurement instruments, etc.) are considered to be minor or negligible in the sense that they do not exert any systematic influence on the research results. The experiments can also be called *strict replications* here. Though such strict replications are only rarely or never conducted in the social sciences, they are assumed for matters of convenience in the presentation at this point.

Furthermore, suppose there is *one* effect size θ giving rise to all effect size estimates. This is a case where effect sizes are often called *homogeneous*, because they all are assumed to represent the same parameter of interest.

However, in general each of the ten replications will report a different observed effect size, so there is a nonzero variance of observed effect sizes. One important question to be answered is how such differences may arise. In the FE model, differences between reported effect sizes are ordinarily conceived as resulting only from sampling error, and sampling error results from different person sampling in the studies. The variance of the observed effect sizes, however, is assumed *not* to be caused by substantive differences between studies, like differences in treatment nuances, validity of measurement instruments, and so forth. This is a very strong assumption for which usage of the FE model has been heavily criticized in recent years (Erez et al., 1996; Hunter & Schmidt, 2000; National Research Council, 1992). As a consequence of the assumptions, one would expect the conduct of 10 more studies of the same type as the first ten studies to result in different estimates of θ only because of varying samples of participants.

The observed effect size measures will be denoted as T_i ($i = 1, \ldots, k$). Usually, different studies also have a different number of participants so that the estimates vary in precision[1] of estimating the parameter θ. The variance of each

---

[1]In a strict statistical sense estimates do not vary in precision but only estimators do. Hence, one could also conceive each observed estimate as a realization from a different estimator when n is different between studies and the precision of the estimator depends on n. However, in the present context it may be confusing to use the term estimator when all effect size measures are of the same family. As a consequence, the term estimate will be used in what follows.

effect size estimate T_i will be denoted as v_i and is a measure of this precision. The crucial point is that the estimates might differ in their precision of estimation though they all estimate the *same* constant θ (i.e., $\theta_1 = \theta_2 = \ldots = \theta_k = \theta$). In other words, the universe effect size is *fixed* for all studies.

In order to form a precise pooled estimate based on the observed effect sizes, it seems natural to consider the so-called pooled estimator in the FE model

$$\hat{\theta} = \frac{\sum\limits_{i=1}^{k} w_i T_i}{\sum\limits_{i=1}^{k} w_i}. \tag{4.1}$$

This is also often called the *mean effect size (estimate)*. The connotation implied by this label is that $\hat{\theta}$ is a weighted mean (with weights w_i) of the observed effect size estimates. When all observed effect size estimates are unbiased, then $\hat{\theta}$ is also unbiased. As already shown in the previous chapter, not all measures of effect size of interest are indeed unbiased.

The remaining question is what specific weights are to be inserted in Equation 4.1. From a statistical point of view, the optimal weights are the reciprocals of the variances of the estimates, because they minimize the variance of the pooled estimate $\hat{\theta}$ (for a proof, see Böhning, 2000, pp. 96–97).[2] Therefore, the optimal weights are given by

$$w_i = \frac{1}{v_i}. \tag{4.2}$$

Intuitively, these weights also make sense, since they give the largest weight to the most precise estimate (i.e., with smallest v_i). Since the meta-analytical approaches to be presented in Chapter 5 differ with respect to the choice of weights, a more detailed discussion is postponed to the presentation of the approaches. Note, however, that variances used to compute the weights are usually unknown and have to be estimated. Ordinarily, an estimate for this variance $\hat{v}_i$ is available and plugged into Equation 4.2.

No distributional assumptions have been made up to this point. For the next step of inference based on the estimates of θ, it is often assumed that the T_i are normally distributed (e.g., Hedges & Vevea, 1998). However, this is not a necessary assumption to show that

$$v_{\hat{\theta}} = \frac{1}{\sum\limits_{i=1}^{k} w_i}$$

---

[2]It is noteworthy that a justification of the weights can also be given by the maximum likelihood method (see Böhning, 2000, pp. 101-103).

gives the variance of the pooled estimate (see Böhning, 2000), provided every T_i is unbiased. Additionally drawing on the central limit theorem, it is possible to construct confidence intervals via

$$\theta_L = \hat{\theta} - g_\alpha \sqrt{v_{\hat{\theta}}}$$
$$\theta_U = \hat{\theta} + g_\alpha \sqrt{v_{\hat{\theta}}} ,$$

where g_α denotes the critical value for a prespecified α-level from a standard normal distribution to construct two-sided confidence intervals.[3] The index "L" designates the lower limit and "U" the upper limit of the interval, respectively.

In addition to the construction of a confidence interval, the null hypothesis $\theta = 0$ can also be tested by using $v_{\hat{\theta}}$, so that

$$g = \frac{\hat{\theta}}{\sqrt{v_{\hat{\theta}}}}$$

provides a g-value to be compared with a critical value from the standard normal distribution for a prespecified level of α.

As a last step in the FE model, one can test the basic assumption of equal universe effect sizes underlying all studies by computing the following statistic

$$Q = \sum_{i=1}^{k} \frac{(T_i - \hat{\theta})^2}{v_i}.$$

Essentially, this is the sum of squared standard normal values, which follows a χ^2-distribution with $k - 1$ degrees of freedom when the null hypothesis of equal universe effect sizes for all k estimates is true. Hence, by comparing the value of Q with the respective critical value from a χ^2_{k-1} distribution, one tests whether the assumption of equal universe effect sizes for all studies holds.[4] This makes the computation of the Q-statistic a very important step in the application of the FE model. When the test result is significant, one is forced to reject the null hypothesis, and this amounts to rejecting the tenability of the FE model. One of the consequences of such a result is that the mean effect size estimate $\hat{\theta}$ has no simple interpretation anymore within the framework of the FE model as presented up to this point.

Of course, it is still the weighted mean of observed effect sizes but the parameter to be estimated is not a single universe effect size constant for all studies. Instead, one is forced to switch to a different model which incorporates differences in universe effect sizes between k studies.

---

[3] The unusual symbol g_α is used here to avoid confusion with the values of Fisher-z which play a prominent role in the present book.
[4] For convenience, such tests will be labeled as Q-tests.

One possibility to deal with the result of a significant Q-statistic is to build subgroups of studies that are assumed to be homogeneous in the sense of the basic assumption of the FE model and compute as many estimates of mean effect sizes as there are groups. Subgrouping in such a procedure can be based on coded characteristics of the studies, for example. These characteristics may be suggested by theoretical reflections or may also be methodological features of the studies (e.g., experimental vs. quasi-experimental studies). In any case, the pursued aim of subgrouping is to find groups that satisfy the assumption of homogeneity in the FE model. A more efficient procedure than subgrouping would be to fit a categorial or continuous (linear) model to the effect size measures as proposed by Hedges (1982a, 1982b, 1994a). In type, these procedures are akin to familiar techniques such as the general linear model (e.g., ANOVA and regression models). A very general framework for this type of analyses is provided by hierarchical linear models, which will be introduced in Section 4.4.

As is well-known, there are also fixed effects models in ANOVA. Indeed, fixed effects models in ANOVA and in meta-analysis are analogous in the sense that the parameter to be estimated is conceived as fixed instead of being a random variable as in the model to be presented next (see, e.g., Scheffé, 1959/1999; for details on the analogy between ANOVA and meta-analysis, see Hedges & Vevea, 1998). It is important to recognize at this point that although the starting assumption of a universe effect size equal for all k studies is rejected, the fixed effects model can still apply.

Nevertheless, the analogy to ANOVA models suggests an interpretational consequence pertaining to the pooled estimate $\hat{\theta}$. Just like in ANOVA, it now has to be interpreted as an estimate of the grand mean of the observed effect sizes. Against this background, the assumption of equal universe effect sizes stated at the outset can be considered as a special case of ANOVA where a factor *study* with k levels has no effect.

Interpretation of results from inferential procedures as outlined above also have to be refined in this model. They now relate to the grand mean built on the basis of a set of k studies which differ in universe effect sizes. The differences between universe effect sizes are now modeled and are considered to be constant (fixed) over replications. If, for example, a meta-analysis is used to aggregate results from ten studies with a certain grand mean, then another set of ten studies must estimate the same grand mean. In this situation one can think of replicating sets of studies with the same grand mean. Hence, inference relates to a *universe* of studies that is characterized by the grand mean to be estimated. The term universe (of studies) is used here again, to underscore the different level of sampling in comparison to primary studies (see also Chapter 2). To reiterate, a first level of sampling can be considered as sampling of persons in the studies, so that there is a population of persons. The second level is considered as sampling of studies form a universe of studies.

Another possibility to deal with the result of a significant test result for the Q-statistic can be to completely give up the fixed effects assumptions and switch to the random effects model to be presented next.

4.2 RANDOM EFFECTS MODEL

The main difference between the FE model and the random effects model (RE) in meta-analysis is the introduction of a random variable Θ instead of an effect in the universe of studies that is conceived as constant (Hedges, 1983b; Raudenbush, 1994). The objects of main focus in RE meta-analyses are the expected value μ_Θ and the variance σ_Θ^2 of the random variable Θ. In comparison to the FE model, the expected value of Θ replaces θ as the mean effect size. The variance of Θ is a new object of interest that has no counterpart in FE models. Hence, it is acknowledged in RE models at the outset that universe effect sizes may vary between studies. It is easily seen from this conceptualization that the FE model can also be viewed as a special case of the RE model where the variance of the universe effect sizes is zero and the expected value of Θ and the effect size θ in the FE model coincide.

As a consequence of the model assumption, the variance of observed effect sizes is not only explained by sampling error of persons in studies as was the case in the FE model, but also by *true variability* of studies in meta-analyses. That is, variance of effect size measures is decomposed into two components

$$\sigma_{T_i}^2 = \sigma_\Theta^2 + v_i,$$

where it is assumed that Θ and the error component are independent. The sampling error v_i of the studies is interpreted as is done in the FE model.

Although there is ordinarily no explicit sampling scheme implied by collecting the studies, it is usually assumed to be a random sampling process. The additional variance component σ_Θ^2 — also called heterogeneity variance — introduces an additional source of uncertainty, because apart from sampling n participants at a first level there is also a sampling of k studies with different universe effect sizes at a second level.

The procedures applied in the RE model to estimate a mean effect size first require an estimate of σ_Θ^2. There are different estimators of this variance component that will not be given here, however presentation of specific estimators will be given in the introduction of the refined approaches in Section 5.4 of the following chapter. Assume for the moment that a variance estimate $\hat{\sigma}_\Theta^2$ were available. This estimate is used to compute new weights by

$$w_i^* = \left(\frac{1}{v_i} + \hat{\sigma}_\Theta^2\right)^{-1},$$

which are employed in the same way as in the FE model to estimate the mean effect size in the RE model by

$$\hat{\Theta} = \frac{\sum\limits_{i=1}^{k} w_i^* T_i}{\sum\limits_{i=1}^{k} w_i^*}.$$

As can be seen from the weights, results for the mean effect size estimate in the RE model will differ from those in the FE model when the variance estimate $\hat{\sigma}^2_\Theta$ is different from zero, which will generally be the case. Note that $\hat{\sigma}^2_\Theta$ is the same for all k studies so that the effect of the additional component in the weights is to homogenize the weights between studies as compared to the FE model. This also seems plausible since in a situation in which $\hat{\sigma}^2_\Theta$ is much larger in comparison to the v_i this gives a larger impact on the weight to uncertainty due to sampling of studies. In extreme cases where there is practically no estimation error in the individual studies, variability of effect sizes would totally reflect uncertainty due to sampling of studies from the universe. Due to the fact that all studies are ordinarily considered to be equal with respect to sampling from the universe of studies, homogenization is desirable. However, this also makes the estimation of the mean effect size more uncertain and widens the confidence intervals accordingly. This can be seen in the following equations for the construction of confidence intervals

$$\Theta_L = \hat{\Theta} - g_\alpha \sqrt{v_{\hat{\Theta}}}$$
$$\Theta_U = \hat{\Theta} + g_\alpha \sqrt{v_{\hat{\Theta}}}$$

where, again, g_α is the critical value from a standard normal distribution. The estimate of the variance of $\hat{\Theta}$ is denoted by $v_{\hat{\Theta}}$ and given by the reciprocal of the sum of weights

$$v_{\hat{\Theta}} = \frac{1}{\sum\limits_{i=1}^{k} w_j^*}.$$

In the same fashion as in the FE model but with the new weights, a significance test for the hypothesis $\Theta = 0$ can also be performed by

$$g = \frac{\hat{\Theta}}{\sqrt{v_{\hat{\Theta}}}}.$$

As can easily be seen by considering computation of the weights in the RE model, the tests are — ceteris paribus — generally less powerful than those of the FE model. This is due to the additional component $\hat{\sigma}^2_\Theta$ which makes the weights larger, and as a consequence, standard errors $v_{\hat{\Theta}}$ also become larger.

The estimates $\hat{\Theta}$ are always clear to interpret in the RE model. They represent estimates of the expected value of the distribution of universe effect sizes. This is an important point to note since the distribution of effect sizes in the universe of studies represents the distribution of all possible studies. The universe comprises the k studies in a meta-analysis as a sample but also all other studies that could not be retrieved (see Hedges & Vevea, 1998). This suggests a very attractive interpretation of the mean effect size estimate in RE models, namely that the effect size estimate may be generalized to an entire research domain. This is one of the reasons why some authors have argued strongly in favor of the application of the RE instead of FE models (e.g., Hunter & Schmidt,

2000). In other methodological areas in psychology, like generalizability theory (Cronbach, Gleser, Nanda, & Rajaratnam, 1972), there is also an analogous transition in models where the RE model is strongly favored.

However, there is always some ambiguity left in interpretation when the sampling process is somewhat obscure as will mostly be the case in applications of meta-analysis. A random sampling process would require the specification of the whole universe of studies and a procedure that guarantees a random sample of k studies from this universe. This is not feasible in practice and may represent a critical point for the application of RE models. In a similar vein, some authors have noted that the assessment or decision as to whether study samples are indeed representative for an entire research domain is not an easy task, if possible at all (Kavale, 1995). Yet this is not a problem specifically pertaining to meta-analysis but also arises in ordinary research practice in psychology or other fields where random samples are scarcely available. On the other hand, random sampling is considered not to be a necessary prerequisite in general for valid interpretations by some authors (e.g., Frick, 1998). Furthermore, a Bayesian perspective on the research problem in meta-analysis also does not necessitate a formal random sampling procedure for the justification of random effects (Raudenbush, 1994).

In addition, when not many studies are available in a field of interest generalization to a whole domain of research may be unfounded or at least risky because few studies are scarcely representative for a universe of studies. Furthermore, problems arise also in the application of RE models to a set of only few studies with respect to estimation of the heterogeneity variance σ_Θ^2 (Raudenbush, 1994; see also Hunter & Schmidt, 1990, who discuss such issues under the heading of *second-order sampling error*). It may be more sensible in such cases to restrict interpretation only to studies like those in the sample as is done with the FE model. Therefore, it is of great interest how applications of the RE model perform in situations with very few studies which is one of the aims that will be pursued in the empirical part of this book.

Unfortunately, there seems to be considerable confusion as how to conceptualize and interpret the random effects model of meta-analysis. For example, Erez et al. (1996) draw a distinction between the fixed and random effects model in a way that the fixed effects model is interpreted as an intercept-only regression model, whereas the random effects model is regarded as a regression where the heterogeneity of observed effect sizes is additionally accounted for by covariates (Erez et al., 1996, p. 278). The difference between the FE and RE model, however, is not one of differences in predictors in regression models but whether universe effect sizes are conceived as random variables or not. In both models it is possible to apply linear models for the explanation of variation in study findings with any desired set of predictors as long as the basic assumptions of the models are met.

As already noted, the homogeneity test based on the Q-statistic in the FE model is often used in practice to make a decision between the random and the fixed effects model. Although this decision does not require such a test, the decision is often made conditionally on the result of the test. Such a procedure is also called the *conditionally random effects procedure*. This hybrid procedure has been reported to have properties in between FE and RE procedures with respect to test results (Hedges & Vevea, 1998). As has been outlined in this section, there are important differences in interpretation associated with the choice of a model. Therefore, it seems reasonable to require the Q-test to perform quite well as one of the most important decisions in meta-analysis hinges on its results. The present study will also present an empirical evaluation of the Q-test as used in various approaches to assess its quality (see also Alexander, Scozarro, & Borodkin, 1989; Cornwell, 1993; Field, 2001; Hardy & Thompson, 1998; Harwell, 1997; Hartung, Argaç, & Makambi, 2003; Sánchez-Meca & Marín-Martínez, 1997).

4.3   MIXTURE MODELS

Mixture models provide a very general framework for the meta-analytic situation that embrace and extend the fixed and random effects models presented in the previous two sections. Since mixture analyses are not part of the Monte Carlo procedures to be presented in later chapters, only a brief sketch of the main characteristics is given here. The concepts introduced in this section will nevertheless be taken up in later sections because they provide a very concise way to describe the meta-analytical situation in a well-founded statistical theory. For an in-depth treatment of the subject with application to meta-analysis the reader is referred to the work of Böhning (2000) and also to one of the first applications of these methods to meta-analysis in psychology by Thomas (1989a, 1989b, 1990b). Because the present study is mainly occupied with the application of meta-analysis to correlational data, the following presentation will be given with the correlation coefficient as effect size data.

Suppose again, there are $k = 10$ studies given and each of the ten studies reports a correlation coefficient r_i for two variables that are bivariate normal in distribution. Now the following concepts and notation are introduced. Observed correlations are regarded as realizations of random variables denoted by R_i with a certain n_i per study and universe correlation ρ_j. For matters of convenience, it is assumed that all n_i are equal[5] and can be denoted by n. The index j is used to indicate potentially different universe correlations for a set of i correlations. That is, there may be subsets of the i studies with different universe correlations, for example. In mixture models, such j universe parameters — universe correlations in the present case — are also called *components*. The total number of components is denoted by c, so that $j = 1, \ldots, c$.

What the meta-analyst wants to understand, explain, and model, is how the distribution of observed correlation coefficients arises. If there is only one $\rho_j = \rho$ common to all studies, a homogeneous case is given. In mixture models

---

[5]It would not be difficult to conceive the number of participants also as a random variable. However, this would not add much to understanding the concepts here and there is no loss in generality by assuming equal n.

this is also called a case with one component. The distributions of the R_i only differ when the sample sizes n_i of the studies are different. Otherwise, all variables have the same distribution, characterized by a probability density function $f(r; \rho, n)$. In this case, knowledge of ρ and n suffices to characterize the sampling distribution of the observed correlation coefficients.

Now suppose, two components with $\rho_1 \neq \rho_2$ and therefore a heterogeneous case is given. As mentioned in the previous sections, such a situation could be modeled by procedures of the general linear model when it is known for each of the k studies which of the two ρ_j is underlying each study. Assume such knowledge is not available to the meta-analyst and membership of the observed correlations to the different components can be said to be unobserved or latent. In this situation, the distributions of the R_i differ only because of the different ρ_j. The ρ_j can now themselves be considered as realizations of a random variable P (large Greek Rho)[6]. The distribution of P is called the *mixing distribution* in the present context and is not yet specified. For the present case of only two different components ρ_1 and ρ_2, the distribution of P is characterized by the two components and the according weights λ_j. The weights give the probability of belonging to the jth component and therefore conform to the usual constraints $\lambda_j \geq 0$ and $\sum_{j=1}^{c} \lambda_j = 1$ when there are c components (in the present example, there are only two).

Under these conditions, the correlation coefficient R_i of interest in study i can be said to have a *conditional density* denoted by $f\left(r_i | P = \rho_j, n\right)$. That is, given the universe effect size parameter ρ_j and the number of participants per study n, the correlation coefficient has a density as given in Equation 3.1 (see page 21). For purposes of illustration, assume that for the two components in the example all studies have equal probability of belonging to one of the components. That is, $\lambda_1 = \lambda_2 = .50$. For this example, the unconditional density of R, the variable representing all observed correlation coefficients r, is given by

$$f(r|n) = .50 \times f(r; P = \rho_1, n) + .50 \times f(r; P = \rho_2, n),$$

and for the more general case of c components the unconditional density is

$$f(r|n) = \sum_{j=1}^{c} \lambda_j \times f(r; P = \rho_j, n).$$

This is also the density of the so-called *mixture distribution* with *kernel* $f(r; P = \rho_j, n)$ for the present case. Of course, the kernel of the mixture distribution depends on the effect size under investigation when mixture models are applied in the context of meta-analysis.

---

[6]Not to be confused with the symbol for probability $\mathcal{P}$ used in the following. In any case, it will also always be clear from the context which symbol is used.

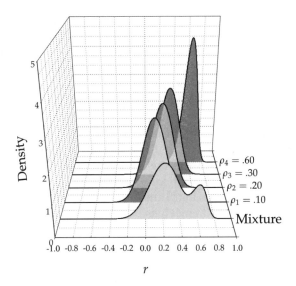

Figure 4.1   Example of a mixture distribution with four components, $n = 50$.

As a further example, consider a situation with $n = 50$ where the distribution of P is uniform on the four points $\rho_1 = .10$, $\rho_2 = .20$, $\rho_3 = .30$, and $\rho_4 = .60$. Then a situation like the one depicted in Figure 4.1 is given.

The four darkly shaded densities are the conditional densities for each of the components, with a fixed n of 50. The resulting mixture distribution filled in light grey is depicted in the front and illustrates the density of R in this situation. In meta-analysis, a number of k correlation coefficients are given which are considered as arising from the mixture density given in Figure 4.1. That is, the mixture distribution is similar in shape to what one would expect as a frequency distribution of k observed correlations in a meta-analysis (given the four components and a fixed n of 50).

As already mentioned, the number of components is usually unknown so that it has to be estimated along with the component weights. Conventionally, this is done by maximum likelihood estimation but details on estimation and algorithms will not be presented here (see Böhning, 2000).

The attractive options offered to the meta-analyst by an application of mixture models are manifold. Mixture models provide a general and flexible framework of conceptualizing as well as statistically modeling the object of interest in meta-analysis, namely the distribution of observed effect size measures. Furthermore, procedures to estimate the number of components as well as their weights are offered. This makes it possible to address the problem of heterogeneity of effect sizes even after attempts to apply linear models with observed variables have been undertaken. When the number of components and their weights are estimated, it is also possible to classify the k studies under investigation by posterior Bayes classification (see Böhning, 2000). The fit of the model applied to effect size data can also be assessed to give an impression of how well the estimated parameters serve to explain heterogeneity.

Of course, the application of mixture models to effect size data does not guarantee that the user can easily interpret the composition of the components suggested. Interpretation of results requires theorizing as well as speculation about the nature of the latent variable. Replications and further research may well be indicated to support or to question interpretation of results from mixture analysis.

Evaluations of an early mixture approach to meta-analytic databases by Thomas (1989b, 1990b) on the basis of Monte Carlo study results were quite encouraging (see Law, 1992). In several situations of Law's study, the procedures proved to be quite accurate with respect to estimation of the weights and the actual values of ρ_j. However, in identifying the proper number of components there seemed to be room for enhancement of the procedures. Given that improved algorithms and procedures have become available in recent years, updated and more in-depth evaluations of the procedures seem to be desirable.

To conclude, as with many statistical techniques newly introduced to a field of application, mixture models involve relatively complicated procedures and estimation is by far not as easily done as with the procedures outlined for the FE and RE models. However, in the case of mixture models there are easy-to-use programs available so that estimation is feasible in practice and therefore not really much more complicated than with all other models (Böhning, Schlattmann, & Lindzey, 1992; Schlattmann, Malzahn, & Böhning, 2003).

4.4   HIERARCHICAL LINEAR MODELS

In addition to the more standard FE and RE models and the more advanced mixture distribution analysis presented in this chapter, there are other models available as well. These will not be treated in detail, but at least a rough idea of their basics of conceptualization will certainly help in gaining a deeper understanding of meta-analysis and potential modeling approaches. This section describes the HLM approach. For a comprehensive overview of models, (estimation) methods, and issues in HLM that also includes meta-analysis as a special case, the reader may consult the book by Raudenbush and Bryk (2002). A more focused and succinct presentation on multilevel models for meta-analysis is given by Hox and de Leeuw (2003), for example.

Hierarchical linear models (HLM) are a very general class of models that may be applied not only in meta-analysis, but in a very large number of situations, all of which are characterized by different levels of data. The lowest level of data in HLM is ordinarily the individual units level, that is, persons in an observational or experimental study, for example (Level 0; see Figure 2.1). As a result of primary analyses, some estimates for parameters of interest are obtained and these are considered to constitute another level of data (Level 1). As conceptually outlined in the previous sections, such estimates are the data for meta-analysis. If modeling of the study parameters (θ_i) is of interest, then we have yet another level of data. This is the case, for example, in mixture modeling as presented in the previous section, where study parameters are thought to arise from a mixing distribution. In sum, it is important to recognize and differentiate levels of data as conceptualized in HLM.

Yet, the situation of meta-analysis is somewhat special from the perspective of HLM. The data of individual units are not available and if they were, one would most probably try to conduct secondary analyses or more specifically a three-level analysis in HLM. The first level of interest in meta-analysis is therefore at the study level and modeling takes place at a second level in order to explain potential heterogeneity of effects (i.e., $\sigma_\Theta^2 \neq 0$), for example.

To explain how the meta-analytical situation is modeled with HLM, consider once more the situation a meta-analyst is confronted with. There are a number of k study results, extracted from the literature on a certain research question, and the task is to summarize them in a theoretically sound and — for the research question — appropriate way. The following equation specifies a model for the individual effect size data of the ith study, that is, a so-called *within-studies* or Level 1 model by

$$T_i = \theta_i + e_i. \tag{4.3}$$

The observed effect size is a realization of T_i for the ith study. It is conceived as the sum of the corresponding universe parameter θ_i and an error component denoted by e_i. The error component represents random fluctuations, whereas the universe parameter θ_i is a constant per study and hence specific for every study i. As an alternative, one might as well assume $\theta_1 = \cdots = \theta_k = \theta$ as is done in FE models. This additional assumption makes the FE model a special case of HLM. The error component is ordinarily assumed to be normally distributed with expected value of zero, that is, $e_i \sim \mathcal{N}(0, v_i)$. The variance of the error component v_i can therefore be identified as error variance of the estimator T and is assumed to be *known* in HLM of meta-analysis. This latter assumption results from the situation given in meta-analysis, where the available data have to be gained from research reports and original data at the individual level are not available.

For the case of correlational data, Equation 4.3 may be stated as $r_i = \rho_i + e_i$. What is already known from the previous chapters is that for correlations as effect sizes, the assumption of a normal distribution for the error component is not tenable for sample sizes less than approximately 500. For this reason, the correlation coefficient is ordinarily transformed into z-space by the Fisher-z transformation for which the assumption of normally distributed errors may be reasonable even for modest sample sizes. In addition, assuming the error variance to be known is also well-founded in z-space since it only depends on n_i and no estimation is needed. Note, however, that v_i would have to be estimated for correlations and the error component variance involves the universe parameter (see Equation 3.6 on page 26). Furthermore, correlations are biased and the assumption $E(e_i) = 0$ is not correct in a strict sense, though the bias may be negligible, especially for ρ_i close to zero (see Chapter 3). The same is true for values resulting from the Fisher-z transformation. As will be shown in later chapters, however, this transformation has some undesirable properties making its use a problematic feature in HLM and meta-analysis in general.

In addition to the Level 1 model, the following Equation is of importance in HLM. It specifies the Level 2 — or *between studies* — model as

$$\theta_i = \gamma_0 + \gamma_1 X_{1i} + \cdots + \gamma_L X_{Li} + u_i. \tag{4.4}$$

The linear model stated in this equation includes a set of L regressors X all of which are considered to be *observed* study characteristics in meta-analysis. Examples for such variables include methodological quality scores and other attributes coded in step 3 of a meta-analysis (see Chapter 2), like intensity or duration of an experimental treatment, type of measurement instruments used, and so forth, which are more of substantive interest. The parameters in the equation are the intercept γ_0 and the weights for the regressors $\gamma_1, \ldots, \gamma_L$. These components of Equation 4.4 represent the explanatory part for the variability in θ_i. Additionally, there is a random effect component for each study denoted by u_i. This random effect represents each study's universe parameter θ_i deviation from the value predicted by the explanatory part of the model. The random effect component is ordinarily assumed to be normally distributed as $U \sim \mathcal{N}(0, \sigma_U^2)$ in HLM. This makes clear that the study parameters θ_i are conceived as realizations of a random variable θ. Due to the fact that the model includes fixed effects (the regressors) and a random effect (u_i) the model is referred to as a mixed model.

Substituting Equation 4.4 in Equation 4.3 results in

$$T_i = \gamma_0 + \sum_l \gamma_l X_{li} + u_i + e_i. \tag{4.5}$$

In this equation it becomes clear how variability of the observed effect size measures T_i is decomposed in HLM. There is variance explained by the study characteristics, there is residual variability due to a random effect, and also variability due to sampling error. HLM is quite an attractive model for meta-analysis that goes beyond the more standard models of fixed and random effects as outlined in Sections 4.1 and 4.2 by incorporating explanatory variables. It includes, however, these more popular models as special cases. The generality of HLM is thus recognized by considering some special cases of Equation 4.5.

First, the FE model without explanatory variables was already shown to be a special case. Second, consider Equation 4.5 without a random effect u_i. This basically is the fixed effects model in meta-analysis with regressors as described by Hedges and Olkin (1985). Note that in such models there is, of course, the supposition of variability in the T_i, but it is assumed to be explained by the regressors so that only variability due to the error component remains. Hence, σ_U^2 is assumed to be zero. One of the important features of HLM is that such assumptions are testable. HLM therefore offers statistical tests in meta-analysis — in this specific case akin to the Q-test — to test critical assumptions. Third, imagine there were no explanatory variables in Equation 4.5, so that

$$T_i = \gamma_0 + u_i + e_i.$$

In this case, the model is equivalent to the RE model as presented in Section 4.2. The intercept γ_0 represents the mean effect size across all studies, the variability of σ_U^2 would correspond to σ_Θ^2, and the variability of e_i is v_i. As alluded to before, tests and the construction of confidence intervals are possible by using HLM to analyze a meta-analytic database.

However, HLM does not include all models presented in this chapter as special cases. An important exception are mixture models. Although both models aim at explaining potential heterogeneity of effect sizes, HLM incorporates observed explanatory variables, whereas in mixture models such variables are considered as latent. Hence, both models should be considered as complementary rather than competing.

Apart from their theoretical attractiveness, how well do HLM perform in comparison to the more simple and much more popular standard FE and RE models? Since different — likelihood-based — estimation algorithms are used in HLM, it can not be taken for granted that they lead to the same or better results as compared to standard models. Available Monte Carlo studies focusing on the standardized mean difference as an effect size show that HLM methods compare quite favorably under some simulated conditions. Van den Noortgate and Onghena (2003) have made such a comparison and showed that HLM lead to very similar results vis-à-vis RE models for parameter estimates, for example. Interestingly, they also pointed to some deficiencies in the testing procedures, for instance, and concluded that HLM procedures do not unequivocally lead to better results in comparison to standard models. Nevertheless, this does not belittle the virtue of model generality of HLM.

Finally, as important extensions of the basic HLM for meta-analysis, there are multivariate models available which enable the meta-analyst to deal with the otherwise difficult situation of multiple effect sizes per study, a case quite often encountered in practice. Another important problem in meta-analysis, namely missing data for regressor variables, can also be handled in a statistically sound way with HLM. All of these extensions are well beyond the scope of interest in the present context. In addition to the book by Raudenbush and Bryk (2002), the interested reader is referred to Kalaian and Raudenbush (1996) for multivariate extensions.

4.5   CLASSES OF SITUATIONS FOR THE APPLICATION OF META-ANALYSIS

The following presentation serves several purposes. It provides a taxonomy of classes of situations that will more clearly elucidate potential forms of distributions in the universe of studies when correlation coefficients are used as effect sizes. Furthermore, the conceptual distinctions to be introduced will also serve to concentrate the subsequent presentation on some of the members of the classes of situations. Finally, the presentation specifies the distributions in the universe of studies of concern in the third part of the book.

Against the background of the models introduced in the previous sections, several distinct situations, henceforth denoted by $\mathfrak{S}$, can be identified. The term *situation* is used throughout the present and the following chapters in a generic sense to indicate distinct classes of universe effect size distributions. In analogy to the presentation of mixture models in Section 4.3, the universe effect sizes of the studies to be aggregated can be regarded as realizations ρ of a random variable P. The expected value of this variable will be denoted by $E(P) = \mu_\rho$ and its variance by σ_ρ^2. Suppose there is a total number of k studies, so that we have $\rho_1, \ldots, \rho_k$. Then the situations to be described in the following two paragraphs will be distinguished by the form and parameters of the distribution of P, that is, the parent or mixing distribution. Two broad types of classes can be differentiated here: discrete and continuous mixing distributions.

Discrete Distributions.   There is one important special case among the discrete distributions that defines the first situation $\mathfrak{S}_1$, namely a one-point distribution with probability mass 1 at the point of a single ρ_0 in $[-1, 1]$. That is,

$$P(\rho) = \begin{cases} 1 & \text{if } \rho = \rho_0, \\ 0 & \text{otherwise} \end{cases}$$

This is the most simple distribution, where the universe of studies is characterized by a *single* constant effect size $\rho = \rho_0$ that gives rise to *all* observed effect sizes. As a consequence, no variation of universe effect sizes is present here (i.e., $\sigma_\rho^2 = 0$), a situation for which the FE model is appropriate. Since all studies are identical with respect to ρ, a *homogeneous* situation is given. To illustrate one instance of $\mathfrak{S}_1$, assume $\rho_0 = .40$. In this situation, the universe parameter for all studies is .40 with probability 1 and the sampling distribution of the observed correlation coefficients r_i is exactly the same for all studies if all studies have the same number of persons n_i, that is, $n_1 = n_2 = \ldots = n_k = n$ (see Figure 4.2).

In the upper panel of Figure 4.2, a graph of the discrete density of the mixing distribution is depicted. The probability mass is concentrated at the point $\rho_0 = .40$ and all other values of the interval from -1 to 1 have zero probability. This universe parameter is underlying all studies so that the density of the observed coefficients is the same for all studies. This density is depicted in the lower panel of Figure 4.2. Here it is assumed that in all studies an n of 50 is given. The conditional density $f(r|P = \rho_0)$ depicted in the lower panel is — although it looks like a normal distribution at first glance — the exact density given by Hotelling (1953) (see page 21). Accordingly, the distribution of the random variable R_i for the observed effect sizes is fully determined by ρ_0 and the number of participants n in the k studies to be aggregated. In effect, one can argue that there is nothing to differentiate on the level of the universe in

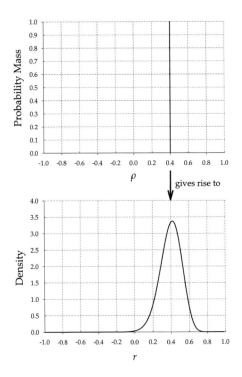

Figure 4.2 Example of $\mathfrak{S}_1$, $\rho_0 = .40$ and $n = 50$.

the upper panel and there is also no need to set sampling distributions apart as long as all the studies have the same n. This is entirely true for a fixed effects model and it will become evident that the differentiations were made for conceptual reasons.

The situation depicted in Figure 4.2 is highly restricted with respect to the distribution of the values in the universe and one might wonder whether $\mathfrak{S}_1$ is relevant at all for the present study. However, as already noted it is actually the most often assumed model in published meta-analyses. Although this assumption is rarely explicitly stated, it is implied by the application of FE methods in meta-analysis as described in Chapter 5. Furthermore, albeit not plausible as a model for most research situations in psychology, there may be cases for which the FE model seems appropriate for theoretical reasons or based on research experience. Even though strict replications — for which the FE model would be a perfectly reasonable model — regrettably are exceptions in the social sciences, there are at least some fields like personnel selection for which a homogeneity "at the level of substantive population parameters" can be assumed on the basis of research experience (Hunter & Schmidt, 2000, p. 276; see also Schmidt et al., 1993).

In the second class of situations with a discrete distribution $\mathfrak{S}_2$, *two* subpopulations are present at the the universe level. They are characterized by two

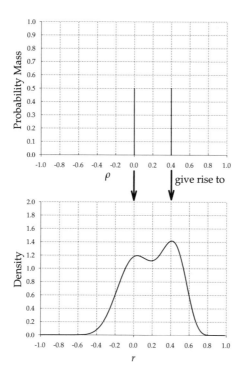

Figure 4.3   Example of $\mathfrak{S}_2$, $\rho_1 = .00$, $\rho_2 = .40$, and $n = 32$.

discrete and distinct values ρ_1 and ρ_2 in $[-1, 1]$. Specifically,

$$
P(\rho) = \begin{cases} .50 & \text{if } \rho = \rho_1, \\ .50 & \text{if } \rho = \rho_2, \\ 0 & \text{otherwise} \end{cases} \tag{4.6}
$$

The variance of P is different from zero in this situation but P can only take on two values. This is clearly a heterogeneous case. The following presentation will exclusively be restricted to instances in which $P(P = \rho_1) = P(P = \rho_2) = .50$, so that $P(P = \rho_1) + P(P = \rho_2) = 1$, of course. Both values ρ_1 and ρ_2 are therefore equally likely to occur. Hence, it is assumed that the k studies to be aggregated are sampled with equal proportions from one of the two classes, respectively. Of course, different cases of discrete two-point distributions with unequal probability masses can easily be imagined but for convenience the presentation will be restricted to the special case indicated. An example for $\mathfrak{S}_2$ with values $\rho_1 = .00$, $\rho_2 = .40$ and $n = 32$ for the studies in both groups is depicted in Figure 4.3.

The upper panel of Figure 4.3 again shows the distribution of the effect sizes in the universe of studies, now with equal probabilities of .50 for both components. The mixture distribution arising from this mixing distribution is depicted in the lower panel of Figure 4.3. Here, it becomes evident how multiple mode or extremely skewed empirical distributions of correlation coefficients may arise in practice. Again, the mixture distribution is derived from the exact density of the correlation coefficient given by Hotelling (1953). Drawing on the notation introduced in Section 4.3, a variable P is given taking on two possible values ρ_1 and ρ_2. It describes the membership of the subgroups in the universe of studies as in Equation 4.6. As usual in mixture distribution analysis, the unconditional density is given by

$$f(r|n) = \mathcal{P}(\rho_1) \times f(r|\rho_1, n) + \mathcal{P}(\rho_2) \times f(r|\rho_2, n)$$

This density is depicted in the lower panel of Figure 4.3 for $n = 32$ in the studies of both classes.

As an interpretation from a substantive viewpoint, the heterogeneous case of $\mathfrak{S}_2$ can be interpreted as corresponding to research situations in which there is an unobserved discrete variable P that moderates the research results. Of course, if one knew about this variable — especially if it could be represented or approximated by observed characteristics of the studies under investigation — efforts to model effect size differences within the framework of HLM or to identify the subgroups by mixture analyses would certainly be indicated. However, it is *not* the aim of the present investigation to evaluate explanatory models[7] in meta-analysis (for a Monte Carlo study on this topic, see Overton, 1998). Instead, it will be assessed how the most often applied methods of meta-analysis perform when data is collected in the heterogeneous situation $\mathfrak{S}_2$. It is argued that it is far from an uncommon situation that a moderator goes unrecognized in a meta-analysis or that estimates of mean effect sizes using the FE model are presented in heterogeneous situations (for a series of examples, see Hunter & Schmidt, 2000).

The question arises in such cases whether an estimate of a mean effect size is sensible at all and if so, how such reported mean effect sizes are to be interpreted. This is not an easy question to answer because it depends on the parameter one intends to estimate and the kind of inference to be made. The presence of heterogeneity per se as in the given situation does not necessarily preclude the reasonable application of fixed effects analysis (Hedges & Vevea, 1998) and the computation of a mean effect size. If one wishes to characterize the study sample with the given characteristics and no further inference is intended, then it is perfectly reasonable to apply fixed effects methods, but the interpretation of test results has to be restricted to studies like those in the sample (see also Section 4.2). The mean effect size that results from applying these procedures is intended to estimate the expected value of the effect size distribution in the universe of studies, just like the grand mean in ANOVA analyses, and has to be interpreted in a similar way in heterogeneous situations. Thus, it

---

[7]Such regression-type models are also known as "moderator analysis" in the social sciences literature. Most often, such regression-type models do not include a random component (u_i) and can therefore be considered to be a special case of the more general HLM for meta-analysis. These special cases are known as "meta-regression" in the medical literature.

has to be conceived as a mean of potentially very different values of universe effect sizes. Any of such mean effect sizes is therefore ambiguous in the sense that vastly different ρ_1 and ρ_2 might yield the same mean effect size. Nevertheless, though ambiguous, a value of .45 for the relationship between attitudes and behavior, for example, can be considered as informative when the additional assumption that the values in the universe of studies are not very different is tenable. Hence, the question whether such values make sense is not a statistical one but has to be answered by the researcher who applies such procedures. Consider yet another example. If interest lies in the predictive validity of a personnel selection procedure in country A in comparison to country B, then one would synthesize all results from applications in these countries separately and make a comparison of estimated mean validities at this level of aggregation. Of course, there may be differences in validities *within* countries, but these are not of interest for the comparison as long as differences within countries occur equally in both groups.

These remarks are definitely not intended to argue in favor of fixed effects analyses or in any way against the application of explanatory models within HLM, for example. Instead, they only illustrate that an estimate of a mean effect size can indeed make sense in heterogeneous situations like $\mathfrak{S}_2$ in the way just described.

Continuous Distributions. The third class of situations $\mathfrak{S}_3$ is characterized by a continuous distribution of the correlation coefficients in the universe of studies. The realizations of P do not take on any restricted or discrete set of values in the universe but are spread over the entire interval from -1 to 1. The kind of spread is described by a continuous density f. The form of this distribution is ordinarily unknown but it is often assumed to be a normal distribution (Lau et al., 1998). There may be several reasons why the normal distribution is chosen. First, lack of prior knowledge about the exact composition of a presumed myriad of influences that determine the effect sizes in a class of research situations, and arguments in analogy to the central limit theorem let the normal distribution appear as a good guess for the distribution at least. Second, especially in situations where effect sizes that can be shown to have a normal sampling distribution are of concern it seems reasonable, again by way of analogy, to assume the same distribution for the universe effect sizes as for its sampling counterpart. Finally, familiarity with and ease of statistical tractability of the normal distribution also contribute to the fact that it is chosen quite often as the distribution of universe effects sizes. Although none of these reasons is essentially compelling there are no cogent alternatives available in such a state of lack of knowledge.

However, for the present case of correlations as effect size data it would be implausible to assume a normal distribution for the universe correlations, due to the fact that the range of these coefficients is bounded by the values -1 and 1. Especially when high absolute values are of particular interest, the normal distribution would provide invalid values larger than 1 or less than -1. The normal distribution has nevertheless been used in simulation studies of meta-analyses to generate values of the universe correlation coefficient (e.g., Overton, 1998).

The question arises which continuous distribution might be considered instead of the normal distribution. Several such distributions were considered as candidates which had to — as was the case with the normal distribution — appear as reasonable for the distribution of the effect sizes in the universe. They also had to conform to the requirement of being supported by the interval $[-1, 1]$. The family of beta distributions was finally considered to be the most sensible choice. It was chosen because its parameters can be adjusted to yield a series of very different distributions on the desired interval. The great flexibility of the beta distribution and the ease of its tractability also made it particularly useful for the present purpose (see also Hedges, 1989). Moreover, the parameters of the beta distribution can be chosen so that the distribution is symmetrical at $\rho = 0$ with an increasing skew for larger values of ρ (in absolute terms). Such distributions resemble the sampling distribution of the correlation coefficients r_i (see Section 7.3). To illustrate, Figure 4.4 depicts a series of beta distributions which show the properties just mentioned.

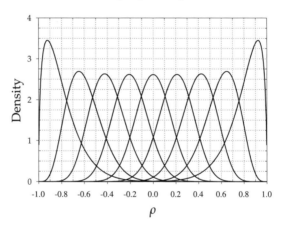

Figure 4.4   Beta-Distributions in $\mathfrak{S}_3$ with varying μ_ρ from $\mu_\rho = -.80$ to $\mu_\rho = .80$ in increments of .20, $\sigma_\rho = .15$ for all distributions.

The parameters of the beta distributions shown in Figure 4.4 were chosen to have different expected values μ_ρ from $-.80$ to $.80$ in increments of $.20$ but with a constant standard deviation of $\sigma_\rho = .15$. As is evident from the distributions given, their forms do at least seem plausible for the given range of ρs.

In the Monte Carlo study to be presented, the family of beta distributions will be considered as the distribution of effect sizes in the universe of studies in $\mathfrak{S}_3$. The following theoretical examinations will often abstract from the specific distributional form but sometimes the beta distribution will be used for illustration purposes.

5

Statistical Approaches to Meta-Analysis

After having outlined the more general characteristics and procedures in the analysis of effect sizes, the present chapter will provide an overview of more specific procedures and formulae proposed in the literature. As introduced in Section 2.2, comprehensive treatments of meta-analysis associated with different author names and at least partially comprising different sets of procedures and formulae are labeled approaches. The approaches of interest in the present context are widespread predominantly in the social sciences and especially in the psychological literature. Furthermore, the focus of this chapter is narrowed down to the statistical details of the approaches. Whereas the models presented in the previous chapter are also well-known in other areas of research, there are some distinctive features of the following approaches that have to be explicated in detail before an empirical evaluation is undertaken.

After considering the presentation of the models, the question arises why sets of procedures and techniques are subject to a comparative evaluation at all. Why not always choose the most proper model and corresponding estimators, considered as optimal from a statistical point of view for a specific research problem? First, the introduction of meta-analysis as a new statistical tool for the social sciences has been associated with proponents from the beginning of its history. This lead to idiosyncrasies of approaches and preferences of authors becoming entrenched in research practice. For example, the correction of correlation coefficients before their aggregation has become almost mandatory in the field of I/O psychology, whereas in the field of educational psychology, these corrections are only considered optional (see also Section 2.2).

Besides historical reasons, properties of the correlation coefficient as an effect size also require specialized techniques. Transformations of the correlation coefficient as presented in Section 3.3 represent such specialized techniques that are not of relevance when a different effect size, like the odds ratio for example, is given in the studies under investigation.

In this book, major approaches for correlations as effect sizes in the field of psychology are evaluated. Further, a series of refinements are introduced for a more comprehensive evaluation of the available procedures. The following sections are structured in correspondence with this classification and all necessary formulae for computation are given. This entails some redundancies in the presentation of formulae but they are nevertheless completely given for reference and to document the procedures as employed in the Monte Carlo study. In addition, the approaches will also be presented in the same order as the meta-analytical steps in the presentation of the FE and RE model, with estimation first and inference thereafter.

As a final remark with respect to the approaches, the reader may wonder why there is also one section that provides computational formulae for the aggregation of d as an effect size when the focus should be on correlations. These procedures are given because one of the aims of the Monte Carlo study is also to evaluate the results of procedures that are based on transformed effect sizes (see Section 3.3). Thus, the common assumption that the transformation of effect sizes — specifically from r to d — is, in essence, inconsequential for the meta-analytical results will be tested. To do this, procedures for the aggregation of transformed effect sizes (i.e., d in the present context) have to be specified. Of course, the prominent set of procedures proposed by Glass et al. (1981) could have been added as another approach. This was not done in order to keep the number of approaches at a manageable level, keep the focus on approaches for correlation coefficients as effect sizes[1], and to maintain comparability to similar examinations of approaches in the literature (e.g., Johnson, Mullen, & Salas, 1995). The question remains which procedures should be used to aggregate the effect sizes d_i when there are many procedures available. Of the major approaches under examination, any could have been chosen for this task. The approach proposed by Hedges and Olkin (1985) presented in the following section was chosen to provide the procedures for this aggregation. The reason for this choice was that it seemed the statistically best founded set. All other major approaches also provide details on the aggregation of d as an effect size so that the choice may also be considered as somewhat arbitrary.

5.1   HEDGES AND OLKIN

The first approach is most comprehensively explicated in Hedges and Olkin (1985) and will be labeled HO in what follows. Technical details of the approach and further procedures proposed by the authors are scattered across a series of articles that may also be consulted for reference (Hedges, 1982a, 1982b, 1982c, 1983a, 1983b, 1991).

The presentation is divided into two subsections. The first one will give details on the aggregation of correlation coefficients and the second one on ag-

---

[1]The approach by Glass et al. (1981) does not provide procedures specifically designed for a meta-analysis of correlations.

gregation procedures for d. It should be noted at the outset that the authors of this approach do *not* explicitly advocate the transformation of r to d when the database only consists of correlation coefficients, as will be the case in the Monte Carlo study in Part III of this book. However, they do provide transformation formulae for effect sizes, so that it is possible to apply their procedures as presented. To distinguish between the r-based and d-based procedures, the symbol HOr represents the r-based and HOd the d-based variant, respectively.

In addition to the d-based approach there is also one refinement in procedures introduced that goes back to the work of Hotelling (1953). To differentiate HOr from this refinement, the latter will conveniently be denoted by HOT.

5.1.1   Procedures for r as Effect Size

In the HOr approach, the observed correlation coefficients are first transformed by using the Fisher-z transformation (see also Section 3.1)

$$z_i = \frac{1}{2} \ln \frac{1 + r_i}{1 - r_i}$$

(Hedges & Olkin, 1985, p. 120, Equation 19; p. 227, Equation 4).

Next, the variances of the transformed effect sizes are given by

$$\hat{\sigma}^2_{z_i} = \frac{1}{n_i - 3} \tag{5.1}$$

(Hedges & Olkin, 1985, p. 227). Note that there is no uncertainty in determining these variances since n_i of every study is given and the parameter estimate does not influence the weights as is the case in approaches not using the Fisher-z transformation.

Estimation of Mean Effect Size.   The mean effect size estimate in z-space is computed by using

$$\bar{z} = \frac{\sum\limits_{i=1}^{k} (n_i - 3) z_i}{\sum\limits_{i=1}^{k} (n_i - 3)}$$

(Hedges & Olkin, 1985, p. 231, Equation 12). This exactly corresponds to the general procedure outlined for the FE model, where the reciprocals of the (estimated) variances of the estimates are used as weights.

Due to the fact that the aim of estimation presumably is never a mean effect size in z-space in practice, the estimate is transformed to an $\bar{r}$ by the inverse Fisher-z transformation

$$\bar{r} = \frac{\exp(2\bar{z}) - 1}{\exp(2\bar{z}) + 1}$$

(Hedges & Olkin, 1985, p. 227, Equation 8). This results in the estimate of the mean effect size in the HOr approach.

Significance of Mean Effect Size.   The next step of testing the mean effect size begins by determining the standard errors for the mean effect size with

$$\hat{\sigma}_{\bar{z}} = \frac{1}{\sqrt{N - 3k}} \tag{5.2}$$

(Hedges & Olkin, 1985, p. 231). In Equation 5.2 and in what follows, N denotes the total number of participants in all studies, that is, $N = \sum_{i=1}^{k} n_i$.

Using the standard error, one can test the null hypothesis of zero mean universe effect sizes by using

$$g = \bar{z}\sqrt{N - 3k} \tag{5.3}$$

(Hedges & Olkin, 1985, p. 231), where g is ordinarily assumed to approximately follow a standard normal distribution.[2]

Approximate lower and upper limits of the confidence interval are constructed by

$$\begin{aligned} z_L &= \bar{z} - g_\alpha \hat{\sigma}_{\bar{z}} \\ z_U &= \bar{z} + g_\alpha \hat{\sigma}_{\bar{z}} \end{aligned} \tag{5.4}$$

and are customarily transformed by the inverse Fisher-z transformation when reporting results.

Homogeneity Test Q.   The test statistic is provided — as described in the context of the FE model — with Fisher-z transformed effect sizes as

$$Q = \sum_{i=1}^{k} (n_i - 3)(z_i - \bar{z})^2 \tag{5.5}$$

(Hedges & Olkin, 1985, p. 235, Equation 16). It is noted that if $\rho_1 = \ldots = \rho_k$ and $N \to \infty$, Q asymptotically follows a χ^2_{k-1}-distribution.

Hotelling's (1953) Adjustment.   In his seminal paper Hotelling (1953) proposed several improvements of Fisher-z with the aim to correct the bias in Z and also to stabilize its variance (see also Section 3.1). Of these, the following correction proposed to be applied to an average z seems to be especially attractive

$$\bar{z}_{\text{Hot}} = \bar{z} - \frac{\tanh \bar{z}}{(2n - 9/2)} \tag{5.6}$$

(Hotelling, 1953, p. 219). In Equation 5.6, n denotes a constant sample size across studies. In practical meta-analyses this will rarely be the case, so that the mean of the sample sizes across studies might be used instead.

One reason why the correction given in Equation 5.6 is used instead of others proposed by Hotelling is the fact that it was constructed to be applied to an average z and therefore perfectly fits into procedures of meta-analysis.

---

[2]To reiterate, the somewhat unusual symbol g is used throughout the text to avoid confusion of standard normal deviates with values of Fisher-z.

Another reason is that with this correction, a reported mean z (or transforms thereof) can be corrected to yield an improved estimate of the mean effect size. An evaluation of this procedure is therefore of relevance for the conduct of meta-analyses as well as their reception. Previous results of a Monte Carlo study conducted by Donner and Rosner (1980) who used the HOT approach as outlined here and compared its performance to HOr, a maximum likelihood estimator and an estimator similar to the one proposed by Hunter and Schmidt (see Section 5.3), suggest a good performance of HOT. They recommended the use of HOT (and the Hunter and Schmidt procedures) for the estimation of μ_ρ in $\mathcal{G}_1$ in comparison to the other approaches they have evaluated, especially when n is small. For a Monte Carlo study on a different modification of the Fisher-z transformation proposed by Hotelling (1953, p. 223), see Paul (1988) (see also Section 3.1).

A significance test can be performed by using the standard error formula given in Equation 5.2 and applying the procedures outlined in Equations 5.3 and 5.4 for the significance test and the construction of confidence limits, respectively.

5.1.2   Procedures for d as Effect Size

As was outlined in Section 3.3, correlation coefficients may also be transformed to d by the following transformation

$$d_i = \frac{2r_i}{\sqrt{\left(1 - r_i^2\right)}}.$$

Of course, there would be no need to apply this transformation if all effect sizes were given as correlation coefficients because procedures to aggregate this type of effect size have just been outlined. In practice, however, it is scarcely the case that all retrieved studies are of the same design and some may be experimental studies, so that only d may be available for some studies. Conventionally, effect sizes are then converted to r or d, depending on convenience. The result is a database that is a mix of converted and non-converted effect sizes r or d. Though not explicitly stated, the usual assumption is that the conversion does not have any influence on the results of the meta-analysis. If this was true, then the application of the following procedures to d values that result from a conversion from r should lead to the same results as the application of the procedures outlined in the previous subsection to the original correlation coefficients r.

Finally, it should be noted that the conversion formula given in the equation above is not the form of effect size that Hedges and Olkin (1985) advocated. Instead, they proposed an unbiased estimator of δ that was already introduced in Section 3.2 and that is considered preferable from a statistical point of view. The conversion formula that represents the d statistic according to Cohen (1988) given here was nevertheless used because of its much more widespread use in the literature and therefore relevance for actual research.

Estimation of Mean Effect Size.   The first step is estimation of the estimate's variance. This variance was already given on page 29 in Equations 3.9 and 3.10 for equal n in all studies, respectively.

The reciprocals of these variance estimates can be taken as weights to yield a mean effect size estimate by

$$\bar{d} = \frac{\sum\limits_{i=1}^{k} d_i/\hat{\sigma}_{d_i}^2}{\sum\limits_{i=1}^{k} 1/\hat{\sigma}_{d_i}^2}$$

(Hedges & Olkin, 1985, p. 111, Equation 6).

Significance of Mean Effect Size.   The null hypothesis test follows the general logic outlined for the FE model and can be accomplished by using

$$g = \frac{\bar{d}}{\hat{\sigma}_{\bar{d}}}$$

as the test statistic with $\hat{\sigma}_{\bar{d}}$ given by

$$\hat{\sigma}_{\bar{d}} = \left(\sum_{i=1}^{k} \frac{1}{\hat{\sigma}_{d_i}^2} \right)^{-\frac{1}{2}}$$

(Hedges & Olkin, 1985, p. 112, Equation 9).

Approximate lower and upper limits of the confidence interval are constructed by the following equations

$$d_L = \bar{d} - g_\alpha \hat{\sigma}_{\bar{d}}$$
$$d_U = \bar{d} + g_\alpha \hat{\sigma}_{\bar{d}}$$

The results for the confidence interval limits are transformed to r by Equation 3.11 when results are reported in Chapter 8 to make them comparable to the estimated limits of the other approaches.

Homogeneity Test Q.   As for the HOr approach, it is also possible to conduct a homogeneity test by using the Q-statistic

$$Q = \sum_{i=1}^{k} \frac{\left(d_i - \bar{d}\right)^2}{\hat{\sigma}_{d_i}^2}$$

(Hedges & Olkin, 1985, p. 123, Equation 25). Again, Q is supposed to asymptotically follow a χ_{k-1}^2-distribution when the null hypothesis is true. It will be particularly interesting to evaluate the performance of this test in comparison to the HOr approach in the Monte Carlo study to be presented. Differences between these tests will reflect potential problems concerning the conversion of effect sizes.

5.2   ROSENTHAL AND RUBIN

The methods proposed by Rosenthal and Rubin (RR) are described in Rosenthal (1978, 1991, 1993) as well as Rosenthal and Rubin (1979, 1982). As will become evident from the following presentation, the procedures are very similar or almost identical to those given for HOr.

Estimation of Mean Effect Size.   In the RR approach, correlations are also transformed via Fisher-z prior to further processing

$$z_i = \frac{1}{2} \ln \frac{1 + r_i}{1 - r_i}$$

(Rosenthal, 1991, p. 21, Equation 2.22).

For aggregation, it is not entirely clear what form of weights should be used. With reference to Snedecor and Cochran (1967), Rosenthal (1993, p. 534) proposes for the weighted aggregation of Fisher-z values to use the degrees of freedom as weights "or any other desired weight". For the current case this would be $n_i - 3$, so that the mean effect size estimate for RR would be *identical* to the one presented for HOr. As an alternative to the degrees of freedom, the sample sizes n_i were chosen as weights but it is noted that these weights are not explicitly recommended by Rosenthal and Rubin. The following computational procedure is given for the mean effect size estimate

$$\bar{z} = \frac{\sum\limits_{i=1}^{k} n_i z_i}{\sum\limits_{i=1}^{k} n_i}$$

(Rosenthal, 1991, p. 74, Equation 4.16; p. 87, Equation 4.32 and 4.33).

In the same way as for the HOr approach, the resulting estimates have to be transformed back to $\bar{r}$ by

$$\bar{r} = \frac{\exp(2\bar{z}) - 1}{\exp(2\bar{z}) + 1}.$$

Significance of Mean Effect Size.   For significance testing of the mean effect size, the following statistic is proposed

$$g_i = r_i \sqrt{n_i}$$

(Rosenthal, 1991, p. 19, Equation 2.18; see also p. 29). That is, correlations are transformed to standard normal deviates which are aggregated subsequently by applying the weights as proposed in the context of estimating the mean effect size

$$g = \frac{\sum\limits_{i=1}^{k} n_i g_i}{\sqrt{\sum\limits_{i=1}^{k} n_i^2}}$$

(Rosenthal, 1991, p. 86, Equation 4.31). Recall again that the authors originally proposed to use the degrees of freedom as weights (i.e., $n_i - 3$).

After having computed the standard normal deviates, approximate lower and upper limits of the confidence interval are constructed by

$$z_L = \bar{z} - g_\alpha \hat{\sigma}_{\bar{z}}$$
$$z_U = \bar{z} + g_\alpha \hat{\sigma}_{\bar{z}}$$

Again, such confidence interval limits are transformed by the inverse Fisher-z transformation when results are reported.

Homogeneity Test Q.   The homogeneity test Q is the same as proposed in the HOr approach and given by

$$Q = \sum_{i=1}^{k} (n_i - 3)(z_i - \bar{z})^2$$

(Rosenthal, 1991, p. 74, Equation 4.15).

5.3   HUNTER AND SCHMIDT

In contrast to the RR approach, the procedures introduced by Hunter and Schmidt (1990) as well as Hunter et al. (1982) offer a series of new features in comparison to HOr. The approach, labeled HS in what follows, is detailed in a very large series of articles of which only a few are referenced (e.g., Burke, 1984; Hunter, Schmidt, & Pearlman, 1982; Schmidt & Hunter, 1977; Schmidt, Hunter, & Pearlman, 1982; Schmidt, Hunter, Pearlman, & Hirsh, 1985). There have also been a series of refinements that are not dealt with in the present context, so the reader is referred to the relevant literature (e.g., Callender & Osburn, 1980; Callender, Osburn, Greener, & Ashworth, 1982; Raju, Burke, Normand, & Langlois, 1991; Schmidt et al., 1993) and also to a recent assessment of the impact of the methods on research and practice in personnel selection (Murphy, 2000), as well as a discussion of the quality of these so-called validity generalization methods from various perspectives (see Murphy, 2003).

The latter two references signify the close connection of this approach with the field of I/O psychology and personnel selection in particular. Though not limited to this field, the main developments and applications have been done in the field of personnel selection. The approach is also often called *validity generalization* which expresses its main characteristics.

First, the preoccupation of applications using the approach with correlation coefficients that represent (predictive) validities of personnel selection methods is indicated. Hence, most of the procedures and their refinements proposed are concerned with correlation coefficients as an effect size measure, but procedures for coefficients from the *d* family have also been proposed (see, e.g., Hunter & Schmidt, 1990). The approach is therefore not limited to correlation coefficients.

Second, one major question in personnel selection is whether validities can be generalized. The designation of *generalizable* is done in a binary fashion, that is, either test validity generalizes or not. Hence, the term *validity generalization* denotes a classification of tests in two groups. This seems to be a quite specific use of the word "generalization" in comparison to more popular ones (see, e.g., Shadish et al., 2002) and might be understood only by considering the legal circumstances in the United States of America (for a review, see Landy, 2003). A common misinterpretation of the term is that it is used to characterize the variability in (predictive) validity coefficients for a certain test across situations. If the validity coefficients are not stable across situations, one might easily use a phrase like "test validity does not generalizes (across situations)" to describe this fact. However, in the HS terminology, a different term is used in this case, namely *situational specificity*. It is considered as quite an important question for practice whether a personnel selection method has to be validated in every new situation of application on the one hand. On the other hand, validities might have been demonstrated to be stable across a series of situations so that it can reasonably be assumed that they hold in a new situation without the need for collecting new evidence. The former case describes a test which is situationally specific, and in the latter case validities are not specific for situations.

Whereas the proponents of this approach have always strongly argued in favor of generalizability and situational non-specificity, and also presented evidence to support these claims in the field of personnel selection (e.g., Schmidt & Hunter, 1998), the approach and its procedures has also been severely criticized (e.g., James et al., 1986; James, Demaree, Mulaik, & Ladd, 1992). Because such issues are not of utmost importance for the statistical quality of the approach, the reader is referred to the book edited by Murphy (2003) for a comprehensive overview.

One further important and distinctive feature of the HS approach is the authors' strong recommendation to correct correlations for various so-called *artifacts* before they are aggregated (for the pros and cons of applying the corrections, see, e.g., Schmidt & Hunter, 1999b). A series of research scenarios to illustrate the relevance of correcting artifacts is given by Schmidt and Hunter (1996). It might be noted, however, that proponents of other approaches have provided similar corrections of effect sizes (e.g., Hedges & Olkin, 1985), though not as elaborate as has been developed within the HS approach. Nevertheless, this feature of the HS approach is not of relevance in the Monte Carlo study of Part III, thus only the basic idea is given here.

One of the potential so-called artifacts which influence the correlation between two variates X and Y is measurement error, another potential artifact is restriction of range[3]. If both artifacts apply in a certain situation, the correlation in the population is attenuated. Let ρ_a be the attenuated correlation and ρ its unattenuated counterpart. Then

$$\rho_a = \rho \times A^{-1}$$

describes the relationship between these two, where A denotes a so-called *artifact multiplier*. The artifact multiplier is considered as a constant which results from one or multiple artifacts operating in a specific situation. For example, if one of the correlated variables has a reliability of $r_{tt} = .81$, then — drawing on results from classical test theory (Lord & Novick, 1968, p. 69) — the artifact multiplier for the correction of unreliability in the predictor is $A = \sqrt{r_{tt}} = .90$. Thus, ρ_a is attenuated by a factor of .90 in this example.

Meta-analysis based on artifact corrected correlations are certainly useful — at least as an addendum to analyses based on uncorrected correlations — to shed light on "what effect size we might expect to find in the best of all possible worlds" (Rosenthal, 1994, p. 240). What the implications and interpretations of meta-analytic results including artifact corrections are, is, however, debatable. In the literature on validity generalization it has been repeatedly argued that analyses based on such a corrected database can lead to estimates of the relationship between *constructs* (e.g., Schmidt & Hunter, 1999b). Unfortunately, this is not the case as Boorsbom and Mellenbergh (2002) have convincingly argued.

In sum, artifact corrections are an important feature of a "full-blown" HS approach but they are neither necessary to evaluate the core of the HS procedures as outlined in the following paragraphs nor do they unequivocally lead to refined interpretations of meta-analytic results as proposed by Hunter and Schmidt. For more details on corrections for artifacts, the reader is again referred to the pertinent literature (Hunter & Schmidt, 1990, 1994a) and also previous Monte Carlo studies that incorporated and partly also evaluated these corrections (e.g., Aguinis & Whitehead, 1997; Callender et al., 1982; Cornwell & Ladd, 1993; Duan & Dunlap, 1997; Law, Schmidt, & Hunter, 1994; Raju, Anselmi, Goodman, & Thomas, 1998).

After these preliminaries, the focus of the following outline of the HS approach will be on the proposed statistical procedures for aggregating the available research database. In the HS terminology, this would be called *bare-bones* meta-analysis.

---

[3]For a more complete list of potential artifacts, see Hunter and Schmidt (1990).

Estimation of Mean Effect Size.   The aggregation of correlation coefficients in the HS approach is done by applying

$$\bar{r} = \frac{\sum\limits_{i=1}^{k} n_i r_i}{\sum\limits_{i=1}^{k} n_i}$$

(Hunter & Schmidt, 1990, p. 100). It can be seen by inspecting this equation that in contrast to the previous approaches HOr and RR, the correlation coefficients are not transformed before the coefficients are aggregated. A negative bias is therefore expected in contrast to the (uncorrected) Fisher-z based approaches which exhibit a positive bias (see Section 3.1). Furthermore, the coefficients are weighted by n_i and not by the optimal weights represented by the reciprocals of the squared standard errors of the estimates. From a statistical point of view, this leads to larger standard errors of the mean effect size estimate and therefore less power in testing.

Significance of Mean Effect Size.   The estimate for the standard error of the mean effect size is a hotly debated issue in the HS approach (cf. Callender & Osburn, 1988; Duan & Dunlap, 1997; Hunter & Schmidt, 1994b; Osburn & Callender, 1992) and has also lead to some confusion when evaluating the HS approach (Johnson, Mullen, & Salas, 1995; Schmidt & Hunter, 1999a). Indeed, confusion may stem from the various forms of computational formulae that have been proposed in the HS approach. This issue is taken up by evaluating the four most prominent versions for the standard error presented in the following formulae.

The formula recommended for estimation of the sampling variance of the mean effect size estimate by (Schmidt et al., 1988; see also Osburn & Callender, 1992; Whitener, 1990) is

$$\hat{\sigma}_{\bar{r}1}^2 = \frac{\left(1 - \bar{r}^2\right)^2}{(N - k)} \tag{5.7}$$

(Osburn & Callender, 1992, p. 115, Equation 3). The index 1 in $\hat{\sigma}_{\bar{r}1}^2$ signifies that it is the first version presented here. When this version of the sampling variance is used in what follows, it will be labeled HS1. This version is supposed to yield the best results when a homogeneous situation like $\mathfrak{S}_1$ is given (Osburn & Callender, 1992).

The second version HS2 is given by

$$\hat{\sigma}_{\bar{r}2}^2 = \frac{\sum\limits_{i=1}^{k} \left(1 - r_i^2\right)^2 / (n_i - 1)}{k^2} \tag{5.8}$$

(Osburn & Callender, 1992, p. 116, Equation 4). Except for very small and divergent sample sizes, HS1 and HS2 are expected to yield similar results (Osburn & Callender, 1992). The terms summed in the numerator of equation 5.8 are essentially the estimated variances of the individual correlations. These estimates in the numerator have attracted considerable attention in the literature on validity generalization (e.g., Callender & Osburn, 1988; Fuller & Hester, 1999; Hunter & Schmidt, 1994b; Osburn & Callender, 1992) and it has been shown that they depend on several characteristics of the research situation like range restriction, for example (Aguinis & Whitehead, 1997), for which it may also be corrected (e.g., Duan & Dunlap, 1997).

The third version for the sampling variance HS3 is given by

$$\hat{\sigma}_{\bar{r}3}^2 = \frac{1}{k}\left(\frac{\left[\sum_{i=1}^{k} n_i\,(r_i - \bar{r})^2\right]}{\sum_{i=1}^{k} n_i}\right) \tag{5.9}$$

(Osburn & Callender, 1992, p. 116, Equation 5; see also Hunter & Schmidt, 1990, p. 100). This version of the sampling variance is supposed to "hold" for the heterogeneous case and should also perform well for the homogeneous case (Osburn & Callender, 1992, p. 116).

The fourth and last form HS4 proposed to estimate the sampling variance is given by

$$\hat{\sigma}_{\bar{r}4}^2 = \frac{(1 - \bar{r}^2)^2}{(N - k)} + \frac{1}{k}\left(\frac{\left[\sum_{i=1}^{k} n_i\,(r_i - \bar{r})^2\right]}{\sum_{i=1}^{k} n_i}\right) - \frac{\sum_{i=1}^{k}(1 - r_i^2)^2 / (n_i - 1)}{k^2}$$

$$= \hat{\sigma}_{\bar{r}1}^2 + \hat{\sigma}_{\bar{r}3}^2 - \hat{\sigma}_{\bar{r}2}^2$$

(Osburn & Callender, 1992, p. 116, Equation 7). It is explicitly recommended for the heterogeneous case (Whitener, 1990).

In principle, each of these formulae discussed in the cited literature can be used for tests and to construct confidence intervals. In the Monte Carlo study presented in Part III all four versions will be evaluated with respect to their performance in the various situations described in Section 4.5 (for an evaluation with real data, see Fuller & Hester, 1999).

The formula to compute a standard normal deviate to test the mean effect size estimates is given for all versions by

$$g = \frac{\bar{r}}{\hat{\sigma}_{\bar{r}}}.$$

As in the previous approaches, the approximate lower and upper limits of a confidence interval are constructed by

$$r_L = \bar{r} - g_\alpha \hat{\sigma}_{\bar{r}}$$
$$r_U = \bar{r} + g_\alpha \hat{\sigma}_{\bar{r}}$$

(Hunter & Schmidt, 1990, p. 121). Both for the test as well as for the construction of the confidence interval $\hat{\sigma}_{\bar{r}}$ stands for one of the four versions of the sampling variance. Although it is well-known that the correlation coefficient is not normally distributed unless n is very large (see Section 3.1), the tests may nevertheless perform as suggested by the formulae, which is due to the central limit theorem. In Chapter 8 the corresponding results on the performance of the four versions will be reported.

Homogeneity Test Q.   A homogeneity test is conducted in the HS approach by using

$$Q = \frac{\sum\limits_{i=1}^{k} (n_i - 1)(r_i - \bar{r})^2}{\left(1 - \bar{r}^2\right)^2}$$

(Hunter & Schmidt, 1990, p. 111). Though not labeled as such in the cited source, in essence, the above equation enables a Q-test as included in the other approaches. The tendency of the proponents of the HS approach to deny situational specificity is expressed by their suggested interpretation of the test results. They state that "if the chi square is not significant, this is strong evidence that there is no true variation across studies, but if it is significant, the variation may still be negligible in magnitude" (Hunter & Schmidt, 1990, p. 112). Thus, the result of the test is taken as informative when in favor of "no true variation", that is, situational specificity, and devalued when indicating heterogeneity.

Estimation of Heterogeneity Variance.   The estimation of heterogeneity variance only makes sense within the framework of a random effects model, hence it might be considered as obvious that the HS approach assumes a RE model. However, the procedures outlined above suggest the HS approach to assume a FE model because estimated heterogeneity variance is not incorporated in estimation and tests. Thus, a somewhat ambiguous case is given here, as is also evidenced by an inconsistent classification of the HS approach with respect to the FE-RE model distinction in the literature (cf. Erez et al., 1996; Field, 2001; Hedges & Olkin, 1985). The ambiguity may result for several reasons. First, the procedures outlined do not fit clearly in one of the model schemes introduced in Chapter 4. Second, the assumption of differences in universe effect sizes and therefore nonzero σ_ρ^2 is an integral part of the HS approach (Hunter & Schmidt, 1990). At the same time the authors of the approach provide procedures and many arguments to reduce observed variability in effect sizes. They do this up to a point where they conclude that universe variance is negligible and generalization of effects (across situations) is therefore possible. Additionally, they have stated that "…applications of our methods have usually used the fixed effects model described in Hedges and Olkin (1985)" (Hunter & Schmidt, 1990, p. 405) on the one hand, and also "The methods described in Hunter et al. (1982), Hunter and Schmidt (1990) […] are RE models" (Hunter & Schmidt, 2000, p. 275) on the other hand. Such statements have certainly contributed to the ambiguity. As a result, it is not entirely clear how the HS approach is to be classified with respect to models in meta-analysis because it is a "hybrid" type in procedures. By taking the answer to the question of whether population correlations are considered as random variables in an approach as an anchor to make the classification, the HS approach qualifies as an RE approach. Thus, it does make sense to estimate heterogeneity variance.

The procedure to estimate heterogeneity variance σ_ρ^2 as proposed in the HS approach is drawing on simply taking the following difference between variance estimators

$$\hat{\sigma}_\rho^2 = \hat{\sigma}_r^2 - \hat{\sigma}_e^2 \qquad (5.10)$$

(Hunter & Schmidt, 1990, p. 106), where $\hat{\sigma}_r^2$ is used to estimate the variance of r and $\hat{\sigma}_e^2$ denotes an estimator for the sampling error variance. The reasoning to arrive at this relationship includes the assumptions that r is an unbiased (and consistent) estimator of ρ, and that an error component e and ρ in the relationship $r = \rho + e$ are independent.[4] None of these assumptions is correct in a strict sense. Nevertheless, violations of the assumptions are ordinarily not considered to be reasons for concern in practical applications of meta-analysis (see, e.g., Hedges, 1988).

A little rearrangement of Equation 5.10 shows that the variance of r is decomposed into two parts. One is the heterogeneity variance σ_ρ^2 and the other is the sampling error variance σ_e^2, where estimators are represented in Equation 5.10. Estimation of heterogeneity variance is done by computation of the following terms

$$S_r^2 = \frac{1}{N} \sum_{i=1}^{k} n_i \left(r_i - \bar{r}\right)^2$$

and

$$\hat{\sigma}_{e1}^2 = \frac{\left(1 - \bar{r}^2\right)^2 k}{N},$$

where the observed variance of correlations S_r^2 is used as an estimator for the variance of r. Again, there have been several estimators proposed for σ_e^2 in the literature, so that $\hat{\sigma}_{e1}^2$ is indexed by 1 to signify that this is a first estimator of σ_e^2. According to Hunter and Schmidt (1990, p. 107), this represents an "almost perfect first approximation". Note that this is the formula used by Johnson, Mullen, and Salas (1995), who conducted one of the first comparison between approaches. They used this estimator in the context of significance testing when conducting their comparative evaluation of the HOr, RR, and HS approaches. Of course, it is the wrong estimator of the variance of $\bar{r}$ as it estimates the expected variance in observed effect sizes due to sampling error. If k had been placed in the denominator as in Equation 5.7, it would have

---

[4]Note the close similarity of this basic equation to those in HLM models, which shows again that many standard meta-analytic models can be considered as special cases of the more general HLM.

been an appropriate estimator of $\sigma_{\bar{r}}^2$ in the HS approach. Thus, the resulting estimated variances were much too large in the Johnson, Mullen, and Salas study. The negative results reported by Johnson, Mullen, and Salas (1995) for the HS approach and the corresponding conclusions are therefore useless (see also Schmidt & Hunter, 1999a).

A second estimator is given as

$$\hat{\sigma}_{e2}^2 = \frac{\left(1 - \bar{r}^2\right)^2}{(N/k) - 1}.$$

According to Hunter and Schmidt (1990, p. 108; see also Hunter & Schmidt, 1994b, p. 171) this is supposed to be "an even better estimate of the sampling error variance", that is, for the estimation of σ_e^2. Hence, only the second estimate was actually used in the Monte Carlo study presented in Part III. For a previous Monte Carlo study on the robustness, bias, and stability of σ_ρ^2, see Oswald and Johnson (1998) who report a negative bias of the estimators presented here under various distributional conditions.

There have been presented further estimators within the framework of the HS approach that claim to be applicable also for databases with dependent correlations and to correct for a potential underestimation in the methods presented above. However, they are not presented here (see Martinussen & Bjørnstad, 1999).

Equation 5.10 can also be regarded as the basic equation of the HS approach since many arguments pertaining to developments of the model rest on this equation. As with many procedures in the HS approach, Equation 5.10 has stimulated much criticism in the literature but arguments will not be repeated here. The interested reader is referred to the pertinent literature (e.g., Osburn & Callender, 1990; Thomas, 1989a, 1990a).

75%-Rule.   A procedure unique to the HS approach is the so-called 75%-rule originally proposed by Schmidt and Hunter (1977). The reasoning behind this rule is as follows. Recall that the development of the HS approach was done with validity coefficients as the main effect size of interest and personnel selection as the most important field of application in mind. Validity coefficients are supposed to be influenced by a series of mainly methodological factors of which many can in principle be corrected for (see Hunter & Schmidt, 1994a). However, in most applications of meta-analysis all the information necessary to correct for the artifactual factors is not available so that variance in observed effect sizes due to uncorrected artifactual influences is always presumed to remain. The component supposed to account for the largest amount of observed variance (S_r^2) is sampling error. If observed variance is larger than expected by sampling error, then there may be variance in effect sizes left to be explained (i.e., $\sigma_\rho^2 \neq 0$). This would represent a challenge to the hypothesis of validity coefficients not being specific to situations, where generalization across situations is a desirable state of affairs for most researchers. Consider in this context the following fraction

$$x = \frac{\hat{\sigma}_{e2}^2}{\hat{\sigma}_{\bar{r}3}^2 k}.$$

An estimator of the sampling error variance in observed effect sizes is given in the numerator and the observed variance in the denominator ($S_r^2 = \hat{\sigma}_{\bar{r}3}^2 k$). Clearly, if there is no artifactual variance in the observed effect sizes left and no explanatory variables exist, observed or unobserved, to explain variability in effect sizes, then this fraction should lead to a value of one because observed variance is totally accounted for by sampling error. As already mentioned, not all artifactual influences can be corrected for, so the following rule of thumb has been proposed

- Homogeneity, if $x \geq 0.75$

- Heterogeneity, if $x < 0.75$

(see e.g., Hunter & Schmidt, 1990, p. 68). That is, effect sizes are considered to be homogeneous, if sampling error accounts for at least 75% of the observed variance in effect sizes, hence the name *75%-rule*.

As examples for previous Monte Carlo studies on this rule, consider Spector and Levine (1987) who found that with small k the ratio as given above is biased (i.e., larger than 1) in homogeneous situations. The ratio quickly increases as the number of k decreases, irrespective of n. In a critique of this article, Callender and Osburn (1988) showed that this result was an artifact stemming from the extremely skewed distribution of the ratio so that the expected value of the distribution of ratios, on which Spector and Levine focused, has an expected value larger than 1 although the individual comparison of estimated error variance and observed variance resulted in no bias.

Like the homogeneity test based on the Q-statistic, the 75%-rule is also taken as indicant in the HS approach of whether there are unsuspected moderators (i.e., explanatory variables) (Hunter & Schmidt, 1990, p. 440). A Monte Carlo investigation on the comparative evaluation of these tests for the detection of heterogeneity will be presented in Part III of this book (see also Cornwell & Ladd, 1993; Koslowsky & Sagie, 1993; Sackett, Harris, & Orr, 1986; Sánchez-Meca & Marín-Martínez, 1997). For a critical appraisal of the rationale of the 75%-rule, the reader is referred to James et al. (1986).

As an addition to the 75%-rule, there has also been proposed a 90%-rule with the same rationale as outlined above, but with a cut-off value of .90 for x that is supposed to be more suitable for Monte Carlo studies in which no artifactual variance exists (Sackett et al., 1986). This rule is also considered in the results to be reported in Chapter 8.

5.4 REFINED APPROACHES

Up to this point, the three main approaches to meta-analysis in the field of psychology have been presented. In the present section, two further sets of procedures will be introduced, one approach for RE models and another that is suitable both in the FE as well as RE model.

5.4.1 DerSimonian-Laird

The most prominent RE approach in psychology draws on the derivations as given by DerSimonian and Laird (1983, 1986) and will be labeled DSL in the present context. Although it is almost identical with the procedures outlined in Section 4.2, computational procedures are given in this section for completeness and reference.

Estimation of Heterogeneity Variance. The heterogeneity variance is presented first for this approach. This is due to the fact that it is used in the estimator of the mean effect size and significance testing, both of which are presented subsequently. Note that the Fisher-z transformation is used in this approach, so that the variance σ_ζ^2 is of interest, that is, the variance of the universe parameters in z-space. The heterogeneity variance is estimated for correlations as effect size data by the moment estimator

$$\hat{\sigma}_\zeta^2 = \frac{Q - (k-1)}{a},$$

where

$$a = \sum_{i=1}^{k} w_i - \left[\sum_{i=1}^{k} w_i^2 \middle/ \sum_{i=1}^{k} w_i \right].$$

This estimator is unbiased by construction. Ordinarily, $\hat{\sigma}_{\zeta+}^2 = \max\{0, \hat{\sigma}_\zeta^2\}$ is used in applications because $\hat{\sigma}_\zeta^2$ may be negative. $\hat{\sigma}_{\zeta+}^2$ can be called a *truncated estimator* which is no longer unbiased (see also Böhning et al., 2002). There have been published several tests of the quality of this estimator and also alternative estimators have been proposed. They will not be dealt with here and the reader is therefore referred to the relevant literature (e.g., Böhning, 2000; Biggerstaff & Tweedie, 1997; Friedman, 2000; Malzahn, 2003; Malzahn, Böhning, & Holling, 2000).

Estimation of Mean Effect Size. The mean effect size is estimated in the DSL approach by a weighted estimator as follows

$$\bar{z} = \frac{\sum_{i=1}^{k} w_i^* z_i}{\sum_{i=1}^{k} w_i^*},$$

where

$$w_i^* = \left(\frac{1}{n_i - 3} + \hat{\sigma}_\zeta^2 \right)^{-1}.$$

Estimation of the mean effect size follows the procedures as outlined within the general framework of the RE model in Section 4.2. As was shown, the procedures of the RE and FE model differ mainly with respect to the weight used in computations. For the present case, note that there is a special case for which the mean effect size as given above for the DSL approach would be *identical* to the one resulting from the application of FE model procedures as specified for the HO*r* approach. This would be the case if the number of persons per study were constant across studies because both parts of the sum to compute the weights (i.e., $(n_i - 3)^{-1}$ and $\hat{\sigma}_\zeta^2$) are the same for all studies to be aggregated. In other words, in situations of equal n for all studies the estimate of the mean effect size of DSL will not differ from HO*r*. This is due to the fact that the variances of the Fisher-z transformed estimators *only* depend on n. When n is equal for all studies, the weights do not differ. However, when n is different for the studies under investigation the weights will mostly differ between HO*r* and DSL estimators and different estimates may result in practical applications. This should be borne in mind since the design of the Monte Carlo study in Part III will be characterized by a constant n for all studies.

Significance of Mean Effect Size.   Significance tests are performed in a usual form by using the test statistic

$$g = \frac{\bar{z}}{\hat{\sigma}_{\bar{z}}}$$

with

$$\hat{\sigma}_{\bar{z}} = \sqrt{\frac{1}{\sum\limits_{i=1}^{k} w_i^*}},$$

so that g can be compared with the critical value from the standard normal distribution for a desired level α.

Approximate lower and upper limits of the confidence interval are constructed by

$$z_L = \bar{z} - g_\alpha \hat{\sigma}_{\bar{z}}$$
$$z_U = \bar{z} + g_\alpha \hat{\sigma}_{\bar{z}}.$$

Again, the confidence limits are customarily transformed into *r*-space subsequently by the inverse Fisher-z transformation.

5.4.2   Olkin and Pratt

The last approaches to be presented are based on an early publication by Olkin and Pratt (1958) on the unbiased estimation of the correlation coefficient (see also Section 3.1), which was applied to the problem posed in meta-analysis by Hedges (1988, 1989; see also Hedges & Olkin, 1985).

Estimation of Mean Effect Size.   The estimation of the mean effect size draws on the UMVU estimator G proposed by Olkin and Pratt (1958) (already given in Equation 3.5 on page 26). The following formula repeats the approximation of G also given in Section 3.1.

$$G_i = r_i \left(1 + \frac{1 - r_i^2}{2(n_i - 1 - 3)} \right).$$

As a first version of an estimator for the mean effect size, consider

$$\overline{G} = \frac{\sum\limits_{i=1}^{k} n_i G_i}{\sum\limits_{i=1}^{k} n_i}.$$

The estimator and further computational procedures using this estimator will be labeled as OP approach.

A second version of the estimator is established in analogy to the procedures in the FE model. To compute the weights for aggregation according to the FE model the variance of this estimator is needed. The variance of G is given by Equation 3.7 on page 27. Defining the weights $w_{i(FE)}$ as usual in the FE approach as $\hat{\sigma}_G^{-2}$, the weighted estimator is given by

$$\overline{G}_{FE} = \frac{\sum\limits_{i=1}^{k} w_{i(FE)} G_i}{\sum\limits_{i=1}^{k} w_{i(FE)}}.$$

Since the weights are constructed as is common in the FE model, this will be labeled the OP-FE approach. Recall that in contrast to z-based approaches and HS, the variance strongly changes across values of ρ. This may have a profound influence on the results when applying this approach. Especially when n is small and estimates thus vary strongly, biased results may emerge. This is due to the facts that, first, the variances are smaller for larger absolute values of ρ (see Figure 3.4) and, second, the (strongly varying) r_i are plugged into Equation 3.7 to obtain estimates of the variance of G. Hence, in applying this procedure high correlations emerging by chance will receive a high weight and an upward bias may result in mean effect size estimation.

A third estimator that draws on the general procedures for the RE model is presented next. It uses weights that incorporate an estimate of heterogeneity variance that is given in the last paragraph for this approach. The weights in the random effects version are designated as $w_{i(RE)}$ and are given by $(\hat{\sigma}_\rho^2 + \hat{\sigma}_G^2)^{-1}$. They are used to estimate $\overline{G}_{RE}$ as follows

$$\overline{G}_{RE} = \frac{\sum\limits_{i=1}^{k} w_{i(RE)} G_i}{\sum\limits_{i=1}^{k} w_{i(RE)}}.$$

This estimator as well as related computational procedures employing it will be labeled the OP-RE approach.

Significance of Mean Effect Size. The test for the OP approach draws on the fact that G has the same asymptotic distribution as r (Olkin & Pratt, 1958; Hedges & Olkin, 1985). As a result, approximately the same standard error is assumed which is estimated by

$$\hat{\sigma}_{\overline{G}} = \frac{1 - \overline{G}^2}{\sqrt{N - k}}. \tag{5.11}$$

The authors also state that G has larger variance than r so that the proposed estimator can be considered to be only an approximation. Interestingly, this approximation has already been used in a Monte Carlo study on combined estimators for the universe correlation by Viana (1982).

For the OP-FE approach, the standard error is computed by

$$\hat{\sigma}_{\overline{G}_{FE}} = \left(\sum_{i=1}^{k} w_{i(FE)} \right)^{-\frac{1}{2}}$$

and correspondingly for the OP-RE approach by

$$\sigma_{\overline{G}_{RE}} = \left(\sum_{i=1}^{k} w_{i(RE)} \right)^{-\frac{1}{2}}.$$

Therefore,

$$g = \frac{\overline{G)}}{\sigma_{\overline{G}}}, \qquad g = \frac{\overline{G}_{FE}}{\sigma_{\overline{G}_{FE}}}, \qquad g = \frac{\overline{G}_{RE}}{\sigma_{\overline{G}_{RE}}}$$

are g-values to be compared with a critical value from the standard normal distribution for the OP, OP-FE and OP-RE approach, respectively.

The confidence limits are constructed by

$$r_L = \overline{G} - g_\alpha \hat{\sigma}_{\overline{G}}$$
$$r_U = \overline{G} + g_\alpha \hat{\sigma}_{\overline{G}}$$

for the OP approach, for the other approaches they are constructed analogously.

Homogeneity Test Q.   For the homogeneity test, only OP-FE is considered. For this approach, the test statistic is computed as

$$Q = \sum_{i=1}^{k} w_i \left(G_i - \overline{G}_{\text{FE}} \right)^2.$$

Estimation of Heterogeneity Variance.   The estimated variance of G is used to estimate the heterogeneity variance by

$$\hat{\sigma}_{\rho}^2 = S_G^2 - \frac{1}{k} \sum_{i=1}^{k} \hat{\sigma}_{\overline{G}_{\text{FE}}}^2 ,$$

where S_G^2 is the observed variance of the Olkin-Pratt estimator

$$S_G^2 = \frac{1}{k} \sum_{i=1}^{k} \left(G_i - \overline{G}_{\text{FE}} \right)^2$$

(Hedges, 1988, p. 198; see also Hedges, 1989, pp. 473–474). Again, estimation is restricted to usage of the estimated variance of the OP-FE approach.

5.5   CONSEQUENCES OF CHOOSING AN APPROACH: DIFFERENT ESTIMATED PARAMETERS

After having outlined statistical details of several approaches, some consequences of choosing between approaches will be examined in this section. The common assumption that the choice of an approach is largely inconsequential for the results is thereby scrutinized and challenged. The treatment will be restricted to a theoretical examination. An empirical Monte Carlo study will be presented in the subsequent Part III of the book to validate some predictions derived from theoretical results presented in the present section and to comparatively evaluate the performance of the procedures as proposed in the approaches.

In the present section, the focus will be kept on the expected value and variance of the mixing distribution as parameters of interest in meta-analysis. It will become evident that one of the main differences between the approaches as outlined in this chapter are differences in the use of effect sizes. That is, whether correlation coefficients are used without any transformations or transformed to Fisher-z or d, respectively. Also, the focus will be laid on $\mathfrak{S}_2$ because, on the one hand, there are no relevant modifications of universe parameters in a homogeneous case ($\mathfrak{S}_1$), and, on the other hand, the general problems outlined in the current section readily generalize to $\mathfrak{S}_3$.

There are two different values ρ_1 and ρ_2 in the universe of studies in $\mathfrak{S}_2$. As specified in Section 4.5, both values have equal probability so that for estimators of the expected value of the mixing distribution based on r values it would be natural to consider the mean of the two universe correlations given by

$$\mu_\rho = \frac{\rho_1 + \rho_2}{2} \tag{5.12}$$

as the parameter to be estimated. This is simply the mean of the two different universe correlations. Of course, it would be reasonable in such a situation not only to estimate a single parameter of the effect size distribution, but — if possible — to identify the classes and estimate ρ_1 and ρ_2 separately in an analysis with HLM, for example. As already stated, an evaluation of such procedures is not the aim of the present context. Instead, the focus will be on an evaluation of the weighted mean effect size as an estimator of the expected value of the mixing distribution.

With regards to the expected value of the mixing distribution, it would intuitively be equally natural to expect the estimators of all approaches to estimate the parameter μ_ρ. To the best of the author's knowledge, all applied meta-analyses on issues of substantive interest which used any of the approaches applying a transformation of the correlation coefficient, seem to presume this. That is, mean effect size estimates are interpreted as if they estimated a mean universe correlation. What this exactly means in applications of meta-analysis is rarely explicated but it seems as if in every case a mean correlation as given in Equation 5.12 was implied. The question to be dealt with here is whether such an interpretation is valid. This is not the case because in contrast to estimators based on r, estimators based on the Fisher-z transformed correlation coefficients (HOr, HOT, RR, DSL) do not estimate a "mean ρ" in the universe of studies but

$$\begin{aligned}
\mu_{\rho z} &= \tanh \mu_\zeta \\
&= \tanh \left(\frac{\zeta_1 + \zeta_2}{2} \right) \\
&= \tanh \left(\frac{\tanh^{-1}(\rho_1) + \tanh^{-1}(\rho_2)}{2} \right).
\end{aligned} \tag{5.13}$$

It is important to note that $\mu_{\rho z}$ is the expected value *in the space of* ρ that results from the inverse Fisher-z transformation of the expected value μ_ζ of ζ. Hence, the computation of the expected value is carried out in z-space and the result is transformed via the inverse Fisher-z transformation to arrive at an expected value of ρ. To distinguish the expected value of ρ for which computations are carried out in r-space (i.e., μ_ρ) from the one for which computations are done in z-space, a double index is used in $\mu_{\rho z}$ to indicate the origin from another space.

As shown in Equation 5.13, for the given case $\mathfrak{S}_2$ the mean of ζ_1 and ζ_2 transformed to a mean ρ using the inverse Fisher-z transformation is $\mu_{\rho z}$. The focal question is: Is it true for all combinations of ρ in $\mathfrak{S}_2$ that $\mu_\rho = \mu_{\rho z}$? If it were true, then a differentiation of μ_ρ and $\mu_{\rho z}$ would not be necessary and the aforementioned interpretation of mean effect size estimates based on Fisher-z transformed correlations would be correct.

As already stated, this is not the case and it is quite important to make this distinction since an inverse Fisher-z transformation of μ_z does *not* lead to μ_ρ in general. Only when $\rho_1 = \rho_2$, that is in the homogeneous case $\mathfrak{S}_1$, does $\mu_\rho = \mu_{\rho z}$ hold. For the case of only two different ρs, Equation 5.13 can equivalently be expressed as

$$\mu_{\rho z} = \frac{\sqrt{1+\rho_1+\rho_2+\rho_1\rho_2} - \sqrt{1-\rho_1-\rho_2+\rho_1\rho_2}}{\sqrt{1+\rho_1+\rho_2+\rho_1\rho_2} + \sqrt{1-\rho_1-\rho_2+\rho_1\rho_2}} \tag{5.14}$$

in terms of the original ρs. This equation makes it clearer that μ_ρ equals $\mu_{\rho z}$ *only* when ρ_1 and ρ_2 are the same. It may be noted that Olkin (1967, p. 116) has already provided an expression similar to the one given above when considering the weighted average of correlation coefficients from two independent populations with a *common* ρ, a problem not exactly the same as in the present context.

It is important for meta-analysis in general that Equation 5.14 is not restricted to $\mathfrak{S}_1$ and can be generalized beyond this restricted situation. In fact, it can be generalized to an arbitrary number of different values ρ. The following result provides such a general expression for which Equation 5.14 can be regarded as a special case.

By induction we have the following

Lemma. *For all c and* $\rho = (\rho_1, \ldots, \rho_c)$ *we have*

(i) $\prod_{j=1}^{c} (1+\rho_j) = \sum_\alpha \rho^\alpha$

(ii) $\prod_{j=1}^{c} (1-\rho_j) = \sum_\alpha (-1)^{|\alpha|} \rho^\alpha$

where summation extends over all $\alpha \in \{0,1\}^c$ *satisfying* $|\alpha| \leq c$.

Note that $\alpha = (\alpha_1, \ldots, \alpha_c)$, $|\alpha| = \sum \alpha_j$, and $\rho^\alpha = \rho_1^{\alpha_1} \times \cdots \times \rho_c^{\alpha_c}$. Now, let $\rho = (\rho_1, \ldots, \rho_c)$ and $z = (z_1, \ldots, z_c)$ be the vector of corresponding Fisher-z values. Define $h(\rho) = \tanh(\bar{z})$. Then

Theorem.

$$h(\rho) = \frac{(\sum_\alpha \rho^\alpha)^{1/c} - (\sum_\alpha (-1)^{|\alpha|} \rho^\alpha)^{1/c}}{(\sum_\alpha \rho^\alpha)^{1/c} + (\sum_\alpha (-1)^{|\alpha|} \rho^\alpha)^{1/c}}$$

Proof.

$$h(\rho) = \frac{\left(\prod_{j=1}^{c} \frac{1+\rho_j}{1-\rho_j}\right)^{1/c} - 1}{\left(\prod_{i=j}^{c} \frac{1+\rho_j}{1-\rho_j}\right)^{1/c} + 1} = \frac{\left(\frac{\prod_{j=1}^{c}(1+\rho_j)}{\prod_{j=1}^{c}(1-\rho_j)}\right)^{1/c} - 1}{\left(\frac{\prod_{j=1}^{c}(1+\rho_j)}{\prod_{j=1}^{c}(1-\rho_j)}\right)^{1/c} + 1}$$

The result then is a consequence of the above given Lemma. □

As an example to see how the generic form of the expression $h(\rho)$ works for cases other than the two-point distribution of focal interest, consider the case of three different ρ. Let $\rho = (\rho_1, \rho_2, \rho_3) = (.10, .50, .90)$. Then $(\sum_\alpha \rho^\alpha)^{1/c}$ and $(\sum_\alpha (-1)^{|\alpha|} \rho^\alpha)^{1/c}$ expand to

$$\left(\sum_\alpha \rho^\alpha\right)^{1/c} = \sqrt[3]{1 + \rho_1 + \rho_2 + \rho_3 + \rho_1\rho_2 + \rho_1\rho_3 + \rho_2\rho_3 + \rho_1\rho_2\rho_3} = \sqrt[3]{a}$$

$$\left(\sum_\alpha (-1)^{|\alpha|} \rho^\alpha\right)^{1/c} = \sqrt[3]{1 - \rho_1 - \rho_2 - \rho_3 + \rho_1\rho_2 + \rho_1\rho_3 + \rho_2\rho_3 - \rho_1\rho_2\rho_3} = \sqrt[3]{b},$$

so that

$$\begin{aligned} h(\rho) &= \frac{\sqrt[3]{a} - \sqrt[3]{b}}{\sqrt[3]{a} + \sqrt[3]{b}} \\ &= \frac{\sqrt[3]{3.135} - \sqrt[3]{0.045}}{\sqrt[3]{3.135} + \sqrt[3]{0.045}} = .61. \end{aligned}$$

The resulting value of $h(\rho) = .61$ shows that the use of Fisher-z yields an overestimation in comparison to $\mu_\rho = .50$, but now for the case of a three-point mixing distribution. As can also be easily recognized, the task to explicitly specify the expression for cases with more than three different ρ becomes rather laborious, though widely available computing resources make it accomplishable.

To give a more comprehensive impression of how large the differences can get in $\mathfrak{S}_2$, a series of differences $\mu_\rho - \mu_{\rho z}$ for varying positive ρ_1 and ρ_2 were computed and are depicted in Figure 5.1. The differences in μ_ρ and $\mu_{\rho z}$ for varying ρ_1 and ρ_2 are portrayed with a surface to enhance visibility of the trends.

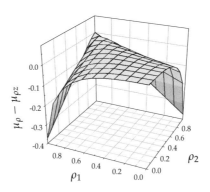

Figure 5.1   Differences between μ_ρ and $\mu_{\rho z}$ by different ρ_1 and ρ_2.

As is evident, μ_ρ is always smaller than $\mu_{\rho z}$ when $\rho_1 \neq \rho_2$. For the homogeneous case there is a ridge from the lower corner of the graph to the upper at a height of zero, indicating the equality of μ_ρ and $\mu_{\rho z}$ for this parameter constellation. With growing differences between the two ρs, differences in expected values become increasingly larger up to values of approximately $-.35$ in extreme cases.

There are several implications of this observation. Most importantly, the estimated parameters in the universe are indeed *different* for the estimators. That is, the Fisher-z transformation introduces a different estimated parameter through its nonlinear transformation of the correlation coefficients in heterogeneous situations. In general, approaches that employ the Fisher-z transformation will always result in higher absolute values for the estimate of the mean effect size in such situations. This may not be entirely clear to every research consumer of meta-analyses when interpreting the results. Second, as a result Fisher-z based estimators may be regarded as inappropriate as estimators of μ_ρ because estimates will necessarily differ from this parameter as illustrated in Figure 5.1. Although the differences as large as the extreme cases depicted in the figure will probably be easily identified in applications of meta-analyses for a two-point mixing distribution in the universe, by simple inspection of the effect size distribution, smaller differences may remain undetected. Furthermore, simple detection of such cases may become quite difficult with discrete mixing distributions with more support points than two, especially when these are fairly close to each other. The application of the Fisher-z transformation will in these cases inflate the mean effect sizes in relation to μ_ρ, a fact that underscores the importance of homogeneity tests.

Another implication of the fact that Fisher-z based procedures estimate $\mu_{\rho z}$ and not μ_ρ in heterogeneous cases is that it would be somewhat unfair to judge the quality of z-based estimators by comparison with μ_ρ, a parameter they are not supposed to estimate. Rather than discarding Fisher-z based estimators from analyses in $\mathbb{S}_2$ to be reported for the Monte Carlo study in Part III, the parameters for comparisons of the estimators correspond to the value they actually estimate, with μ_ρ as the value for estimators based on r and $\mu_{\rho z}$ for estimators based on Fisher-z transformed values. The parameters thus will be chosen to match the parameter to be estimated when reporting results of the Monte Carlo study in Chapter 8.

Basically the same is true for estimators based on d. A similar terminology is used to examine this issue. Hence, the expected value in the space of r that results from transforming an expected value computed in d-space and subsequently transformed into r-space by way of Equation 3.11 will be denoted by $\mu_{\rho d}$. As was shown in Section 3.3, the transformation of r to d has a similar functional form in comparison to the Fisher-z transformation. Accordingly, also a similar form for the difference between μ_ρ and $\mu_{\rho d}$ is expected and indeed will be given as shown in Figure 5.2.

The graph depicted is slightly steeper in the tails of large ρ differences as the transformation suggests. The values for $\mu_{\rho d}$ were computed in analogy to Equation 5.13 with the r to d transformation applied to ρ_1 and ρ_2 and the inverse transformation from d to r applied to the mean δ resulting in $\mu_{\rho d}$. As was the case for the Fisher-z transformation, a ridge for equal values of ρ_1 and ρ_2 indicates the equality of μ_ρ and $\mu_{\rho d}$ in the homogeneous case.

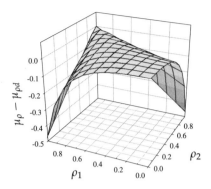

Figure 5.2 Differences between μ_ρ and $\mu_{\rho d}$ by different ρ_1 and ρ_2.

However, values for the mean effect size using HOd are not very close to $\mu_{\rho d}$ as the general logic outlined here would suggest. Actually, they are much closer to μ_ρ. How can this be the case if HOd is assumed to be an estimator of $\mu_{\rho d}$? The reason for this effect lies in the confoundation of the employed weights with δ when aggregating the d values. Holding n constant, the weights are dependent on the parameter δ or estimates thereof, respectively (see Section 3.2). The effect of using these weights is to downweight higher d. Assume equal n in two groups and recall that the weights are the reciprocals of σ_d^2, then by holding n constant, σ_d^2 increases with d, and the weights, being reciprocals of σ_d^2, decrease. The form of the relationship between σ_d^2 and d is illustrated in Figure 5.3.

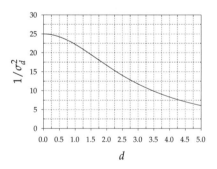

Figure 5.3 Reciprocals of σ_d^2 by d.

In this figure, an n of 100 was assumed for computing the weights and values are depicted up to $d = 5$, which corresponds to $r \approx .93$. There is a clear trend for decreasing weights with increasing d. This leads to mean d values being much closer to, but not exactly at, μ_ρ in comparison to $\mu_{\rho d}$. A selection of varying values for $\mathfrak{S}_2$ is presented in Table 5.1 along with values for μ_ρ, $\mu_{\rho d}$ and a weighted version of $\mu_{\rho d}$. The latter was computed by applying the weights to the population parameters when aggregating.

Table 5.1   Comparison of Theoretical Values of μ_ρ and $\mu_{\rho d}$ in $\mathfrak{S}_2$

ρ_1	ρ_2	μ_ρ	$\mu_{\rho d}$	$\mu_{\rho d}(w)$
.00	.10	.05	.0502	.0501
.00	.20	.10	.1015	.1005
.00	.30	.15	.1553	.1517
.00	.40	.20	.2132	.2039
.00	.50	.25	.2774	.2575
.00	.60	.30	.3511	.3123
.00	.70	.35	.4401	.3675
.00	.80	.40	.5547	.4191
.00	.90	.45	.7183	.4470

Note. The n was fixed at 100 for all values of w. $\mu_{\rho d}(w)$ is the weighted version of $\mu_{\rho d}$.

It is evident by comparison of columns three to five that the weighted version of $\mu_{\rho d}$ leads to results much closer to μ_ρ for larger differences between ρ_1 and ρ_2. Since the weights are not chosen to produce this effect it can be described as somehow incidental. However, recognizing this effect, it would not be reasonable to compare mean effect sizes based on d with an unweighted version of δ, at least not for larger differences. Hence, the results for the bias of the estimators, for example, to be presented in Chapter 8 are based on comparisons between μ_ρ and mean effect size estimates based on d.

Although the estimated parameter for r-based approaches is μ_ρ, there may also arise problems for some approaches in estimating this parameter when the variances of r or G are used in computing the weights for aggregation. The approaches for which this problem may be relevant are OP-FE and to a smaller degree also for OP-RE. The latter also employs estimates of the heterogeneity variance that are equal for all studies to be aggregated so that weights depend on the variance of the estimate to a lesser degree. As already mentioned, this homogenizes the weights.

The problem of this dependency is exacerbated when n is low. In such situations, observed correlation coefficients are highly variable. Theoretically, the variances of estimates are the same in this situation. However, due to the fact that the (highly variable) estimates of the universe parameter (r or G) are used in estimating their variances, the variances also vary strongly and therefore so do the weights. Because there is a relationship of high or low weights occuring along with high or low estimates, a bias in the pooled estimate may be introduced by plugging in the estimates of the variances in the computation of the weights. In cases with (nearly) equal n, it would thus be sensible to estimate the variance of the estimates based on an n-weighted pooled estimate of all effect sizes available. Such a procedure is employed, for example, in the HS approach as outlined in this chapter. Moreover, the problem does not pertain to HS at all for the reciprocals of the variances are not used as weights for the pooled estimate.

In sum, the choice of an approach is often associated with a choice of effect size measures for computations. As shown here, this may have profound effects in heterogeneous situations. The generally applied interpretation of mean effect sizes based on correlation coefficients as estimates of the expected value μ_ρ of the mixing distribution only holds for r-based procedures but not in general for procedures based on transformations of r, since transformations have also to be applied at the level of parameter values (universe of studies).

With regard to the commonly applied Fisher-z transformation this places some remarkable constraints on its usefulness in the context of meta-analysis. It is essential when this transformation is applied for aggregating effect sizes to guarantee the homogeneous case on theoretical or empirical grounds. Otherwise, the mean effect size does not in general estimate what is mostly intended to be estimated, namely μ_ρ. Of course, it may not be an easy task to interpret mean effect sizes in the heterogeneous case without explicitly modeling the situation adequately by application of HLM or mixture modeling, for example. But cases are not uncommon at all in which explanatory variables are not available and the effect size database remains heterogeneous. When using r-based approaches, interpretation of mean effect sizes as estimates of μ_ρ is theoretically founded, whereas for approaches that apply transformations it is not. In the case of HOd, the situation is much more complicated in comparison to HOr because weights also have to be taken into account. To be sure, the expected value μ_ρ is more adequate for most cases in Θ_2 treated here, but it is not the parameter to be estimated by HOd from a theoretical point of view. In the Monte Carlo study in Part III an evaluation of the precision of estimates will be reported with respect to the parameters to be estimated as reported in this section.

5.6   COMPARISONS OF APPROACHES: STATISTICAL PROCEDURES

The approaches presented in previous sections are a set of procedures and techniques that has become very common in the application of meta-analysis in psychology and other social science disciplines. The procedures outlined are not the only available. There are even more *statistical* refinements and procedures to be found in the literature (e.g., Kraemer, 1983; Viana, 1980, 1982) than have been presented and referenced up to this point. However, the focus of the following paragraphs will be laid on the more common procedures and their properties. Furthermore, the comparison largely implies correlation coefficients as effect sizes. Some of the following statements might have to be altered when comparing proposed procedures for other effects sizes.

The first characteristic used to distinguish the approaches is the assumed model. Among the approaches considered, the majority can be classified as FE approaches. This also mirrors current research practice, in that procedures based on the FE model are still the most often applied. Approaches based on RE models have been repeatedly called for (Hunter & Schmidt, 2000; National

Research Council, 1992) but this does not yet seem to have had a profound effect on research practice. The FE approaches are HOr, HOT, RR, HOd, OP, and OP-FE whereas the RE approaches are DSL and OP-RE. Being a hybrid type, the HS approach is not easy to classify for various reasons (see Section 5.3) but it seems to be more of an RE approach in nature. Yet, it is noteworthy that others have classified it as an FE approach (e.g., Erez et al., 1996; Overton, 1998).

The HS approach also stands out somewhat for its peculiar procedures, like the 75%-rule, which is not included in other approaches. A feature of this approach that is very much emphasized by Hunter and Schmidt (1990) are the various techniques to correct for artifacts. These are not of concern in the present context but it should be recognized that an important research problem is addressed with such corrections. Although distinctive in emphasis and elaboration, corrections of effect sizes are not unique to the HS approach (see also Hedges & Olkin, 1985, pp. 131).

With the FE and RE model as outlined in Chapter 4, it is easy to recognize the common structure of the approaches as far as estimation of the mean effect size and inferential procedures are concerned. The commonalities go so far that, in fact, HOr and RR are largely indistinguishable and may not count as different approaches at all. Again, it is recognized that they have been classified as such in previous comparisons (e.g., Johnson, Mullen, & Salas, 1995).

A second characteristic for comparing the statistical procedures of the approaches is the effect size measure used in synthesizing correlation coefficients. As has been outlined in the previous section, important differences exist when transformations of the correlation coefficient are applied. This makes the aggregated effect size measure a quite important characteristic, at least in heterogeneous situations. The r-based approaches are HS, OP, OP-FE, and OP-RE. The Fisher-z-based approaches are HOr, HOT, RR, and DSL, whereas HOd uses another transformation that also leads to a different estimated parameter in the universe of studies in heterogeneous situations. Regarding bias of the estimators it is expected that the approaches may lead to quite accurate results only with respect to the corresponding estimated parameters.

The third characteristic to compare or classify approaches is the weighting scheme. Whereas some approaches use so-called optimal weights (i.e., reciprocals of squared standard errors), others simply use the individual study sample size as weights in their procedures. To classify the approaches with respect to this attribute, recall that the optimal weights for the approaches using the Fisher-z transformation are in essence determined by the sample sizes. This can be seen by inspecting Equation 5.1 on page 57 for HOr, for example. Hence, in these cases, approaches can as well be classified as using n_i as weights because the differences are minuscule in general. As a consequence, almost all of the presented approaches use the sample size as weights, except for OP-FE, OP-RE, and HOd.

Now, does the weighting scheme really make a difference? At least some expectations retrievable in the literature suggest that this is not the case. For example, Huffcutt (2002) clearly states that "it is unlikely that the choice of weighting method has any real influence on the mean effect size [...] estimates" (p. 209). Furthermore, Sánchez-Meca and Marín-Martínez (1998b) have not reported any striking differences between weighting methods for d as an effect size measure on the basis of their Monte Carlo study results. It is nevertheless argued that the weighting does make difference.

The reasons for this are, first, that the empirical evidence available is based on the effect size d, and this is a special case as has already been scrutinized. The theoretical analysis in Section 5.5 has revealed an effect of the weights which might have obscured a profound effect of weighting in the Monte Carlo study by Sánchez-Meca and Marín-Martínez (1998b). Their results may therefore not generalize to the present case of interest, correlation coefficients. Second, recall the dependency of the weights for the UMVU estimator on ρ and also bear in mind the potential variability of effect sizes due to sampling error. Taking further into account that the observed effect sizes have to be plugged into the estimator for the standard error reveals that using such weights will lead to an upward bias in mean effect size estimators. This is exactly what can be expected for the estimators in OP-FE and OP-RE.

Hence, the weighting scheme *is* an important classification aspect for approaches, at least in cases for which a similar plug-in procedure is used as in OP-FE and OP-RE. How, then, can these be the statistically optimal weights? The reason is simply that to prove the optimum properties of this weighting scheme, one has to assume that the weights are *known*. Because this is almost never the case, one has to use the plug-in procedure which causes the problem and makes the weighting scheme suboptimal. For a theoretical analysis and empirical demonstration of the considerable effect of using plug-in estimates in the context of estimating heterogeneity variance, see Böhning et al. (2002).

Of the approaches introduced, HOd is somewhat special. It is hardly comparable to the other approaches because in the way it is used in the present examination it would almost never be used in practice (i.e., a database consisting only of r would ordinarily not be converted to d). Remember that the approach was introduced to show how correlation coefficients converted to d would be aggregated. It is intended to enable a test of the common assumption that the well-known conversion of r to d does not have an effect on the results of meta-analysis.

There are some empirical comparisons of meta-analytical approaches in the literature available to date. One quite influential early comparison that has raised serious doubts on the quality of the HS approach was conducted by Johnson, Mullen, and Salas (1995). They compared the approaches HOd, RR, and HS by analyzing a small database which they also transformed by adding constant values, for example. Hence, they have not conducted a Monte Carlo study but analyzed a specific dataset and its transformations to examine the quality of the approaches. Unfortunately, there are several problems with this comparison. First, they stated with reference to the techniques proposed by Hedges and Olkin (1985) that "...study outcomes usually are converted into standard deviation units..." (Johnson, Mullen, & Salas, 1995, p. 95). Hedges and Olkin actually do not advocate transformations of r to d as a standard technique applied to correlation coefficients. Instead, they provide elaborate procedures for the analysis of correlation coefficients, as can be seen in Section 5.1. Although sometimes approaches as presented in this book are associated with certain effect sizes, it is not true for any of the approaches outlined that they can *only* be applied to a certain kind of effect size family. Admittedly, the HS approach has a main focus on correlations, but is not limited to the analysis of this effect size measure. It is therefore important to recognize that the present examination evaluates the procedures of the approaches that are proposed for correlational data and may not generalize to other procedures proposed. Second, the formula for standard error in the HS approach as used by the authors (Johnson, Mullen, & Salas, 1995, Formula 12, p. 97) is wrong and leads to strong overestimates of the standard error of the mean effect size (see also Schmidt & Hunter, 1999a). Third, Johnson et al. tried to vary certain "parameters of the databases [. . .] while attempting to hold all other variables constant. . . " (Johnson, Mullen, & Salas, 1995, p. 99). Unfortunately, there was a (linear) relationship in the database between r and n ($r = .158$) that influenced the results of their comparisons between the approaches. In sum, their comparison is only of limited value for a comparative evaluation of the approaches under consideration.

Despite these problems, the Johnson et al. study may have had a profound effect on other researchers and may have led them to abstain from using the HS approach. Others even tried to "explain" the divergence from conventional statistical expectations that was reported in the Johnson et al. study for the HS approach (e.g., Erez et al., 1996, p. 283). Nevertheless, the Johnson et al. study had at least the beneficial effect of drawing the attention of researchers to the potentially diverging approaches in psychology.

Another more recent comparison of approaches focusing on correlation coefficients as effect sizes was done by Field (2001). This study was not plagued with the problems of the Johnson et al. study and developed this work by conducting a Monte Carlo study. Field (2001) reported a series of results on the estimation of the mean effect size, significance test for the mean effect size, and homogeneity test performance. In separate Monte Carlo studies the performance of the approaches in homogeneous as well as heterogeneous situations was examined. Interestingly, his results indicated a bias in estimating the mean effect size in heterogeneous situations being very much larger for the approach using the Fisher-z transformation (DSL) in comparison to the HS approach. In contrast, such effects were not observed in homogeneous situations (here, HOr was compared to HS). A clear theoretical rationale for this effect was, however, lacking.[5] For more detailed results the reader might wish to consult the original article. Overall, the reported results seemed to favor the

---

[5]It might be noted that Hunter et al. (1982, p. 42) already pointed to the excess bias resulting from the Fisher-z transformation. In later work (Hunter & Schmidt, 1990, pp. 216–217), they repeated this observation but still without providing an elaborate statistical argument. They only pointed to an (still) unpublished paper which was referenced by Field (2001) to support his prediction. Hence, an elaborate theoretical argumentation as given in the previous chapter has not yet been available.

HS approach over other approaches mainly on the grounds of larger bias in heterogeneous situations for Fisher-z based approaches.

A further comparison, namely of the DSL and HS approach, was conducted by Hall and Brannick (2002). Although large parts of the study focused on artifact corrections, which are not of interest here, they reported some results worth noting in the present context. In a comparison between the approaches based on Monte Carlo study data, a similar pattern of results with respect to the bias of the mean effect size estimators was observed as in the Field (2001) study. That is, in homogeneous situations both approaches lead to approximately equal results and in heterogeneous situations the results differed. Differences grew bigger the larger the variance of universe parameters was, with DSL leading to overestimates. This result is perfectly compatible with expectations on the basis of the theoretical analyses of the estimators' properties outlined in this chapter. Hall and Brannick (2002), however, attributed this observation to some peculiarity of their Monte Carlo procedure. Most interesting for the present examination of approaches are reanalyses of four published meta-analyses. The authors reported higher estimates of the DSL approach in comparison to the HS approach on the basis of the four real datasets, though in one case the estimates were virtually identical. The maximum difference was between a value of .237 (HS) and .286 (DSL) for one study. This difference is remarkable and might have been even bigger if the mean effect size level and the variance of universe correlations would have been larger. These additional results in the Hall and Brannick (2002) study point to the fact that the theoretical analyses of this chapter are not only statistical gimmicks but can have a real impact. For further theoretical and empirical comparisons of approaches with different models and effect size measures, the reader is referred to the pertinent literature (e.g., Overton, 1998; Brockwell & Gordon, 2001).

To summarize, the approaches under examination have many attributes in common as can be recognized from the perspective of the general frameworks of meta-analysis. HOr and RR, for example, are different in a minor detail at best. Nevertheless, important differences between approaches lie in the underlying model (FE vs. RE), the effect size measures used in aggregation (r vs. Fisher-z) and also in the weights employed in aggregation. Previous comparisons of approaches — most of which were based on Monte Carlo study results — show convergence as well as differences in results, where differences can at least partly be attributed to properties of the estimators as outlined in this chapter.

6

Summary of Statistical Part

In this part of the book, the statistical foundations of several approaches to meta-analysis of correlations have been outlined. The effect size database of interest in the present context was restricted to two families, the correlation coefficient and standardized mean effect sizes with a strong focus on the former. They still represent the most often used effect sizes in the social sciences and properties of estimators for both were therefore examined.

For the correlation coefficient as an effect size, the sample correlation coefficient and its properties were examined. The approximation introduced by Fisher (1921) was presented as a transformation of the correlation coefficient that shows a much more rapid convergence to a normal distribution in comparison to the correlation coefficient. Both estimators are biased and approximate formulae suggest a larger bias in absolute value for Fisher-z. However, the approximate variance of Fisher-z is independent of the population parameter to be estimated whereas the approximate variance of the correlation coefficient is not. For the latter, illustrations of this dependency were given. In addition to the common estimators r and Fisher-z, the unique minimum variance unbiased estimator introduced by Olkin and Pratt (1958) and its variance were presented. The variance was also shown to be dependent on the population parameter to be estimated.

From the d family, three estimators were presented of which d is considered the most important in the present context. It is, however, not the one which best attains desirable statistical properties like unbiasedness. The variance of d was also shown to depend on the the population parameter it is supposed to estimate, but the relationship is very different from the one presented for the correlation coefficients.

A brief examination of the conversion of the effect sizes presented along with revised formulae was given. It was concluded that available formulae may not hold for the nonnull case. The Monte Carlo study in Part III will provide evidence on this subject.

The methods of aggregating effect sizes were first presented in a general framework by specifying the statistical models of fixed effects and random effects. One important difference between the models lies in their assumptions about the distribution of effect sizes in the universe of studies. In the fixed effects model, homogeneity of all effect sizes or subgroups of effect sizes is often assumed. The fixed effects case represents a common assumption made in most applications of meta-analysis in practice but was criticized on various grounds (e.g., Erez et al., 1996; Hunter & Schmidt, 2000; National Research Council, 1992). It was pointed out in this context, that in the presence of heterogeneity application of the fixed effects model demands careful interpretation of the mean effect size. It has to be interpreted like a grand mean in ANOVA and may in some cases be ambiguous. This does not necessarily invalidate statements made on the basis of results from applying fixed effects models in heterogeneous situations. Whether ambiguity is indeed a problem, is a question to be answered by the researcher applying the models in a specific research situation.

In the random effects model, in contrast, heterogeneity of effect sizes is always an integral part of estimation as well as inference (see Hedges & Vevea, 1998). For both models, desired inference is different. In the fixed effects model, interpretation is restricted to studies like those available. In the random effects model, generalization of estimated characteristics of the effect size distribution leads to generalizations of effects to studies different from those examined but from the same research domain (Hedges, 1994b; Hedges & Vevea, 1998). As was pointed out, one important task for a researcher who wants to apply meta-analysis, is to carefully consider the model of the situation of interest and the desired inferences.

Additionally, the principles and concepts of applying mixture models to meta-analysis were outlined. It was pointed out that they provide a very flexible framework for the research situation of meta-analysis and were used to describe the research situations $\mathfrak{S}_1$ to $\mathfrak{S}_3$ that cover many important situations and will be used in Part III in the Monte Carlo study to systematize the design and presentation of results.

As another model class, hierarchical linear models were briefly introduced. These models are often used to assess the effect of observed explanatory variables on the effect size variability. It was shown that these models are very general and most other models can be regarded as special cases of hierarchical linear models.

The specific procedures of the various approaches to meta-analysis were outlined in detail in the subsequent chapter. As the major meta-analytical approaches for correlations as effect sizes, the approaches proposed by Hedges and Olkin (1985), Rosenthal and Rubin (1979), as well as Hunter and Schmidt (1990) were identified. In addition to these approaches, refinements were also presented that draw on the works of Hotelling (1953), Olkin and Pratt (1958), as well as DerSimonian and Laird (1986). All approaches are presented for application to correlations as effect sizes. In addition to these approaches, the procedures for d as an effect size presented by Hedges and Olkin (1985) were also outlined. Distinctions were drawn between the approaches with respect to the effect size to be aggregated (r, Fisher-z or d) and they were categorized according to the general framework introduced. The major approaches as well as OP, HOT, and OP-FE were identified as fixed effects approaches whereas DSL and OP-RE are random effects approaches. HS seemed to be of a hybrid type. Two major approaches, HOr and RR, are indistinguishable and may therefore not count as different approaches at all.

In the penultimate section of the last chapter, it was shown that the choice of an approach is at least consequential in situations $\mathfrak{S}_2$ and $\mathfrak{S}_3$, where heterogeneous situations are given. Fisher-z-based (HOr, RR, HOT, and DSL) and d-based (HOd) approaches were shown to estimate different parameters in comparison to r-based approaches. Since the expected value μ_ρ of the effect size distribution is considered to be the parameter of main interest in meta-analysis of correlations, cautions were raised about the application of Fisher-z based approaches in heterogeneous situations. Furthermore, the use of variances of the estimates in computing weights when the variances are confounded with the population parameters was pointed out to be a potential problem for the pooled estimators of the approaches. For HOd, the effect of applying such a weighting scheme is that the estimates are expected to be closer to μ_ρ than to the theoretically derived parameter without employing weights. In the case of OP-FE and OP-RE problems in estimation may arise. However, the r-based approaches retain the interpretation of the mean effect size estimate for μ_ρ in all situations because n is used in weighting the effect sizes and are therefore preferable in these situations from a theoretical point of view.

Finally, a comparison of approaches was presented that highlighted the major statistical attributes to classify the approaches as presented beforehand. These were the distinction between random versus fixed effects models, the use of transformed correlations, and the weighting scheme. Additionally, a brief overview of previous comparisons of meta-analytic approaches for correlations as effect sizes was presented.

In the following chapters, the design and results for a Monte Carlo study conducted for evaluation of the approaches will be presented. The situations introduced in the present chapter will be incorporated in the design and performance of the approaches with respect to the various estimates they propose will be evaluated.

Part III

Evaluation of Statistical Approaches:
A Monte-Carlo Study

7

Aims, Design, and Implementation

In this part of the book, a comprehensive Monte Carlo study for the comparative evaluation of the statistical approaches will be presented. First, the aims and general procedure will be outlined. Procedural details will be given to enable an assessment of the precision of the study and justify the validity of the results to be presented in Chapter 8. Next, the parameters characterizing the universe from which the effect sizes are drawn will be presented and related to the situations of fixed and random effects as outlined in Chapter 4. This will define the scope of interpretation of the results and shed light on viable generalizations of the results. Finally, technical details on the generation of correlation coefficients in Monte Carlo studies in general are discussed and some specifications for software programming to conduct the Monte Carlo study are given.

Monte Carlo studies are designed to investigate the properties of statistical procedures, techniques, or estimators in particular by conducting a specified number of replications of a statistical procedure when an analytical treatment of the problem is not feasible. In a sense, they can be regarded as experiments conducted to study the behavior of statistics of interests subject to the variation of a set of parameters within the framework of a prespecified model. Accordingly, the design of a Monte Carlo study delimits the scope of interpretation of the results (see Skrondal, 2000). If interest lies, for example, in the performance or robustness of a parameter's estimator, it can only be evaluated with respect to the specific other parameters of the model that have been varied or held constant in a Monte Carlo study. Hence, in the following sections the design of the Monte Carlo study conducted to compare the computational approaches of meta-analysis as outlined in the previous chapters will be described in detail.

7.1 GENERAL AIMS AND PROCEDURE

The main aim of the Monte Carlo study is to *compare* as well as evaluate the various statistical approaches of meta-analysis as presented in Chapter 5. One of the most important questions to be answered based on the results is whether and when the choice of an approach of meta-analysis makes a difference. In the present Monte Carlo study, the effect sizes under scrutiny will be confined to correlations. Only the d-statistic will be of concern insofar as correlations can be transformed to d and the meta-analysis be based on these transformed effect sizes. The correlation coefficient was chosen as an effect size measure to compare the meta-analytical approaches for several reasons. First, it is one of the most often reported effect sizes indices in the empirical literature in the social sciences and psychology in particular. It therefore represents one of the most representative effect size measures in these scientific areas. Second, all the approaches presented in Chapter 5 explicitly propose procedures to aggregate this effect size measure. Third, its various forms can be easily accommodated to express the size of an effect in a wide variety of research situations and also for results from focused hypothesis tests, a fact that lead several researchers to strongly advocate its use (e.g., Rosenthal & DiMatteo, 2001; Rosenthal et al., 2000). The empirical comparison of meta-analytic approaches is thus limited to a research database consisting of correlations.

If present, differences between the results of these approaches will be highlighted and compared to expectations from an analytical point of view. Comparisons of empirical results with the latter type of expectations are also of interest insofar as many of the theoretical results presented and referenced in Part II hold only asymptotically. Thus, it will be investigated whether the application of the proposed procedures yields sufficiently accurate results so that their use is justified under restricted conditions (see Hedges, 1994b). The restriction of conditions predominantly refers to the number of studies to be aggregated and the number of persons in the studies. It is important to recognize and differentiate these two types of asymptotics. On the one hand, holding everything equal, results may be expected to converge asymptotically to some parameter when n grows larger. On the other hand, this might be the case — ceteris paribus — when the number of studies in a meta-analysis grows. It may well be the case that for some estimator of interest, only one of these types is relevant and a growing n or k does not have an effect on the results.

The approaches will be compared with respect to the statistical properties of the proposed procedures for the various meta-analytical tasks. The tasks are estimation, testing, and confidence intervals for the mean effect size, homogeneity tests, and estimating heterogeneity variance. The presentation of the results is structured correspondingly. Special attention will be payed to indices that were developed in individual approaches, like the 75%-rule of the HS-approach), and their usefulness as meta-analytical tools will be assessed in a separate subsection.

Some computational details and specifications on the indices used to make comparisons (e.g., for the mean squared error) will be reported when they are needed, that is, in the relevant sections in Chapter 8. It will then be pointed out which of the respective indices performs best with regards to conventional statistical criteria, like the mean squared error of the point estimators, for example. A possible and hardly surprising result might be that there is no single approach to meta-analysis performing best under all conditions defined by the design. Instead, a newly assembled collection of procedures from various approaches might emerge as a set of meta-analytical techniques performing best under the examined conditions. If the performance of the indices varies strongly in dependence on parameters varied in the Monte Carlo design, the parameter configurations under which single indices perform best will be highlighted. This can be useful information for future meta-analyses to condition their choice of an index on the specific circumstances (e.g., mean n of the studies to be integrated and number of studies k).

The comparison of approaches will be conducted under various parameter configurations that correspond to different models. As mentioned in Section 4.1, the most often applied approaches in meta-analyses on research topics in psychology assume a fixed effects model. This has been severely criticized for various reasons and calls have been made for an increased use of the random effects model (e.g., National Research Council, 1992). Nevertheless, the research practice in meta-analysis has not yet followed this call (for examples, see Hunter & Schmidt, 2000). Hence, a comparative evaluation of the effects of applying the fixed effects procedures of the approaches in heterogeneous cases is of vital interest. This is the case for at least two reasons. First, it will be possible to point out situations in which flaws in the conclusions of such meta-analyses are likely to prevail. Second, it will be possible to assess the tenability of conclusions of such meta-analyses and the potential need for reevaluations. Comparisons of meta-analytical approaches that pursue a similar goal have already been conducted (e.g., Johnson, Mullen, & Salas, 1995), but there are some shortcomings in procedure and design associated with these comparisons that make it reasonable to reinvestigate this topic (see also Section 5.6). Furthermore, most comparisons of procedures referenced in Section 5 have focused on single indices and used different procedures in their simulation studies that complicates and exacerbates the comparison of approaches. The present effort therefore also aims at comparing the approaches within a single simulation framework and to evaluate the approaches *comprehensively* in procedures and design.

7.2   GENERAL EXPECTATIONS AND PREDICTIONS FOR THE RESULTS

On the basis of the many properties of estimators and procedures highlighted in Part II, some more specific predictions for the results can be made. These will be highlighted in the following paragraphs.

Estimation of the Mean Effect Size.   The bias of the correlation coefficient and Fisher-z transformed correlations is a very well investigated topic in the statistical literature. At least since Hotelling's seminal paper in the 1950s, the biases are well-known and can count as *theoretically* well understood. Nevertheless, there is a plethora of articles investigating the comparative biases of the r and Fisher-z transformed r in simulation studies (e.g., Corey et al., 1998; Donner & Rosner, 1980; Field, 2001; Silver & Dunlap, 1987). Adding yet one more Monte Carlo study to demonstrate the biases seems like flogging a dead horse.

Hence, it is expected on the basis of theoretical results outlined in the previous part that in a *homogeneous* situation ($\mathfrak{S}_1$) the approaches, as categorized by type of effect size measure and using n as weights, show slightly different biases in opposite directions, especially when n is small. Corresponding results will only add to the credibility of the simulation procedure and represent nothing new. Yet, additional estimators are included in this Monte Carlo study which have not been investigated as thoroughly as HOr and HS, for example. It is expected that OP will be unbiased and HOT will show a similar behavior. These predictions are expected to hold across all values of n and k in the Monte Carlo design. OP-FE and OP-RE are expected to show positive biases due to the weighting scheme used (see Section 5.6). In comparison, OP-FE will show a larger bias than OP-RE because incorporation of (estimated) heterogeneity variance will level differences in weights in the latter approach. The size of the biases is not easy to predict and will emerge as a result of the Monte Carlo study. Biases for these two approaches will also diminish when n grows larger because of decreasing variability of observed effect sizes for larger n. The bias will stay unchanged across values of k, which will be true for all approaches since biases are not expected to vanish or be exacerbated because more (biased) data points are added. Predictions for HOd can hardly be made due to its strange behavior (see Section 5.5). As a consequence, there are also no good reasons to expect HOd to show similar results as any of the other approaches.

In a *heterogeneous* situation (i.e., $\mathfrak{S}_2$ and $\mathfrak{S}_3$) predictions are quite different. Here, Fisher-z based approaches estimate $\mu_{\rho z}$ and not μ_ρ. Only with respect to the parameter which is estimated, approaches are expected to perform well. It should nevertheless be borne in mind that Fisher-z based approaches have a *positive* bias with respect to μ_ρ the larger the heterogeneity variance. The reasons for this are expounded in Section 5.5. Again, OP is expected to perform uniformly best in the heterogeneous situations because of its UMVU qualities. HOT is now expected to estimate a different parameter in comparison to OP due to its Fisher-z basis. OP-FE and OP-RE are expected to retain their bias in general, but it is again predicted that OP-RE will show smaller bias the larger the heterogeneity variance. This interesting effect is expected because with growing heterogeneity variance the weights will be dominated by the estimates of the heterogeneity variance. Again, it is unclear how HOd will perform.

Overall, OP is expected to perform uniformly best. In some of the situations under investigation other approaches might nevertheless show acceptable performance with the standards of precision in the social sciences in mind.

With respect to another aspect of estimating the mean effect size, namely the estimators' mean squared error, predictions are not easy to make. Of course, there will be a tendency of estimators with large bias to also show large mean squared errors, but it is not necessarily the case that estimators with small bias will perform well with respect to this criterion. These facts notwithstanding, OP is again expected to perform best in relation to all other estimators.

Significance Tests.   With respect to tests of the mean effect size, it is important to discriminate between two cases: when $\mu_\rho = 0$ and when it does not. Of course, the null hypothesis need not be H_0: $\mu_\rho = 0$, any other value of interest might be inserted instead of 0, but this traditional "nil hypothesis" will be focused on here. For the purpose of testing, there is a large set of candidates included in this Monte Carlo study.

Predictions concerning Type I error rates will first be explicated, that is, the performance of the approaches when the null hypothesis is true will be examined. In a *homogeneous* situation $\mathfrak{S}_1$, all approaches are expected to retain an a priori chosen α level to an acceptable degree, except for cases in which small n is coupled with small k and a disadvantageous weighting scheme is used, as for OP-FE, OP-RE, and HOd. This is due to the facts that all testing procedures follow the same basic rationale on the one hand, and deleterious effects of some weighting schemes as already outlined on the other. When the null hypothesis is not true, the power of the approaches' procedures is concerned. Power will be higher for all approaches the larger the effect, that is, the higher the absolute value of μ_ρ. With regards to power it is important to recognize both n and k being relevant for the performance. One of the reasons to apply meta-analysis at all is because of its suspected high power due to aggregating study results (i.e., increasing k and total n). This is indeed a valid suspicion as Cohn and Becker (2003) as well as Hedges and Pigott (2001), for example, have demonstrated. However, in these papers it was also demonstrated that power is not always high in meta-analysis. For example, adding studies with small sample sizes may decrease power (Hedges & Pigott, 2001) for RE approaches. Hence, this effect is expected to occur in the results of the simulation study. Otherwise, FE approaches will tend to reject the null hypothesis more often than the more conservative RE approaches (see Hedges & Vevea, 1998, for example). Because OP is expected to be most precise in estimation, this is expected to generally translate to better performance in testing as compared to other FE approaches.

In *heterogeneous* situations the RE approaches are expected to perform better overall as compared to FE approaches, because the basic model assumption (heterogeneity) is correct and the approaches account for this in their procedures. This will also generally lead to more conservative decisions in comparison to FE approaches. Hence, higher power of FE approaches is expected to come at the cost of excessive Type I error rates. More specifically, the null hypothesis will always be false in $\mathfrak{S}_2$ in the Monte Carlo study due to the design which does not include negative universe parameters. In essence, basically the same results as in $\mathfrak{S}_1$ are expected to emerge with acceptable performance of most approaches in most situations, except for some combinations of the design variables (low n coupled with high k). In $\mathfrak{S}_3$, RE approaches are expected to perform best when the null hypothesis is true (i.e., $\mu_\rho = 0$) because FE approaches do not incorporate heterogeneity variance in the standard error. More specifically, this prediction applies to DSL and OP-RE. However, DSL will retain the prescribed α-level best because it is suspected that the weighting scheme of OP-RE will impair its performance when n is small. With reference to Osburn and Callender (1992), it was pointed out in the context of presenting the HS approach that using the variants HS3 and HS4 may result in good performance in heterogeneous situations (see also Whitener, 1990). Hence, these two approaches are also expected to perform well. If the null hypothesis is false, then the power can again be examined. In these cases DSL is again predicted to show more conservative behavior in comparison to FE approaches. However, it is again predicted that the higher precision of OP will have a beneficial effect on its performance, though at the cost of an excessive Type I error.

Confidence Intervals.   In evaluating confidence intervals of the approaches two aspects have to be accounted for: coverage rates and interval widths. Coverage rates refer to the proportion of intervals covering the universe parameter in a series of replications. High coverage rates may come at the cost of large intervals, so they are not unequivocal indicators of the quality of the procedures. Thus, such rates have to be qualified by simultaneously considering the interval widths.

The most important property of estimators to attain high coverage rates — disregarding interval widths — is low bias. Since OP is expected to show the smallest bias in all situations, it is again predicted to show the best performance. This is anticipated to be true in all situations $\mathfrak{S}_1$, $\mathfrak{S}_2$, and $\mathfrak{S}_3$. RE approaches will show high coverage rates in all situations but these approaches will also have the largest interval widths notwithstanding which situation is examined. This is caused by incorporating estimates of heterogeneity variance in standard errors, which will almost always be positive, even in the homogeneous situation. Coverage rates are expected to become better for all approaches for larger n and k as conventional statistical results would suggest.

Homogeneity Tests.   Two different types of homogeneity tests were introduced in Chapter 5, those based on the Q-statistic and the 75% or 90% rule, respectively. First, focus will be on the Q-statistic, which is available to conduct a test in the approaches HOr, HOd, HS, and OP-FE. For the predictions it is important to recall one of the most important assumptions of this test, namely the normal distribution of the deviates. These are squared, weighted and summed over k studies to arrive at the Q-statistic. Under this assumption and if the null hypothesis is true, the Q-statistic has an asymptotic central χ^2_{k-1}-distribution, that is, when study sample sizes are (very) large.

As a consequence, it can be predicted that HOr will perform best in comparison to the other approaches. The basis for this prediction is the reasonableness of the assumption of normally distributed deviates for Fisher-z transformed correlations. In contrast, it is not wise to assume a normal distribution either in the case of r-based approaches (HS and OP-FE) or for HOd. At least when ρ is moderate to large and/or sample sizes are not huge, the assumption is not tenable. With regards to HOd, the assumption might be sensible if d was not a transformed r as in the present case. In addition to the distributional assumption, the deleterious effects of the weighting scheme are expected to operate again for HOd and especially OP-FE. In sum, HOr is expected to perform best amongst the approaches under examination. However, on the basis of theoretical analyses (see Hedges & Pigott, 2001) and previous evidence from attempts to evaluate this test (e.g., Harwell, 1997; Sánchez-Meca & Marín-Martínez, 1997), it can be expected that at least for some combinations of the design variables Type II errors will occur. More specifically, it is predicted that particularly for situations of small n and large k — which operates to exacerbate the small n problem — low power of the homogeneity test based on the Q-statistic will be observed.

The 75% and 90% rules as homogeneity tests are not expected to represent viable alternatives to the homogeneity test mentioned in the above paragraph. Due to their crude rationale and previous evaluations of these rules (for an overview of results, see Cornwell & Ladd, 1993), a high Type I error rate and relatively low power for combinations of moderate to low n and k is to be expected.

Estimation of Heterogeneity Variance.   A total of three estimators for the heterogeneity variance is available in the Monte Carlo study: DSL, HS, and OP-RE. Of these, DSL is Fisher-z based and therefore in z-space and not directly comparable to the other two estimators based on r. Unfortunately, there is no transformation formula available to date to make these three estimators directly comparable. Nevertheless, some predictions for their comparative performance are possible.

In the *homogeneous* situation $\mathfrak{S}_1$, all estimators are expected to show positive but small bias. This is due to their construction which prescribes negative estimates to be set to zero. If either non-truncated (i.e., negative estimates are not set to zero) or truncated estimators are compared, then DSL and HS are predicted to perform better than OP-RE. Despite the fact that OP-RE is unbiased (see, e.g., Hedges, 1989), the deleterious effects of the weighting scheme are expected to hamper good performance, at least when n is small. DSL is not expected to suffer from any weighting scheme problem and is unbiased by construction, though the weighting scheme might cause problems with the estimator when other effect sizes are used as in the present case (see Böhning et al., 2002). Hence, the DSL estimator is expected to perform best.

Basically the same predictions for relative performance of the approaches can be made for *heterogeneous* situations. DSL is expected to perform best, HS might show negative bias (see Hall & Brannick, 2002), OP-RE will perform worst.

7.3   DISTRIBUTIONS IN THE UNIVERSE OF STUDIES

In line with the differentiation between fixed and random effects models drawn in Chapter 4 and with regard to the importance of assumptions about the distribution of the universe effect sizes to be modeled, the situations introduced in Section 4.5 will be distinguished in the Monte Carlo study. The choice of the situations is mainly oriented on the assumptions that are ordinarily made in published meta-analyses about the universe of studies.

As a consequence, $\mathfrak{S}_1$ is an important situation to include in the design, mostly because of its prevalence in the literature. It represents the homogeneous case where only a single universe effect size is assumed to be estimated by the studies under investigation. Additionally, $\mathfrak{S}_1$ is also included in the design of the Monte Carlo study to test whether the FE methods work properly when their basic assumptions are met and also to explore how RE methods perform in homogeneous situations.

One of the heterogeneous situations included in the design is $\mathfrak{S}_2$. Here, two different values ρ_1 and ρ_2 are present in the universe of studies with equal probability of occurrence. The difference between these values is not yet specified, but is a design aspect. The probabilities of .50 associated with the two values of ρ are the weights of the components in mixture distribution parlance and will *not* vary as part of the design. The Monte Carlo study thus also investigates the performance of the approaches in $\mathfrak{S}_2$ and compares estimates of mean effect sizes, for example, with the expected value of the mixing distribution they are intended to estimate. It should finally be kept in mind that the design of the Monte Carlo study will be limited to situations in which the component weights will also always be equal. Of course, this restriction precludes reliable generalizations to situations in which there are more than two classes and where components weights are very different.

The second type of heterogeneous situation included in the Monte Carlo study is $\mathfrak{S}_3$. Here, a univariate continuous distribution is given in the universe of studies which is the beta distribution in the present study. The normal distribution was not used because it is not bounded by the interval $[-1, 1]$ and to avoid discarding invalidly large values. An alternative procedure was realized by Overton (1998), for example, who randomly set invalid values from the normal distribution to values between .90 and .9999 according to a uniform distribution extending over this range. This is certainly an unsatisfactory state of affairs because the density of the normal distribution is distorted by such trimming of values and a determination of its actual parameters and properties is thus impeded. Hence, such procedures are not considered as satisfactory.

In contrast to an earlier work that also used the beta distribution (Hedges, 1989), using parameters for the beta distribution that yield U-shaped or rectangular distributions was refrained from because they did not appear as plausible for the distribution of effect sizes in the universe. The same is true for distributional forms of a J-shape. Discussion of this issue will be resumed in the following section when the specific parameters values for the Monte Carlo design will be introduced.

The question remains how the particular parameters of the beta distribution were calculated in the Monte Carlo study. To elucidate the procedure, consider the following probability density function of the beta distribution with parameters p and q

$$p_X(x) = \frac{1}{B(p,q)} x^{p-1}(1-x)^{q-1}, \quad 0 \leqslant x \leqslant 1,$$

given in standard form (see Johnson, Kotz, & Balakrishnan, 1995). As is evident, this standard form is bounded by the interval $[0,1]$. Next, the aim is to find values of the parameters p and q that correspond to desired expected values and variances in terms of ρ. For example, how should p and q be chosen to yield a beta distribution with an expected value of $\mu_\rho = .10$ and $\sigma_\rho^2 = .15$? To find an expression for the computation of the parameters it is important to note that a random variable X following a beta distribution still continues to be beta-distributed when linearly transformed. Accordingly, the transformation $P = 2X - 1$ is applied to a standard beta-distributed random variable X to yield a distribution on the interval $[-1, 1]$. Furthermore, the moments of this transformed variable are (see Johnson, Kotz, & Balakrishnan, 1995, p. 219)

$$E(P) = \frac{2p}{p+q} - 1,$$

and

$$\text{Var}(P) = \frac{4pq}{(p+q)^2(p+q+1)}.$$

Equating $E(P)$ and $\text{Var}(P)$ with μ_ρ and σ_ρ^2, respectively, and solving simultaneously for p and q leads to the following equations

$$p = \frac{1 + \mu_\rho - \mu_\rho^2 - \mu_\rho^3 - \sigma_\rho^2 - \mu_\rho\sigma_\rho^2}{2\sigma_\rho^2} = -\frac{(1+\mu_\rho)(-1+\mu_\rho^2+\sigma_\rho^2)}{2\sigma_\rho^2}$$

$$q = \frac{1 - \mu_\rho - \mu_\rho^2 + \mu_\rho^3 - \sigma_\rho^2 + \mu_\rho\sigma_\rho^2}{2\sigma_\rho^2} = \frac{(-1+\mu_\rho)(-1+\mu_\rho^2+\sigma_\rho^2)}{2\sigma_\rho^2}$$

Now μ_ρ and σ_ρ^2 correspond to the desired values for the expected value and variance in terms of the beta-distributed variate on the interval $[-1, 1]$. Applying these equations to the example given above ($\mu_\rho = .10$ and $\sigma_\rho^2 = .15$) yields $p = 23.65$ and $q = 19.35$, respectively. In the Monte Carlo study these equations were applied to compute the parameters of the beta-distribution for a whole set of combinations of μ_ρ and σ_ρ^2. The resulting values are reported in Tables A.1 and A.2 in the appendix. The type of continuous distribution of the random variable P in the universe of studies is now specified and characterizes $\mathfrak{S}_3$ of the Monte Carlo study.

In sum, a total of three situations $\mathfrak{S}_1$ to $\mathfrak{S}_3$ is given of which the first represents a homogeneous case and the second and third are heterogeneous cases. The first two situations $\mathfrak{S}_1$ and $\mathfrak{S}_2$ are characterized by discrete distributions whereas the third is continuous. Of course, one could easily imagine a host of further situations: for example, situations with more than two groups and a discrete distribution, a variety of different component weights in the discrete situations, different parametric continuous distributions in the universe and maybe even mixtures of continuous distributions at the universe level. Thus, although this Monte Carlo study can count as one of the most comprehensive in design on the present research topic up to date, it is necessarily limited. These limits of the design should be borne in mind when examining the results. Having described the types of situations under investigation, the parameter values that were chosen for the various variables of the design will now be specified.

7.4   PARAMETERS

The variables of the design to evaluate the approaches of meta-analysis are

- the values of μ_ρ for all situations $\mathfrak{S}_1$ to $\mathfrak{S}_3$,
- the variance of the beta distribution (σ_ρ^2) in $\mathfrak{S}_3$,
- the number of studies k to be aggregated in a meta-analysis, and
- the number of persons n to compute the effect sizes in the individual studies.

The values for μ_ρ represent one single universe effect size common to all k studies in $\mathfrak{S}_1$ and the expected value of the beta distribution in $\mathfrak{S}_3$. For $\mathfrak{S}_2$, two different values ρ_1 and ρ_2 were chosen. Of course, there is also a corresponding μ_ρ in $\mathfrak{S}_2$, however, it is ambiguous for the specification of ρ_1 and ρ_2.

As specified in Section 4.5, the weights for the components in $\mathfrak{S}_2$ were held constant. Additionally, the number of persons for each effect size is considered to be invariant within each simulated meta-analysis. That is, if in $\mathfrak{S}_1$ there is one universe parameter μ_ρ underlying a number of $k = 32$ studies, for example, then the effect sizes r_i of all 32 studies have some fixed number of persons. Although not representative of published meta-analyses, n is held constant mainly to exclude any interaction effects of n with other aspects of the design. An interaction effect of n and μ_ρ, for example, is indeed a very interesting research topic on its own. The well known publication bias in meta-analysis (Begg, 1994; Rosenthal, 1979) can be regarded as such an interaction and continues to stimulate research efforts to assess and eliminate such influences on the results of a meta-analysis (e.g., Hedges & Vevea, 1996; Iyengar & Greenhouse, 1988; Rust, Lehmann, & Farley, 1990; Schwarzer, Antes, & Schumacher, 2003; Vevea & Hedges, 1995). Thus, the reasons to hold n constant are to ensure exclusion of such interaction effects from the results and to keep the focus on the effects of the design variables as implemented.

The specific values that are used for the design variables listed above are presented in Table 7.1. The first row of Table 7.1 shows that the values for μ_ρ are positive in all simulated cases.

Table 7.1   Parameter Values in the Simulation Procedure

Parameter	Values	Number of Values
μ_ρ	0; 0.1; 0.2; 0.3; 0.4; 0.5; 0.6; 0.7; 0.8; 0.9	10
σ_ρ^2 (σ_ρ)	0.0025 (0.05); 0.01 (0.10); 0.0225 (0.15); 0.04 (0.20); 0.0625 (0.25)	5
k	4; 8; 16; 32; 64; 128; 256	7
n	8; 16; 32; 64; 128; 256	6

Note. μ_ρ = expected value of correlation in the universe, σ_ρ^2 = variance of correlations in the universe, k = number of studies per meta-analysis, n = number of persons per study used to compute the observed correlations (r_i).

Since the distributions in the interval below zero would mirror those simulated on the positive side, only the given set of values is of concern. Note that the values provided for μ_ρ also represent the range of values chosen for ρ_1 and ρ_2 in $\mathfrak{S}_2$. The second row shows the values for the variances and the respective standard deviations in parenthesis for the beta distributions in situation three. The given values are considered to cover the range of plausible variances for the mixing distribution. The third and fourth row show the range of values for the number of studies in a meta-analysis and the number of persons per study, respectively. The values were chosen to yield a higher resolution for small values but also to extend to relatively large values. This was achieved by calculating powers of two beginning with 2^2 for k up to 2^8.

The reader might wonder whether the values used in the Monte Carlo study are representative of published meta-analyses. Unfortunately, investigations of the characteristics of the distributions of the design variables are quite rare, so the main resource to judge adequacy of the values is research experience. At least, there are content analyses of meta-analytic studies of correlations in I/O psychology available (Cornwell, 1988; see also Lent, Aurbach, & Levin, 1971). The results of Cornwell's study on 81 meta-analyses published in seven major journals of I/O psychology provides descriptive statistics for the distributions of n and k, respectively. Since there are extreme values for both variables (Maximum $n = 45,222$ and Maximum $k = 2,162$), the author provided the statistics for a truncated distribution for both variables[1]. The mean value for n was 283 (Median = 102; Mode = 73) and a value of 37 (Median = 12; Mode = 6) resulted for k. Hence, the choice of including a value of $k = 4$ in the present Monte Carlo study seems warranted. An additional argument in favor of the inclusion of such small values is the fact that subgrouping of studies corresponding to the levels of assumed explanatory variables very often leads to very small k in the subgroups (see, e.g., Farrell & Hakstian, 2001). The largest value for k

---

[1]The distributions were truncated at $n \leq 500$ and $k \leq 120$.

included in the design does not occur very often but there are other research areas, like attitude–behavior research, for which a very large number of research articles is available (see, e.g., Eckes & Six, 1994; for an overview, see Schulze & Wittmann, 2003). The values chosen for n in the present design seem to cover the range of values occurring in practice although very small values are not very often reported in the content analysis (however, Minimum $n = 7$). But again, there are research areas for which very small n is customary as Hunter and Schmidt (1994b), for example, have pointed out. The variances chosen in the present design also match those used by Cornwell and Ladd (1993) and those used in other Monte Carlo studies in the field.

In sum, the levels chosen for the design variables seem to cover customary values of research practice, at least in the I/O psychology area. Nevertheless, the criterion of realism should not be overvalued when considering the levels of the design, since research practice might change and in some fields of study totally different characteristics may prevail. Moreover, against the background of the aim to study the properties of statistics that draw on asymptotic statistical theory, it is important to include also low values of the design variables. The inclusion of values for μ_ρ that can be judged as very high in comparison to estimates observed in meta-analyses in any field of psychology is also intended not only to mirror research practice but to study the behavior of procedures also under extreme conditions. However, it is not the case that such high values do not occur in I/O psychology (see Hite, 1987) or social psychology (see Schulze & Wittmann, 2003), for example.

To gain an overview of the large number of design variable combinations under study, it is instructive to review their number. In $\mathfrak{S}_1$, only one of the ten universe effect sizes is given and the variance is zero in all cases. These 10 values are combined with all of the k and n values resulting in a total of $10 \times 7 \times 6 = 420$ meta-analyses to be simulated.

The second situation $\mathfrak{S}_2$ differs from the first in that two different values for ρ are given, resulting in a number of non-redundant combinations of $\frac{(10 \times 9)}{2} = 45$. The differences between the values range from .10 to a maximum of .90. Again, these 45 universe value combinations are combined with all of the k and n values leading to a total of $45 \times 7 \times 6 = 1890$ meta-analyses.

Finally, the values for μ_ρ of the beta distribution were combined with the variances of row two in Table 7.1. The full combination of all values unfortunately lead to J-shaped beta distributions in extreme cases. This is illustrated in Figures A.1 to A.5 in the appendix and can be seen by inspecting the parameter values p and especially q in Table A.2 in the appendix. For values of p or q less than one, the beta distribution turns into a J-shape (Johnson, Kotz, & Balakrishnan, 1995). The utilization of such distribution types would lead to sampling values from the beta distribution that are predominantly very large and close to one, with a few extremely low values to attain the prescribed values for μ_ρ and σ_ρ^2. Two reasons lead to the omission of such distributions from the Monte Carlo design. First, the described problem only applies to very high values of μ_ρ in combination with high values of σ_ρ^2 that are very unlikely to arise in practice. Second, the utilization of these distributions would presumably have an enormous impact on the results of the study, in particular on the tests of homogeneity and estimates of heterogeneity variance. They would lead to biased assessment of the overall performance of estimators due to extreme values that emerge from J-shaped distributions. The following combinations were omitted: $\mu_\rho = .90$ with variances $\sigma_\rho^2 = .0625, .04, .01, .0225$ and $\mu_\rho = .80$ with variances $\sigma_\rho^2 = .0625, .04$. The omission of the six combinations of μ_ρ and σ_ρ^2 resulted in $10 \times 5 - 6 = 44$ combinations and thus a total of $44 \times 7 \times 6 = 1848$ meta-analyses in $\mathfrak{S}_3$.

The sum of the meta-analyses of all situations amounts to a total of 4158. For all these combinations, the statistics and tests of the several approaches to meta-analysis are computed to facilitate a comparative evaluation of the approaches in a wide range of possible situations given by these combinations. For all of the 4158 combinations, the computations were repeated in 10,000 iterations. Correspondingly, the results to be presented in Chapter 8 are either the means of certain statistics computed over all iterations or statistics derived from the iterations, like the standard deviation of the estimators for the mean effects over 10,000 values. The number of iterations in the present study can be considered to be relatively large in comparison to other Monte Carlo studies in the context of meta-analysis. Most previous Monte Carlo studies have chosen 1000 iterations (e.g., Cornwell, 1993; Law, 1995; Sackett et al., 1986; Sánchez-Meca & Marín-Martínez, 1998a; Spector & Levine, 1987) or 5000 iterations (e.g., Harwell, 1997; Sánchez-Meca & Marín-Martínez, 1998b), only a few studies have used 10,000 iterations (e.g., Alexander et al., 1989; Silver & Dunlap, 1987) and rarely were more iterations used (100,000 by Field, 2001). The number of iterations chosen here is therefore regarded as sufficient.

7.5   DRAWING RANDOM CORRELATION COEFFICIENTS

A final important technical aspect of the simulation study will now be discussed in considerable detail because it is one of the most important steps in the Monte Carlo study. Up to this point it has been laid out which variables and values are chosen for the design of the Monte Carlo study. The next task is to generate random correlation coefficients r_i that conform to these prescriptions. For convenience, assume correlations coefficients have to be generated for a single ρ, that is, $\mathfrak{S}_1$ is of concern and $\rho = \rho_1 = \ldots = \rho_k$. Note that the problem to be described is fully equivalent for all other situations and the results of this sections do not only pertain to $\mathfrak{S}_1$.

There are k independent studies with a common sample size n. The observed correlation coefficients r_i provided by the studies are assumed to be based on pairs $(x_1, y_1), \ldots, (x_n, y_n)$ of two variates X and Y having a joint bivariate normal distribution. Drawing random correlation coefficients means that we want to generate a set of k values of r_i for a given ρ. The first procedure that comes to mind is to generate n pairs for the two variates X and Y and compute the sample correlation correlation coefficient. That is, one would use the following equations to generate the values for x and y on an observational level:

$$x = v \times \sqrt{\rho} + e_1 \times \sqrt{1 - \rho}$$
$$y = v \times \sqrt{\rho} + e_2 \times \sqrt{1 - \rho}$$

(7.1)

where v, e_1, and e_2 are realizations of corresponding variates that follow a standard normal distribution and are mutually independent. This procedure has often been used in Monte Carlo studies to generate correlation coefficients (e.g. Corey et al., 1998) and it is easy to show that X and Y have correlation ρ when generated by this procedure.

Unfortunately, this procedure is computationally rather intensive and takes up a great amount of computation time in a large simulation study. This is the case because to generate a single correlation r_i one has to draw $n \times 3$ times for v, e_1, and e_2 from a standard normal distribution and correlate the resulting values of x and y subsequently. To speed up the whole process of generating correlation coefficients it would be much more efficient to directly draw correlations from the sampling distribution of the correlation coefficient or approximations thereof without generating pairs of values for X and Y. Several candidates for a more efficient approach using this strategy are considered now. The reader not interested in technical details may skip the following section and directly go to Section 7.6 without loss of understanding for the subsequent chapter.

7.5.1   Approximations to the Sampling Distribution of r

Alternatives to the computationally intensive procedure are given by using a series of analytical results on the distribution of the correlation coefficient. First, it is well known that when $\rho = 0$

$$\frac{r\sqrt{df}}{\sqrt{1 - r^2}} \sim t_{df},$$

(7.2)

where df are the degrees of freedom ($df = n - 2$) in Equation 7.2. Accordingly, one could draw values from a central t distribution with df degrees of freedom and use the transformation

$$r = \sqrt{\frac{t^2}{t^2 + df}}$$

(7.3)

that results from solving Equation 7.2 for r to simulate a series of r_i values. This procedure would fulfill the need for a more efficient strategy but the question arises how r values can be generated in cases where $\rho \neq 0$.

Ideally, one would draw directly from the sampling distribution of such correlation coefficients but their distribution is unfortunately mathematically rather complex (see Section 3.1). Since it cannot be given in closed form, its usage as a distribution to draw correlations from is obstructed. Nevertheless, it will be considered as a benchmark to judge the quality of the approximations to the distribution of r we will turn to in the following paragraphs. The PDF of r was already given in Equation 3.1 on page 21.

Three approaches that rely on different distributional approximations to the PDF as given by Equation 3.1 are considered and discussed in some detail in the following paragraphs. A comparison and evaluation of these approaches with respect to the proximity to the PDF of r will follow their presentation.

The Fisher Approximation.   A first method to generate r values with a specific ρ in the underlying population is to randomly draw values from a normal distribution $\mathcal{N}(\mu_Z, \sigma_Z^2)$ with the following parameters

$$\mu_Z = \frac{1}{2} \ln \left(\frac{1+\rho}{1-\rho} \right) = \tanh^{-1} \rho \tag{7.4}$$

and

$$\sigma_Z^2 = \frac{1}{n-3}. \tag{7.5}$$

In the next step, the resulting values of z are transformed to sample correlation coefficients r via

$$r = \frac{\exp(2z) - 1}{\exp(2z) + 1} = \tanh r.$$

Although refinements of these formulae have been proposed in intensive investigations of the mathematical properties of the distribution function of r (Hotelling, 1953; Ruben, 1966), the approximation by using Equations 7.4 and 7.5 is a very popular one (see Chapter 3.1) and might therefore be considered as a possible and natural procedure for a simulation study.

The Harley Approximation.   A second approach is based on the analyses reported by Harley (1957) that dealt with an approximation of the noncentral t distribution by the distribution of a transformed correlation coefficient. She showed that in a population with a given ρ of

$$\rho = \sqrt{\left(\frac{2\tau^2}{2n - 3 + \tau^2} \right)}, \tag{7.6}$$

the function

$$\sqrt{\frac{2\,df(1-\rho^2)}{2-\rho^2}} \frac{r}{\sqrt{1-r^2}} \sim t_{df,\tau} \tag{7.7}$$

is distributed as noncentral t with noncentrality parameter τ. Using equation 7.6 and solving for τ leads to

$$\tau = \sqrt{\frac{(2\,df+1)\,\rho^2}{2-\rho^2}}.$$

This result can be used in simulation studies to compute τ of the noncentral t distribution to randomly draw values from. From a rearrangement of Equation 7.7, the resulting values of t can then be transformed back to r using the following equation

$$r = \sqrt{\frac{t^2}{t^2 + \frac{(2\,df+1)\,df}{2\,df+1+\tau^2}}},$$

which is given here in a form remarkably similar to Equation 7.3.

The Samiuddin-Kraemer Approximation. The last approximation to be considered here is based on the work by Samiuddin (1970) that was later refined and extended by Kraemer (1973, 1975; Kraemer & Paik, 1979). Due to the elaborations mainly presented by Kraemer it will be labeled *Kraemer approximation* in what follows. The approximation also draws on the t distribution.

It was shown that

$$\frac{(r - \rho')\,\sqrt{df}}{\sqrt{(1 - r^2)(1 - \rho'^2)}} \sim t_{df} \tag{7.8}$$

has a central t distribution with df degrees of freedom. In Equation 7.8, ρ' is a function of ρ that has to satisfy a series of requirements not repeated here (see Kraemer, 1973). Although Kraemer (1973) proposed that the median of the distribution of r is a good approximation to ρ' and better than ρ at least for small sample sizes while Mi (1990) was able to show that if ρ is taken as ρ' the distributional result stated above holds. Accordingly, the possibility for a simulation study established by this approximation is to draw t values from a central t distribution with df degrees of freedom and convert the resulting t values to r. The conversion can be done by solving Equation 7.8 for r, which leads to

$$r = \frac{(n - 2)\,\rho - (\rho^2 - 1)\,t\sqrt{n - 2 + t^2}}{n - 2 - (\rho^2 - 1)\,t^2}.$$

Of course, it is claimed that all the approximations presented here are satisfactory as compared to the sampling distribution of r. The results reported by the referenced authors seem to support this claim. It is therefore reasonable to consider these approximations when a Monte Carlo study is conducted, in which a large amount of r values has to be randomly generated, as is the case for the present study. It should finally be noted that none of the authors of the approximations advocated their use for the purpose of conducting Monte Carlo studies. The utilization of the approximations can consequently be regarded as an innovative aspect of their usefulness, but their utility has to be scrutinized beforehand. We will now turn to an evaluation of the presented approximations for this purpose.

7.5.2   Evaluation of the Approximations

Among the most important questions within the framework of an evaluation are the procedures of evaluation and provision of according criteria. The approximations presented in the previous subsection will be evaluated by determining the distribution and distributional properties of the rs they produce. As a first criterion, a visual inspection of the probability density function of the r values of the approximations in comparison to the exact density given in Equation 3.1 will be carried out. Additionally, the expected value and variance of the distributions will be compared as a second set of criteria, again with the exact density as a standard for comparisons. The approximations will be considered as satisfactory if the distributions of the r values generated by the procedures very closely match those of the values as given by the exact distribution. To accomplish this type of evaluation, the distributions in question were determined by numerical methods using MATHEMATICA. For details on the specific procedures applied, the interested reader is referred to Section B of the appendix where an annotated MATHEMATICA notebook can be found. It can be used to understand the genesis of the results reported here and to reproduce and possibly extend them.

The general logic underlying the computations is as follows. The characteristic feature of all the approximations is that there is a transformation T of the correlation coefficient R, denoted as $T \circ R$, the distribution of which ($\mathcal{P}_{T \circ R}$) can be approximated by a member of a well-known family of distributions. That is, the values $T \circ R$ are conceived as if they were generated by a variate X with a probability distribution $\mathcal{P}_X$ belonging to that family. Yet in other words, the distributions $\mathcal{P}_{T \circ R}$ and $\mathcal{P}_X$ — or equivalently the random variables $T \circ R$ and X — are equated. For example, in the Fisher approximation the rs are transformed to z values that have an approximate normal distribution as described above. In the proposed procedures to generate r values the first step is to draw values from the hypothesized probability distribution of X and convert the resulting values back to r subsequently by applying the transformation formulae presented in the previous subsection. To be clear, it is thereby assumed that $\mathcal{P}_X$ is not only the asymptotic but the exact distribution of $T \circ R$. In the case of the Fisher approximation $\mathcal{P}_X$ is the normal distribution, whereas for Harley's and the Kraemer-Samiuddin approximation it is the central and noncentral t distribution, respectively. The question to be answered by the evaluation is whether the distribution of the rs, which are generated by the outlined procedure, does indeed show the same properties as R expected by exact theory.

All transformations T are strictly increasing so that the inverse function exists. For an example, consider again the Fisher approximation where it is the inverse Fisher transformation $\tanh z$. That is, for all transformations there is $T(R) = X$, and we also have $T^{-1}(X) = R$. Under these conditions the aim can be restated as to determine the probability density of R when the density $p_{T \circ R}(x)$ is given and the inverse transformation is applied. To achieve this aim, we first consider

$$\mathcal{P}(R \leq r) = \mathcal{P}(T^{-1}(X) \leq r) = \mathcal{P}(T \circ R \leq T(r)).$$

Again, this will be illustrated for the Fisher approximation by

$$P(R \leq r) = P(\tanh(Z) \leq r) = P(Z \leq z).$$

The probability density distributions can therefore be computed as

$$P(R \leq r) = P(T \circ R \leq T(r)) = \int_{-\infty}^{T(r)} p_{T \circ R}(x)dx = \int_{-1}^{r} p_{T \circ R}\left(T(y)\right) T'(y)dy,$$

where the critical step is a change of variables[2] in the equation above. Yet again, this can be illustrated as an example for the Fisher approximation by

$$P(R \leq r) = \int_{-\infty}^{z} \varphi(x)dx = \int_{-1}^{r} \varphi\left(\tanh^{-1}(y)\right) \tanh^{-1'}(y)dy$$

where $\varphi(x)$ is the normal distribution with expected value ζ and variance $(n-3)^{-1}$. The change of variables is extraordinarily useful for the present purpose of inspecting a distribution of a random variable (R) when it is subject to a transformation, since the result of this procedure is of utmost importance for the evaluation of such transformations. Applying this procedure to the present set of transformations allows a comparative inspection of the distribution of R for different cases. The following Figures 7.1 and 7.2 depict examples of the density distributions for the transformations of interest in the present context. In Figure 7.1 the densities are plotted for $n = 32$ and $\rho = .30$. As can be seen, the densities are virtually indistinguishable by inspection in this case. All approximations coincide with the exact density of R and can therefore count as very satisfactory. In Figure 7.2 a more extreme case is depicted, also for $n = 32$ but $\rho = .90$. Note that this case is of interest for the present study as it is part of the design. Here, the curves do not all coincide. The density for the Harley approximation is obviously most "off" from the others. The Fisher and Kraemer approximation are virtually identical but do not perfectly match the exact density of R. Nevertheless, from inspection of the figures they may still count as very good approximations to the exact density. The point to be noted is that graphical comparisons between the densities of the approximations in comparison to the standard distribution allow some of the approximations to appear as quite satisfactory. Of course, up to now only two special cases with a fixed n and two different ρ values were chosen for comparison and for other constellations of the parameters the approximations may be even better or worse

---

[2]As a reminder, a change of variables is given for two continuous functions f and g, where f is continuous and g is continuously differentiable with derivative g', by

$$\int_{g(a)}^{g(b)} f = \int_{a}^{b} (f \circ g) \cdot g'$$

$$\int_{g(a)}^{g(b)} f(u)du = \int_{a}^{b} f\left(g(x)\right) \cdot g'(x)dx.$$

The two equivalent forms for the change of variables are given here for ease of comparison with the equations given in the text (see e.g., Spivak, 1967).

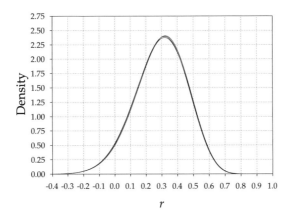

Figure 7.1   Densities for R of the approximations, $n = 32, \rho = .30$.

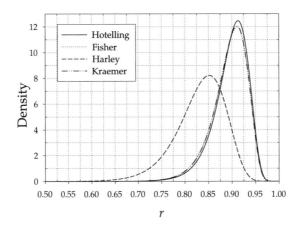

Figure 7.2   Densities for R of the approximations, $n = 32, \rho = .90$.

than indicated in the figures. The parameter constellation was actually deliberately chosen to illustrate a general trend of the value of the approximations. First, all approximations become worse the higher the ρ that is chosen. Second, all aproximations are almost perfect in the region about $\rho = 0$. Third, a point not illustrated by the figures, all approximations perform better the higher the value for n that is is chosen, but they are still visually distinguishable from the exact density for $\rho \gtrsim .90$ when n is not extremely large. In sum, the approximations perform very well for some constellations of the parameters but not for all. As will become evident by the following inspection of the numerical properties, that is, the expected values and variances of the distribution, the visual inspection of such graphs can be quite deceptive insofar as good-looking approximations may nevertheless not achieve satisfactory values for distributional properties.

Table 7.2 Expected Values and Variances for the Approximations and the Exact Density of R, $n = 8$ and $n = 128$, $\rho = 0, \ldots, .90$

		Hotelling		Fisher		Harley		Kraemer	
n	ρ	μ	σ^2	μ	σ^2	μ	σ^2	μ	σ^2
	.00	.000	.1429	.000	.1472	.000	.1429	.000	.1429
	.10	.093	.1409	.085	.1455	.093	.1409	.086	.1412
	.20	.187	.1349	.171	.1403	.186	.1349	.172	.1363
	.30	.281	.1250	.259	.1317	.280	.1251	.260	.1281
8	.40	.376	.1115	.348	.1196	.374	.1116	.349	.1166
	.50	.472	.0945	.440	.1040	.469	.0947	.441	.1017
	.60	.571	.0747	.536	.0851	.563	.0753	.537	.0835
	.70	.672	.0529	.637	.0629	.654	.0547	.638	.0623
	.80	.776	.0305	.745	.0386	.741	.0350	.746	.0388
	.90	.885	.0105	.864	.0145	.820	.0187	.864	.0151
	.00	.000	.0079	.000	.0079	.000	.0079	.000	.0079
	.10	.100	.0077	.099	.0077	.100	.0077	.099	.0077
	.20	.199	.0073	.198	.0073	.199	.0073	.198	.0073
	.30	.299	.0065	.298	.0066	.299	.0065	.298	.0066
128	.40	.399	.0056	.397	.0056	.397	.0056	.397	.0056
	.50	.499	.0045	.497	.0045	.495	.0045	.497	.0045
	.60	.598	.0033	.597	.0033	.589	.0033	.597	.0033
	.70	.699	.0021	.697	.0021	.679	.0022	.697	.0021
	.80	.799	.0010	.798	.0011	.761	.0013	.798	.0011
	.90	.899	.0003	.899	.0003	.834	.0006	.899	.0003

Note. The columns labeled "Hotelling" correspond to the exact density whereas the other columns are labeled in accordance with the approximations introduced in the previous Subsection 7.5.1.

Table 7.2 presents a series of expected values and variances of the approximations and the exact density for comparison. Similar to the visual inspection of the figure, only a small subset of possible combinations of n and ρ is chosen for comparison and presented in Table 7.2, but these values suffice to illustrate the general points to be highlighted[3]. First, the approximations by Fisher and Kraemer seem to fare equally well in comparison to Harley's, which generally leads to inferior values for higher ρ in terms of differences to the Hotelling standard. Second, all approximations get worse for higher ρ and better for larger n. This is what is to be expected from statistical theory, because the distribution of R is central t at zero and all the approximations are expected to be almost perfect in this region. Furthermore, the distributional properties of the approximations hold only asymptotically, so they get better with growing

---

[3]With the notebook presented in Appendix B it easy to compute any desired values to extend the comparisons.

numbers of n. Lastly, none of the approximations seems to provide satisfactorily similar expected values and variances to the standard, except in the case of ρ in the region of zero combined with high n. Although the reported differences may appear quite small in value, they are actually too large for the purpose of generating correlation coefficients by these procedures. To understand this judgment, focus on the Fisher approximation as an example. This approximation leads to generally smaller expected values in comparison to the exact density and somewhat larger variances. This means that a simulation study in which z values are drawn from a normal distribution, these are converted to r by the inverse Fisher transformation, and estimates of the mean effect size are based on these r values, may possibly report flawed conclusions for an assessment of the bias. The reasons for a potential flaw lie in the difference between the expected value of the Fisher approximation and the exact distribution. The expected value for a situation of $n = 64$ and $\rho = .50$ is $\mu = 0.49701$ for the exact density and $\mu = 0.49398$ for the Fisher approximation. Now suppose a comparison between the biases of r and Fisher-z is of interest in this situation. For the exact density, the biases to be anticipated by statistical theory[4] are $\text{Bias}_r = -0.002943384$ for r and $\text{Bias}_z = 0.003987731$ (given in the space of r) (see Hotelling, 1953, p. 212 for r and p. 216 for z), the well known negative bias for r and positive bias for z. But the biases are not to be anticipated when the expected value of the probability distribution is shifted downwards by the simulation procedure as is the case with the Fisher approximation. This downward shift will have the effect that the overestimation of Fisher-z will not be as large as expected by theory and the negative bias of r will emerge as larger in absolute value than it effectively is when assessed in relation to the exact density. In short, the positive bias of z is compensated by using the Fisher approximation in the simulation procedure and incorrect conclusions with respect to biases may result.

It is therefore concluded that the considered candidates for a simulation procedure cannot be used because they produce distortions of the sampling distributions for statistics. This happens to an extent that is of relevance for Monte Carlo studies. Hence, none of the candidates will be used and the computationally more costly procedure introduced at the beginning of this section in the Equations 7.1 will be used instead. The results of the evaluation have relevance not only for a decision in this Monte Carlo study, but also for a reevaluation of previous ones. For example, Spector and Levine (1987) have employed the Fisher approximation to generate r values in a Monte Carlo study on the susceptibility of the HS-procedure to Type I and II error rates. In light of the results presented here, at least some doubt is cast on the results and conclusion of the Monte Carlo study by Spector and Levine and others who have used the approximations.

---

[4]Note that the bias of r given here does not add up with the expected value to ρ exactly. This occurs because the approximation by Hotelling (1953, p. 212) is only given up to the third term of an expansion.

7.6   DETAILS OF PROGRAMMING

A computer program for MS-DOS was designed and programmed in Borland C++ Version 5.02. The procedure to generate the correlation coefficients followed Equations 7.1. Since a very large amount of numbers had to be randomly drawn for these correlations, a random number generator with a very long period length was of interest. Remarkably, standard random number generators in common use appear to have serious deficiencies (Hellekalek, 1998). According to the review of random number generators by Hellekalek (1998), the Mersenne Twister (TT800) (Matsumoto & Nishimura, 1998) was the only random number generator with a flawless performance,[5] and was therefore implemented in the program.

To speed up the draws from the standard normal distributions, an array of two million values was filled from which values were drawn. The array was randomly refilled 8 times in the course of the whole computations.

7.7   SUMMARY

The current Monte Carlo study is designed for a comparative evaluation of the approaches to meta-analysis in common use in the social sciences and the procedures they propose as valuable tools for meta-analysis. To achieve this aim, the design of the Monte Carlo study includes a wide range of different values for the universe correlations ρ in the universe of studies (from .00 to .90 in increments of .10), the number of studies to be aggregated (from 4 to 256), and number of persons in the studies to be aggregated (from 8 to 256). Additionally, different situations are implemented in the design that correspond to the assumptions of the fixed and random effects models in meta-analysis. The situations were distinguished by the form of the distribution of universe effect sizes that were classified as discrete and continuous. For the discrete distributions homogeneous and heterogeneous situations are included where the heterogeneous situations have two distinct values. In the case of a continuous distribution, six different variances of a beta-distribution were additionally varied.

As a result, the whole procedure can be thought of as a two-stage sampling process. In the first step, universe values are drawn from a distribution in the universe of studies with prespecified properties as described above and in the second step, observed values are drawn from distributions with properties that depend on the universe values drawn in step one. For the second step, different forms to generate the observed correlation coefficients were considered and the possibility to draw correlations directly from approximate distributions was rejected as unsatisfactory.

---

[5]The source code of the Mersenne Twister TT800, as well as reviews of the quality of random number generators can be found at http://random.mat.sbg.ac.at

8

Results

The following sections provide an overview of the results for the Monte Carlo study of meta-analytic approaches. First, a brief introduction to the presentation style will be given. This seems necessary because of the complex structure and multitude of results. The intention is to make the presented results more easily comprehensible and to point out how a maximum of information can be gathered from the graphics found in the subsequent sections. The presentation of results diverges from the structure of Chapter 5 in that the focus is kept on the questions to be answered by the statistical analyses. First, Section 8.2 is devoted to questions pertaining to the estimation of the effect size in the universe of studies, for example, issues regarding the bias and relative efficiency of the proposed estimators. Next, the results on the accuracy of homogeneity tests will be reported in Section 8.5. Finally, estimators of the heterogeneity variance — which are important in random effects approaches — are examined in Section 8.6. The sequence of sections thus resembles the conduct of a meta-analysis, while not exactly mirroring it. The situations $\mathfrak{S}_1$ to $\mathfrak{S}_3$ will be separated in all sections to assess the statistics' performance under different conditions.

8.1 PRELIMINARIES

One of the characteristic features of the present study is the wealth of situations, design variables, and number of different approaches to be compared. Most of the results are subject to levels of the dimensions k, n, μ_ρ, or differences of ρ_1 and ρ_2 in $\mathfrak{S}_2$. Additionally, results are compared for levels of variances (σ_ρ^2) in $\mathfrak{S}_3$. The number of dimensions obviously precludes any simple pictorial or tabular presentation. As a consequence, the report of the results needs to be brought into an easily comprehensible form.

The results presented in the text are always selected to represent and illustrate the primary aspects of the respective results. Mostly, results will be collapsed over at least one design variable. More specifically, collapsed means that the *mean* over all levels of such a variable will be computed. The resulting mean values will then be presented for the levels of all other variables in the design. For example, in the presentation of results for the biases of estimators over several levels of n, the mean values computed across levels of k will be presented. The absolute values of biases are then easily interpretable, if biases do not (greatly) vary over levels of k. A more complicated picture emerges in cases where results differ across *all* levels of *all* design variables. This will be highlighted in the presentation and should be borne in mind when inspecting collapsed results. Nevertheless, even in these more complicated cases, a *comparison* of the approaches is still possible.

In general, much more emphasis will be placed on graphical rather than tabular presentation of the results to facilitate illustration of trends and relationships which often go unrecognized in tables. The figures will prevalently be three-dimensional graphs since they often give a better impression of interactions of the design variables and are also very compact ways of representing a wealth of results and general trends. All three-dimensional graphs will display smoothed data or surfaces using negative exponential smoothing. This is a local smoothing technique using polynomial regression with weights.[1] In short, the weights are chosen in this technique so that the influence of points decreases exponentially with the horizontal distance from certain points of the surface.

The following graphs illustrate the effect of smoothing and how graphs produced by this technique can be interpreted. The upper left and right panel in Figure 8.1 depict a three-dimensional scatterplot of the bias of a statistic for varying μ_ρ and n. Both upper panels show the same results, each from a different angle of view. The lower panels depict the same graphs with smoothed surfaces added resulting from negative exponential smoothing. As can easily be seen, the lower set of graphs gives a much clearer and more easy to grasp picture of the relationships between the variables depicted. These types of graphs also supersede series of two-dimensional line graphs as ordinarily presented in the literature, where it is left to the observer to synthesize the graphs cognitively. When inspecting the graphs it is important to recognize — as can be verified in Figure 8.1 — that the intersections of the meshes on the surfaces correspond to the *data points* plotted. The mesh intersections are *not* to be interpreted as projections of the plots' grid intersections onto the surface. Data point dots will therefore be omitted in the graphs of the results sections. Since the data points are not equally spaced with respect to a linear scale on the design variables n and k, the mesh of the surface will also be more tightly interconnected in some areas when the results are plotted by n and k. Additionally, when different shadings occur on the surfaces they can be interpreted

---

[1]For the graphical presentation in this chapter, SigmaPlot for Windows Version 8.02 and its smoothing facilities were used to prepare the figures.

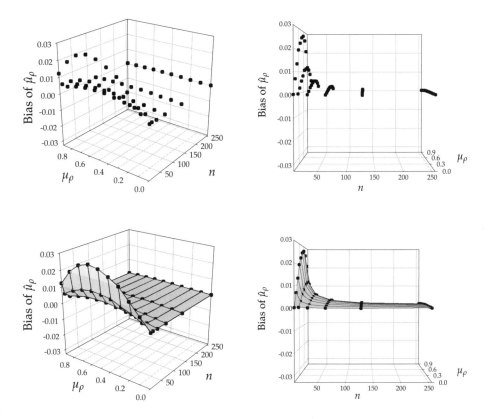

Figure 8.1 Illustration of smoothing in graphical presentations.

as contours with respect to the vertical axis. In the example graphs this is the axis labeled "Bias of $\hat{\mu}_\rho$". This enables the reader to see the height of values on the surfaces even in the middle of a three-dimensional graph. At least rough estimates of the actual values plotted can thereby be gathered from the graphs.

   Unfortunately, the virtues of a concise graphical presentation of the results are accompanied by a loss in numerical precision in the report. More precise results not readily read from the figures are provided by the author to the interested reader upon request.[2]

8.2   ESTIMATION OF THE MEAN EFFECT SIZE IN THE UNIVERSE OF STUDIES

At the core of most meta-analyses is the estimation of a mean effect size. Two connotations are usually associated with this phrase. First, a summary of the available effect size data is intended to be given by the meta-analyst that is a

---

[2]Email: rs@psy.uni-muenster.de

good representation of the data at hand. The weighted mean of the observed effect sizes usually gives such a good summary in a least-squares sense. Second, the phrase also alludes to estimating a parameter of the distribution of effect sizes in the universe of studies. The parameter supposed to be of most concern to meta-analysts is μ_ρ, the expected value of the universe distribution in the space of r. It is this latter sense that will be of concern in the following subsections. The main question to be answered is how well the different r-based estimators of the various approaches are in estimating μ_ρ. Recall from Section 5.5 that z-based approaches do not estimate μ_ρ but $\mu_{\rho z}$. This issue will be elaborated when it is of most concern, namely when presenting the results for heterogeneous situations.

All approaches outlined in Chapter 5 provide procedures that yield estimates either for μ_ρ or $\mu_{\rho z}$. Results on the bias of these estimators and their accuracy are given first, followed by results for the proposed significance tests of the approaches. The two subsections will thus provide an evaluation of the estimators with respect to estimation and inference.

8.2.1   Bias

The bias of an estimator is one important aspect of its statistical quality (see Stuart et al., 1999). The biases were computed for the following presentation so that positive biases indicate estimators for which the mean exceeds the parameter to be estimated. As in most previous studies on the bias of some of the estimators under investigation, the biases will first be examined in a homogeneous situation.

8.2.1.1   Homogeneous Situation $\mathfrak{S}_1$ In $\mathfrak{S}_1$ we have the simple situation of only one effect size in the universe of studies that is estimated by all k studies. Hence, μ_ρ and $\mu_{\rho z}$ are equal and estimators of approaches using r versus its Fisher-z transform need not be differentiated here. The bias of approaches that apply the Fisher-z transformation was computed for the mean effect size transformed into r-space, whereas for approaches that do not apply this transformation the estimators were used directly. For convenience, the value in the universe to be estimated is denoted by μ_ρ in all situations. This notation is used also in describing the results in $\mathfrak{S}_1$ for reasons of consistency. Of course, μ_ρ is a constant ρ in $\mathfrak{S}_1$, and the reader should not be confused by this notation.

The following graphs show the biases of all approaches by the design variables k and n. As mentioned in the introduction of this chapter, statistics have to be combined across levels of other design dimensions (i.e., μ_ρ in the present case) to facilitate the presentation of results. To create the graphs depicted in Figure 8.2, the mean bias of the estimators over the omitted dimension μ_ρ was computed and the data points in the figure represent these mean biases. As will become evident from the subsequent presentation, biases vary substantially over levels of μ_ρ, so that it should be borne in mind for interpretation of the depicted values that the graphs represent aggregates over the omitted dimension.

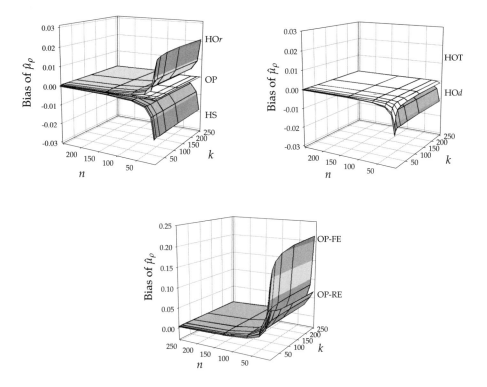

Figure 8.2   Bias of μ_ρ estimators in $\mathfrak{S}_1$ by k and n.

Here and in the following graphs, the three panels show the results of all approaches. The arrangement of approaches is not oriented on theoretical concerns but for clearer representation of the results. The reader may wonder why the results for DSL and RR are omitted. This is due to the fact that the results for both approaches are identical to the results for HOr as far as bias and mean squared errors are concerned. For a recapitulation of the reasons for these identities the reader is referred to Sections 5.2 and 5.4.1. The results for RR are generally omitted from the presentation in the text — except for the subsection on significance testing — because the results for RR and HOr are indistinguishable for theoretical reasons.

The bias of all estimators strongly depends on the sample size whereas biases show practically no variability with respect to k. The strongest change in biases occurs from very small $n = 8$ to approximately $n = 64$. For values larger than 64 the biases for all approaches vanish, as one would expect from consistency of the estimators. Estimators of approaches that use the Fisher-z transformation without corrections (HOr) generally show a positive bias and estimators simply based on r (HS) always show a negative bias. This is to be expected from the theoretical analyses reported in Section 3.1.

Two estimators can be identified in Figure 8.2 that show outstanding performance in biases. The correction of r by Olkin and Pratt (OP) as well as the

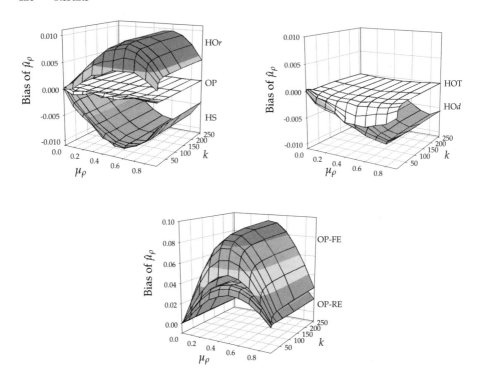

Figure 8.3   Bias of μ_ρ estimators in $\mathfrak{S}_1$ by μ_ρ and k.

correction of z proposed by Hotelling (HOT) show nearly flat planes at a value of zero bias, though OP seems to be slightly better for very small n and k.

In contrast to these extraordinarily good estimators, OP-RE and especially OP-FE stand out with a very poor performance. Whereas both upper panels in Figure 8.2 have a similar scaling on the vertical axis, the scaling of the lower panel had to be strongly extended to show the surfaces for these latter estimators. The surfaces for OP-FE and OP-RE depicted in the figure clearly show the inadequate performance of these estimators of μ_ρ when n is small. The proposed reason for these poor results of the estimators is the weighting scheme they apply. As already mentioned, accidently high values of r receive a very high weight in comparison to lower values and thereby they exert a strong influence on the overall estimate, leading to the high positive bias. OP-RE performs better in $\mathfrak{S}_1$ than OP-FE because it incorporates estimates of heterogeneity variance in its weights that are equal for all aggregated effect sizes. Since these estimates are most frequently non-zero even though the universe variance is zero in $\mathfrak{S}_1$, the deleterious effect of the weights for the biases of OP-FE is somewhat levelled out in OP-RE. The performance of these approaches was expected to be impaired when n is small, however, the magnitude of bias seems surprising. The poor performance of both estimators can also be seen in the graphs shown in Figures 8.3 and 8.4.

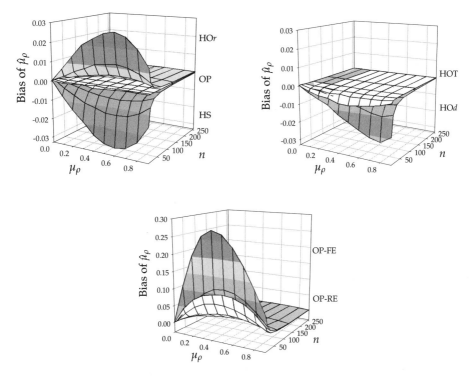

Figure 8.4   Bias of μ_ρ estimators in $\mathfrak{S}_1$ by μ_ρ and n.

Figure 8.3 shows the biases of the estimators for varying μ_ρ and number of studies. Biases are shown not to strongly vary across values of k, only for small values of k below approximately 16 studies do biases show *smaller* values in comparison to higher values of k. This somewhat surprising finding was also reported in a comparison of r and the Fisher-z transformation by Corey et al. (1998) and is not expected from theoretical examinations given in Section 3.1.

The arrangement of estimators in all panels of Figure 8.3 is the same as before and shows the same direction of bias for all estimators. Again, OP and HOT appear as flat planes in the graphs with OP showing slightly better performance for very small values of k. The curvature of the graphs across values of μ_ρ is representative of the general behavior of the estimators. The largest values of bias occur in the region about $\mu_\rho \approx .60$. Scaling of the vertical axis has again to be extended for OP-FE and OP-RE to show the very high values of bias for these estimators.

This has also to be done for the graphs depicted in Figure 8.4, where biases are shown across values of μ_ρ and n. Because the biases do not show substantial variability across values of k and Figure 8.4 shows aggregates over this design dimension, it can be regarded as the best representation of the results on biases in $\mathfrak{S}_1$.

Table 8.1   Descriptive Statistics for the Bias of μ_ρ Estimators in $\mathfrak{S}_1$

			Statistic		
Approach	Max.	Mean	Median	Min.	SD
HOr	.0324	.0053	.0018	−.0008	.0075
HOT	.0008	−.0011	−.0002	−.0174	.0023
HOd	.0009	−.0036	−.0011	−.0240	.0056
HS	.0008	−.0058	−.0025	−.0301	.0077
OP	.0026	.0000	.0000	−.0033	.0004
OP-FE	.3432	.0514	.0184	−.0005	.0740
OP-RE	.1180	.0280	.0146	−.0010	.0303

Note. The total number of values described by these statistics is 420.

The direction of the estimators' biases and their absolute values closely match the results depicted in Figure 8.2. It becomes evident in Figure 8.4 that in contrast to the estimators based on r or its Fisher-z transform, HOd shows its maximum bias not in the region about .50 but at higher values around .80. However, this slight departure from the behavior of the other estimators does not seem to be of great importance for an overall evaluation of the estimator. Nevertheless, it is remarkable that the application of the transformation from r to d and the meta-analytical aggregation of the resulting effect sizes retains the negative bias of r that becomes a positive bias through the application of the Fisher-z transformation.

OP and HOT again appear as the best estimators in terms of bias and can be designated as the best estimators over the design dimensions n, k, and μ_ρ after inspection of the graphs presented up to this point. The proposed refinements of the estimators in common use show a very satisfying behavior at all levels of the design variables.

The graphs presented here also point to two types of convergence. First, biases converge to zero with larger n, as would be expected. The second type is convergence for larger values of k. Biases do not converge to a value of zero for larger k but instead converge to the bias expected from statistical theory. This is important insofar as it makes clear that adding more studies to a meta-analysis does not lead to vanishing biases in the pooled estimator.

The absolute values of the reported biases may seem very small in magnitude. In fact, most descriptive statistics presented in Table 8.1 show relatively small values of bias for all estimators, except OP-FE and OP-RE. The absolute mean values seem to be of trivial magnitude and not of relevance for interpreting meta-analytical results at all.

If the sole purpose of a meta-analysis would be the estimation of μ_ρ in a homogeneous situation this may indeed be regarded as a valid summary statement for the results presented here. Correspondingly, it has been stated that the cases are very rare in which a correction of bias is worthwhile (Hunter & Schmidt, 1990, p. 71). Although the results also indicate that bias can be of substantial magnitude when n is very small, such values of n are rarely encountered in practice.

Nevertheless, when evaluating the results one should also take into consideration the importance of the estimates for other analytical steps in a meta-analysis. They play a prominent role, for example, in the computation of the Q-statistic. Although seemingly of inconsequential magnitude, a small bias transfers to and may add up in other statistical analyses based on these estimators. Apart from the small biases of most approaches, the observed biases for OP-FE and OP-RE are of such magnitude that it does not seem sensible to use them as estimators when n is less than approximately 60.

8.2.1.2 *Heterogeneous Situation* $\mathfrak{S}_2$ The next situation for which performance of the estimators will be evaluated is $\mathfrak{S}_2$. A two-point distribution of effect sizes is given in the universe of studies in $\mathfrak{S}_2$. In analogy to the previous section, mean biases will be computed for several combinations of the design variables.

For better comprehension of the results presented, a reconsideration of the estimated universe parameters seems necessary. In Section 5.5 it was shown that the estimated parameters are different in $\mathfrak{S}_2$ for estimators based on r, Fisher-z transformed r, and d (as resulting from a conversion of r). Recall, however, that in the case of HOd the weights have an effect making it more sensible to use μ_ρ as a universe parameter for comparison. Hence, in the following presentation of results the bias of HOd was not computed with respect to $\mu_{\rho d}$ as the general logic outlined for Fisher-z based approaches would suggest but with respect to μ_ρ. This seemingly inconsistent procedure was applied due to the fact that the values to be presented for HOd are actually much closer to μ_ρ than $\mu_{\rho d}$.

For the approaches using the Fisher-z transformed correlation coefficient, the universe parameters $\mu_{\rho z}$ are higher as compared to μ_ρ. This is illustrated in Figure 5.1 on page 78. To give a more precise impression of this difference consider Table 8.2.

The first two columns in this table provide combinations of the two different parameters in the universe of studies. In the third column the corresponding μ_ρ is given, in the forth column $\mu_{\rho z}$, and the difference between these two parameters can be seen in the fifth column. These differences are actually part of the values depicted in Figure 5.1. It is important to realize that the values in the fifth column are theoretically derived and *not* estimated. As an interpretation of these differences in the context of estimation, one can think of them as providing the biases for Fisher-z based approaches *if* they were *un*biased with respect to $\mu_{\rho z}$ but evaluated with respect to μ_ρ. Hence, it would come as no surprise to observe a "bias" of $-.10$ for the HOr mean effect size estimator in the case as specified in the penultimate row of Table 8.2, for example. Note that this "bias" would be observed (only) if the HOr estimator was indeed *un*biased (with respect to the parameter $\mu_{\rho z}$ it in fact estimates)!

Table 8.2   Comparison of Values of μ_ρ and $\mu_{\rho z}$ in $\mathfrak{S}_2$

ρ_1	ρ_2	μ_ρ	$\mu_{\rho z}$	$\mu_\rho - \mu_{\rho z}$	Est. Bias	$\mu_\rho - (\mu_{\rho z} + \text{Est. Bias})$
.00	.10	.05	.0501	−.0001	.0016	−.0017
.00	.20	.10	.1010	−.0010	.0034	−.0044
.00	.30	.15	.1535	−.0035	.0051	−.0086
.00	.40	.20	.2087	−.0087	.0063	−.0150
.00	.50	.25	.2679	−.0179	.0080	−.0259
.00	.60	.30	.3333	−.0333	.0093	−.0426
.00	.70	.35	.4084	−.0584	.0105	−.0688
.00	.80	.40	.5000	−.1000	.0093	−.1093
.00	.90	.45	.6268	−.1768	.0080	−.1848

Note. The estimated bias is for the HO*r* approach (Est. Bias) and was taken from the results for $k = 16$ and $n = 16$.

As a consequence, the biases for Fisher-z based approaches reported in this section are evaluated with respect to $\mu_{\rho z}$. To facilitate comparisons of these biases with others reported for *r*- and *d*-based estimators, they are given in *r*-space, that is, the inverse Fisher-z transformation is applied. As an illustration, column six in Table 8.2 provides estimated biases for HO*r* from the Monte Carlo study results for the case of $k = 16$ and $n = 16$. As can be seen, the values are small and round off to approximately −.01 in most cases. Thus, it can be concluded that HO*r* has a small bias with respect to $\mu_{\rho z}$ in $\mathfrak{S}_2$. If interest lies in biases with respect to μ_ρ, they can easily be estimated as well by computing values as given in column seven. By inspecting these values it becomes clear that — at least in this case — the biases of HO*r* with respect to μ_ρ are predominantly composed of the theoretically derived values in column five and the estimated biases in column six only account for a small part.

Amongst the available estimators only those based on *r* provide estimates of μ_ρ in $\mathfrak{S}_2$. This is quite an important theoretical result for the estimation of a mean effect size with correlational data in a heterogeneous situation of the given type. Biases for these approaches are not transformed and will be given as they result in the Monte Carlo study.

In sum, when inspecting the following results, the reader should bear in mind that Fisher-z based approaches are evaluated with respect to a different universe parameter as the other approaches. In addition, since μ_ρ was used as the standard of comparison for HO*d*, but μ_ρ can not be considered the estimated parameter when weights are disregarded, its role is somewhat special. To highlight these facts, the following presentation of results is subdivided in accordance with these distinctions.

***r*-Based Estimators in $\mathfrak{S}_2$.**   There are four *r*-based estimators under investigation: OP, OP-FE, OP-RE, and HS. Figure 8.5 gives an overview of the results for these estimators for varying *k* and *n* (upper panels).

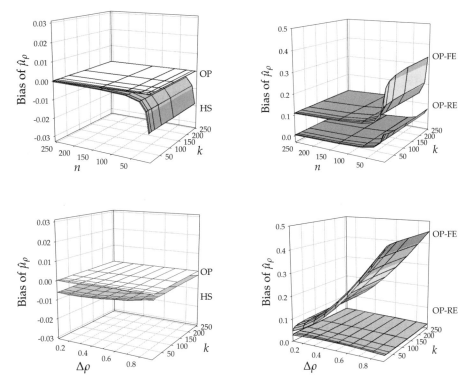

Figure 8.5 Bias of r-based μ_ρ estimators in $\mathfrak{S}_2$ by k and n (upper panels) as well as by $\Delta\rho$ and k (lower panels).

Both upper panels in the figure show similar behavior of the estimators as compared to the results in the previous situation. The only difference is an even worse performance for the OP-FE estimator approximating a value of .10 in bias with growing n. As before, OP is also in $\mathfrak{S}_2$ clearly the best estimator available in this category of estimators, showing almost no bias at all. HS also shows good performance, at least for sample sizes of 32 or larger.

The lower panels in Figure 8.5 depict the biases of the estimators across values of k and differences between ρ_1 and ρ_2, which will henceforth be denoted by $\Delta\rho$, that is, $\Delta\rho = \rho_1 - \rho_2$. The forms of the surfaces differ somewhat more from those in $\mathfrak{S}_1$. The direction of biases is still the same, with the OP-estimator being best across all values of the design. HS is depicted in the same graph and shows small negative biases which are almost invariant across values of $\Delta\rho$. Biases of HS can again be considered as negligible at least when sample sizes are 32 or larger.

The biases of OP-RE are approximately the same as those reported in $\mathfrak{S}_1$. OP-FE shows steadily increasing biases with higher values of $\Delta\rho$ that rapidly reach levels that can be considered to be unacceptable. As is evident from these results, the approximation of an OP-FE bias of .10 in the upper right panel is

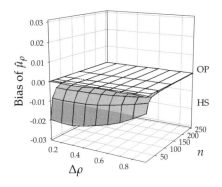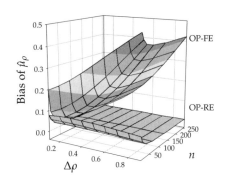

Figure 8.6   Bias of r-based μ_ρ estimators in $\mathfrak{S}_2$ by $\Delta\rho$ and n.

due to very large differences in bias across values for the difference between universe parameters. OP-FE is the only estimator in this class that is strongly affected by $\Delta\rho$. In addition to the strong effect of $\Delta\rho$, small n even amplify the bias depicted in Figure 8.5. This can be seen by inspecting the results shown in Figure 8.6.

The values for biases of r-based estimators across values of n and differences between ρs are depicted in Figure 8.6. The general trends and evaluation of the estimators do not change in comparison to $\mathfrak{S}_1$, as can be seen by inspection of this figure. OP is consistently showing a flat surface of zero bias across all values of n and $\Delta\rho$, hence it is clearly also the best point estimator of μ_ρ in $\mathfrak{S}_2$. HS only shows a small bias for very small n and does not perform as well as OP overall. In marked contrast, OP-RE and especially OP-FE show relatively bad performance, as can be seen in the right panel of Figure 8.6.

The reported biases of OP-FE across the design variables are huge in magnitude. It is remarkable that even with very high n biases do not diminish but actually rise. Such an observation is counterintuitive for at least two reasons. First, the results in the previous figures also show that the k point estimates of OP — on which OP-FE is based — are very accurate and show almost no bias at all in any of the situations and combinations of design variables. Hence, problems with biases of the OP-FE estimator cannot be caused by the point estimates. Second, consistency of estimators suggests that biases do not rise for increasing n but decline (and vanish for very large n). The converse is observed for OP-FE. All this clearly points to an effect of the weighting scheme because point estimates are very accurate on the basis of the UMVU estimator. Since the highest values for the bias of OP-FE are almost as high as the mean effect size in the universe (see the combination of lowest n and highest $\Delta\rho$ in the right panel of Figure 8.6), this shows that the class having higher ρ of the two-point distribution exclusively dominates the estimates. Hence, it must be the case that the correlations arising from the class with a higher ρ receive an excessive weight in comparison to the ones of the lower ρ class. Recall, first, that the weights are the reciprocals of the variances; second, that the variances of the estimator are different across values of ρ (see Figure 3.4); and third, that

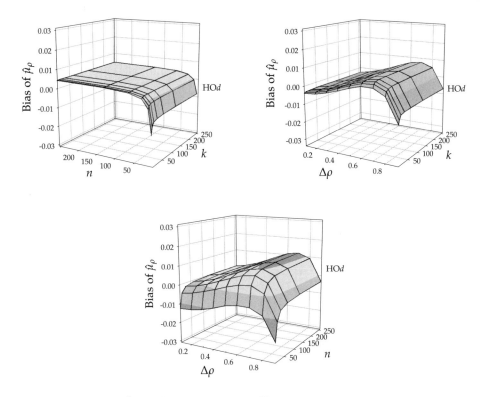

Figure 8.7   Bias of d-based μ_ρ estimators in $\mathfrak{S}_2$.

the estimates are plugged into Equation 3.7 to arrive at the estimates for the variances. Putting these facts together explains the high biases of OP-FE. As an example, consider the case of $\rho_1 = 0$, $n = 256$ and $\rho_2 = .90$, $n = 256$. For simplicity, assume that all r arising from ρ_1 are exactly zero and all r from ρ_2 are .90. As an aside, this is not far from what is actually observed with $n = 256$. In the given case, the weight for the first class is $w_1 = 252.00$, and $w_2 = 7104.54$ for the second. Applying these weights in the given situation and aggregating a total of $k = 256$ studies leads to an estimate of $\hat{\mu}_\rho = .87$. Subtracting $\mu_\rho = .45$ leads to a bias of .42, a value corresponding to the highest biases of OP-FE in the Monte Carlo study as can be observed in Figure 8.6, for example. Hence, large difference in weights lead to the huge biases observed for OP-FE in $\mathfrak{S}_2$.

Overall, the general trends in biases across levels of the design variables are similar to those resulting in $\mathfrak{S}_1$. Biases are fairly stable across values of k, OP clearly shows the best performance, and the weighting scheme emerges as a profound problem for OP-FE making the use of this estimator very unreasonable.

d-Based Estimator in $\mathfrak{S}_2$.   The results for the d-based estimator are depicted in Figure 8.7. As can be seen, biases show a somewhat strange behavior that differs from those of r-based estimators.

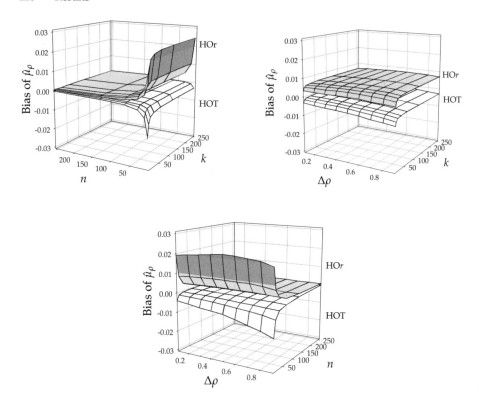

Figure 8.8   Bias of Fisher-z-based $\mu_{\rho z}$ estimators in $\mathfrak{S}_2$.

Although there are regions of the design variables where the d-based estimator shows no bias, it is quite sensitive with respect to differences between
universe parameters in comparison to other estimators. The highest absolute
values occur for combinations of small k and n. Recall again that the bias is
computed with respect to μ_ρ and that varying weights of d also exert an influence on the behavior of the estimator. As a result, HOd shows a different
behavior in bias in comparison to the situation $\mathfrak{S}_1$. Over- or underestimation
of μ_ρ is harder to predict than for other estimators.

Fisher-z Based Estimators in $\mathfrak{S}_2$.   The estimators of this category are HOr
and HOT. To reiterate, as the universe parameter for these estimators $\mu_{\rho z}$ was
used which differs from μ_ρ the larger the difference between ρ_1 and ρ_2 (see
Section 5.5). The upper left panel of Figure 8.8 shows biases for this category
of estimators similar to those in $\mathfrak{S}_1$.

Although HOT shows some deficiencies in bias with combinations of very
small k and n it can still be considered as a better estimator than HOr. The
estimates are therefore also improved in $\mathfrak{S}_2$ by the application of Hotelling's
correction. The upper right panel of Figure 8.8 shows the biases by k and differences between ρs. In contrast to the r-based estimators there is a tendency

Table 8.3 Descriptive Statistics for the Bias of μ_ρ and $\mu_{\rho z}$ Estimators in $\mathfrak{S}_2$

Approach			Statistic		
	Max.	Mean	Median	Min.	SD
HOr	.0323	.0061	.0026	−.0012	.0078
HOT	.0011	−.0019	−.0006	−.0253	.0032
HOd	.0189	.0003	.0003	−.0343	.0078
HS	.0004	−.0058	−.0026	−.0289	.0070
OP	.0041	.0000	.0000	−.0051	.0005
OP-FE	.5175	.1622	.1324	.0011	.1256
OP-RE	.1166	.0297	.0188	.0006	.0283

Note. The total number of values described by these statistics is 1890.

of larger negative biases to occur for small values of k. The biases of estimators by n and differences between ρs are shown in the lower panel of the figure. As can be seen in the upper right and lower panel, biases of HOr do not differ very much across levels of $\Delta\rho$ and the same is true for k. The number of persons shows a strong influence on biases only for very small n. In sum, the Fisher-z-based estimators do not show larger biases of concern in comparison to the results reported in $\mathfrak{S}_1$, but estimators are only precise with respect to $\mu_{\rho z}$. Finally, a highly condensed overview of the descriptive statistics for the estimators in $\mathfrak{S}_2$ is presented in Table 8.3. The values in this table underscore the conclusions for $\mathfrak{S}_2$ already drawn.

In sum, values for biases are relatively small for all estimators, except for OP-FE, and may generally not be of concern at all, as was the case in $\mathfrak{S}_1$. Although OP-RE does not show mean biases in Table 8.3 as high as those for OP-RE, the estimates are highly variable in comparison to those of other estimators. This undesirable property points to the existence of cases in which the biases for this estimator are high. Hence, it does not appear attractive as an estimator even though it is designed for heterogeneous situations.

It must again be emphasized that biases have always to be judged against the background of different universe parameters. From a substantive point of view, r-based estimators address the parameter of interest best. The d-based estimator also performs relatively well in estimating μ_ρ but its bias is less predictable in comparison to r-based estimators. The results from meta-analyses for mean effect sizes in heterogeneous situations of type $\mathfrak{S}_2$ can therefore be interpreted as estimating quite accurately the expected value of the mixing distribution. However, for Fisher-z based estimators it has to be taken into account that it is $\mu_{\rho z}$ that is estimated, a parameter usually *not* of interest to the researcher. Hence, concerns are in order regarding the usage of Fisher-z based in heterogeneous situations like $\mathfrak{S}_2$. The interpretation of the mean effect size as a "mean ρ" is not warranted in a strict sense under these circumstances. Whereas the assumption of homogeneity can be regarded as a prerequisite for an interpretation of the mean effect size of z-based approaches in $\mathfrak{S}_2$, the results from the other approaches can safely be interpreted as estimates of the expected value of the distribution of ρs. Nevertheless, whether such an estimate is of real interest must be decided by the researcher based upon substantive concerns, because a vastly different set of ρ_1 and ρ_2 may have produced the observed mean effect size.

8.2.1.3 Heterogeneous Situation $\mathfrak{S}_3$

The last situation $\mathfrak{S}_3$ for which biases of the estimators will be examined is characterized by a continuous distribution of effect sizes in the universe of studies. Analogous to the introductory remarks made in the previous Subsection 8.2.1.2, the estimated parameters μ_ρ and $\mu_{\rho z}$ used as standards of comparison for the various estimators are considered first. For the case of correlation coefficients not subjected to the Fisher-z transformation, the expected value of the beta distribution is taken as the parameter of interest. For the Fisher-z transformed coefficients, the expected value in z-space (i.e., μ_ζ) given by

$$\mu_\zeta = \int_{-1}^{1} \tanh^{-1}(r)f(r)dr$$

constitutes the standard of evaluation. Here, $f(r)$ is the beta probability density function as described in Section 4.5. The values of μ_ζ are subsequently transformed into the space of r by the inverse Fisher-z transformation $\mu_{\rho z} = \tanh \mu_\zeta$. The resulting values computed for the expected values and variances of the beta distribution are reported in Tables A.1 and A.2 in the appendix. For the same reasons as in $\mathfrak{S}_2$, the expected value μ_ρ was used for the d-based estimator and results are presented separately for the three groups of estimators in the following paragraphs.

r-Based Estimators in $\mathfrak{S}_3$. Biases of the estimators of this category over different combinations of the design variables can be inspected at a glance in Figure 8.9.

Evidently, the biases of the r-based estimators do not differ much from the previous two situations in overall quality. The OP estimator is again characterized by showing practically no biases notwithstanding which parameter constellation is prescribed by the design variables. The behavior of the estimators with respect to n and k is quite the same as before with biases showing practically no variation across values of k and larger biases for smaller n. It can also be seen that except for OP, the biases tend to be slightly smaller for HS as σ_ρ^2 becomes larger. The scaling of the vertical axis, however, shows that overall biases for HS are very small and only grow to a noticeable magnitude for extremely small sample sizes not likely to be encountered in practice. OP-FE again shows unacceptable behavior making it unsuitable as an estimator for situations of type $\mathfrak{S}_3$ as well. Hence, it does not seem reasonable to include OP-FE in all of the following performance evaluations of the various estimators.

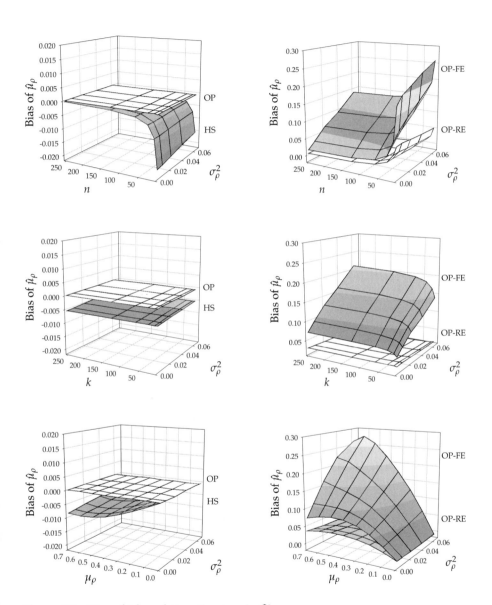

Figure 8.9   Bias of r-based μ_ρ estimators in $\mathfrak{S}_3$.

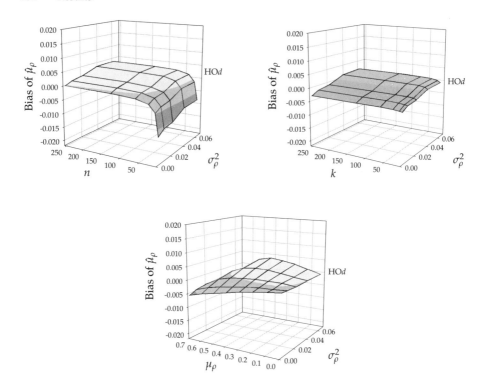

Figure 8.10   Bias of d-based μ_ρ estimators in $\mathfrak{S}_3$.

Note that the present situation is perfectly suitable for random effects approaches like OP-RE, but the performance in estimating μ_ρ is actually best for a fixed effects approach, namely OP. This is proposed to be due to the deficiencies of the weights used for OP-RE as already mentioned. Although the very good performance of OP is remarkable, disadvantages of FE approaches are suspected to lie more in testing, for example, rather than estimation of the universe parameter. The reader is also reminded that DSL, a random effects approach, leads in the present situation to the same results as HOr.

d-Based Estimator in $\mathfrak{S}_3$***.***   The next estimator for which results on biases are presented is the d-based estimator HOd. Again, an ensemble of graphs is given in Figure 8.10 to present results at a glance.

Evidently, biases of this estimator become larger only for very small n. This can be seen in the upper left panel in Figure 8.10. There is a slight tendency for higher values of HOd to occur for larger values of σ_ρ^2 but again, the pattern of relationships of biases across design variables is not as clear as for other approaches. Large values of μ_ρ are accompanied by stronger negative biases (see lower panel). Although all the biases depicted in the three panels are very small in absolute terms, the observed effects are supposed to be due to the weights employed in computing the mean effect sizes using this estimator.

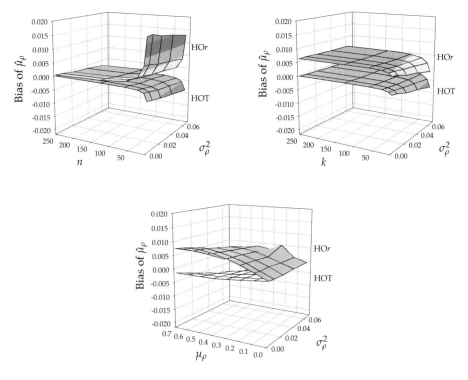

Figure 8.11   Bias of Fisher-z-based $\mu_{\rho z}$ estimators in $\mathfrak{S}_3$.

Because larger values of d are downweighted by using the weights, as already discussed in detail, and such values occur more often with larger variances of the mixing distribution, the negative bias for small σ_ρ^2 visible in the upper right panel of Figure 8.10 seems to be compensated. For large values of μ_ρ, a stronger negative bias results but all in all the values of bias are very small and not of practical concern except for cases of very small sample sizes n.

Fisher-z-based estimators in $\mathfrak{S}_3$.   The biases of the Fisher-z-based estimators are presented in Figure 8.11. The relevant estimators in this class are HOr and HOT.

As in the situations before, HOT performs better than the non-corrected Fisher-z-based estimator HOr. Very small n influences biases of these estimators in a negative way and can lead to a noticeable bias of the HOr estimator. Nevertheless, biases are not large in general and only become discernible for extreme levels of the design variables, especially n (see upper left panel in Figure 8.11. The variance of effect sizes σ_ρ^2 does not have a profound effect on the estimates of $\mu_{\rho z}$. Especially in the lower panel of Figure 8.11 some values for the estimators are hard to inspect precisely. Finally, descriptive statistics for the biases in $\mathfrak{S}_3$ are again presented in Table 8.4 for an overview of the results in $\mathfrak{S}_3$.

Table 8.4 Descriptive Statistics for the Bias of Estimators μ_ρ in $\mathfrak{S}_3$

			Statistic		
Approach	Max.	Mean	Median	Min.	SD
HO*r*	.0325	.0039	.0013	−.0286	.0080
HOT	.0038	−.0025	−.0008	−.0447	.0045
HO*d*	.0090	−.0014	.0000	−.0337	.0060
HS	.0037	−.0053	−.0022	−.0306	.0071
OP	.0037	.0000	.0000	−.0052	.0007
OP-FE	.4545	.1071	.0775	−.0068	.0992
OP-RE	.1161	.0248	.0126	−.0073	.0276

Note. Valid values for all entries are 1848.

Evidently, a similar picture as compared to $\mathfrak{S}_2$ emerges. It can be seen that biases for OP-RE and OP-FE are far more variable in comparison to the other estimators and can produce biases in maximum that are certainly not acceptable. All other estimators fare quite well with respect to the parameters they estimate. OP is clearly the best estimator also in the given situation. It is not only closest on target overall, but also shows the smallest variability in biases. For a comparison of the Fisher-z-based and the other estimators it is quite instructive to also consult Tables A.1 and A.2 in the appendix to gain an impression of how different μ_ρ and $\mu_{\rho z}$ can become.

8.2.2 Relative Efficiency

Besides the bias of an estimator as an expression of how close it is to the estimated parameter, the variance is also an aspect of its closeness to the parameter. However, it is not the variance of an estimator per se that is of concern here but the variance about the parameter of interest. That is, the squared distances from the universe parameter to be estimated are taken and not the ones with respect to the expected value of a potentially biased estimator. The well-known decomposition (see Stuart et al., 1999, p. 24)

$$\text{MSE}(T) = E(T - \theta)^2 = \text{Var}(T) + (E(T) - \theta)^2 \tag{8.1}$$

shows that for unbiased estimators T the mean squared error (MSE) equals the variance of the estimator. In the Monte Carlo study, the values computed are actually

$$\text{MSE} = \frac{1}{\text{Iter}} \sum_{l=1}^{\text{Iter}} (\hat{r}_l - \mu_\rho)^2,$$

where *Iter* signifies the number of iterations (10,000) and $\hat{r}_l$ denotes an estimator based on *r*. That is, the squared distances from the expected value of the distribution of universe effect sizes are summed over all iterations. In the following comparisons, the MSE-ratios of different estimators will be presented.

In $\mathfrak{S}_1$, μ_ρ is used as the universe parameter in the computation of the MSEs, whereas in $\mathfrak{S}_2$ and $\mathfrak{S}_3$ the question of choosing an appropriate universe parameter for comparing the approaches arises again. For the approaches that use the Fisher-z transformation in estimating the mean effect size, there are two possibilities. First, the MSEs can be computed in z-space. That is,

$$\text{MSE}_z = \frac{1}{\text{Iter}} \sum_{l=1}^{\text{Iter}} (\hat{z}_l - \mu_\zeta)^2,$$

where $\hat{z}_l$ is the estimator and μ_ζ the expected value of the mixing distribution in z-space. The additional problem arises that the MSEs for all situations of z-based estimators are not directly comparable to MSEs for r-based estimators. To make the MSEs of the various estimators in $\mathfrak{S}_2$ comparable, the term

$$h(\rho) = \frac{\sqrt{1+\rho_1+\rho_2+\rho_1\rho_2} - \sqrt{1-\rho_1-\rho_2+\rho_1\rho_2}}{\sqrt{1+\rho_1+\rho_2+\rho_1\rho_2} + \sqrt{1-\rho_1-\rho_2+\rho_1\rho_2}} - \frac{\rho_1+\rho_2}{2},$$

which is the difference between μ_ρ and $\mu_{\rho z}$, is used for correction. The correction factor gives the difference between μ_ρ and $\mu_{\rho z}$ *theoretically* to be expected for the various parameter values in $\mathfrak{S}_2$. Subtracting $h(\rho)$ from the Fisher-z transformed values ($\tanh \hat{z}_l$) offers the opportunity to compare the MSEs of the Fisher-z based and r-based estimators on a common scale via

$$\text{MSE} = \frac{1}{\text{Iter}} \sum_{l=1}^{\text{Iter}} \left((\tanh \hat{z}_l - h(\rho)) - \mu_\rho\right)^2.$$

What should become evident here is that in essence the estimator is actually changed by $h(\rho)$ to estimate a different value, namely μ_ρ. For this corrected estimator, the mean squared distances about μ_ρ are computed as for the r-based estimators. Of course, the above equation can be simplified by eliminating the redundant term μ_ρ, resulting in

$$\text{MSE} = \frac{1}{\text{Iter}} \sum_{l=1}^{\text{Iter}} \left(\tanh \hat{z}_l - \mu_\zeta\right)^2,$$

which may be conceived as the natural conception for computing the MSEs for Fisher-z-based estimators in r-space. The derivation given above has just demonstrated that using this conception of the MSE can be justified on theoretical grounds.

Following this general logic, it would be natural to use the expected values of the beta distribution in the computation of the MSEs in $\mathfrak{S}_3$ correspondingly. Unfortunately, numerical integration necessary to compute these values was considered to be computationally too expensive and a correction factor like $h(\rho)$ is not readily available for the continuous case. Hence, the comparison of all approaches is not possible in $\mathfrak{S}_3$.

Table 8.5   Relative Efficiencies of $\hat{\mu}_\rho$ in $\mathfrak{S}_1$

Approach	HOr	HOT	HOd	HS	OP	OP-RE
HOr	1					
HOT	1.1118	1				
HOd	1.1008	.9901	1			
HS	1.0931	.9832	.9930	1		
OP	1.0683	.9609	.9705	.9773	1	
OP-FE	.4741	.4264	.4307	.4337	.4438	1

Note. Table entries are the fraction of the approach found in the column header in the numerator and the row-labeled approach in the denominator. For all approaches mean values were computed over all values of ρ, k, and n.

As in the previous sections, results are presented for $\mathfrak{S}_1$ and $\mathfrak{S}_2$ consecutively, beginning with $\mathfrak{S}_1$. First, it can be noted that all MSEs of the estimators become smaller for larger k, n, and μ_ρ, respectively. Since these general trends apply to all approaches the presentation will be confined to overall results, that is, means of MSEs over all values of k, n, and μ_ρ. Table 8.5 provides a condensed overview of the relative efficiencies of the estimators in $\mathfrak{S}_1$.

Note that in $\mathfrak{S}_1$ the MSEs are comparable for all estimators without any corrections because $\mu_\rho = \mu_\zeta$. The entries in the table can be read as follows. The estimators found in the column are the entry in the numerator and the estimator in the row is the denominator of a fraction of MSEs. Values larger than one therefore represent smaller MSEs for the estimator in the denominator and vice versa. The values in Table 8.5 suggest that HOT is the most efficient estimator in terms of MSE. This is somewhat surprising given that OP has shown remarkably small biases overall, as shown in the previous sections. The reason for this finding lies in the fact that *variances* of the estimators contribute an important part to the corresponding MSEs and also to variation of MSEs across values of the design dimensions. Because the variability across levels of the design variables is very similar for all approaches, no graphical representation is given here.

To facilitate interpretation of the results in Table 8.5, the following remarks seem warranted. As can be seen in Equation 8.1, the MSEs amount to the variances of unbiased estimators and these variances may well be larger for unbiased in comparison to biased estimators. The important distinction between MSEs for these two types of estimators lies in the second term of Equation 8.1 being zero for unbiased and nonzero for biased estimators. Now consider the case of $\mu_\rho = 0$ where the HS (and also OP) estimator actually estimates μ_ρ (see page 121, for example). Here, the variance of the HS estimator is smaller than the variance of the OP estimator and the MSE ratio restricted to this case leads to a value of .9059 in favor of HS. On the other hand, if the comparison is restricted to $\rho = .50$ where the HS estimator performs worst in terms of bias, the same comparison leads to a value for the ratio of 1.0295, now favoring OP in terms of MSE. Of course, this phenomenon pertains to all comparisons in

Table 8.6   Relative Efficiencies of $\hat{\mu}_\rho$ and $\hat{\mu}_{\rho z}$ in $\mathfrak{S}_2$

Approach	HO*r*	HOT	HO*d*	HS	OP	OP-RE
HO*r*	1					
HOT	1.0968	1				
HO*d*	1.0425	.9505	1			
HS	1.0582	.9648	1.0150	1		
OP	1.0290	.9381	.9870	.9724	1	
OP-FE	.4829	.4403	.4632	.4564	.4693	1

Note. Table entries are the fraction of the approach found in the column header in the numerator and the row-labeled approach in the denominator. For all approaches mean values were computed over all values of ρ, k, and n.

Table 8.5 and also what follows. The values reported in the tables for a comparison of estimators regarding their MSEs are therefore to be interpreted with respect to the performance of estimators across the levels of the design variables. Hence, across all values of μ_ρ from zero to .90, HOT is the most efficient estimator. This does not imply that HOT is the most efficient estimator for all possible values of μ_ρ.

Table 8.6 presents the results for $\mathfrak{S}_2$ that closely mirror the results in $\mathfrak{S}_1$. The only notable difference is that HO*d* is slightly less efficient than HS in this situation.

As remarked at the beginning of this subsection, the comparison of estimators with respect to MSE in $\mathfrak{S}_3$ is not possible due to values in different spaces that could not be transformed or corrected. In sum, the surprising result for the MSEs is that OP — which performed uniformly best in all situations with respect to bias — does not also show up as the best estimator in terms of MSE. As a result, it is not more precise in general as compared to HS when all situations under investigation are taken into account (see in this context Hedges & Olkin, 1985, p. 226). Instead, HOT performed best, an estimator that also showed good performance with respect to biases. Taking these two criteria together, it can be recommended for $\mathfrak{S}_1$ to use OP when a relatively small n is given and when μ_ρ is not suspected to be very low. HOT can be considered as an alternative for larger n when μ_ρ is suspected to be small because of its higher efficiency. For $\mathfrak{S}_2$ and $\mathfrak{S}_3$ OP should be considered as first choice for it estimates the parameter usually of interest μ_ρ rather precisely in terms of bias, in contrast to HOT which estimates $\mu_{\rho z}$.

8.3   SIGNIFICANCE TESTS FOR THE MEAN EFFECT SIZE: TYPE I ERRORS AND POWER

Apart from an accurate parameter estimation, significance tests are a common feature of meta-analysis. The significance testing practice in psychology has often been criticized as mentioned in the introductory chapters. Nonetheless, all approaches offer procedures to test the estimates of the effect sizes, although some authors explicitly deemphasize using such tests (e.g., Hunter & Schmidt, 1990). In this section, the proposed procedures are evaluated with respect to their performance in testing the generally adopted null hypothesis $\mu_\rho = 0$. This will be done by examining the rejection rates of the null hypothesis under various conditions and comparing these rejection rates to the α-level a test is supposed not to exceed when the null hypothesis is true. The second case of interest is the performance of the tests when the null hypothesis is false. Both cases will be separated in the following presentation.

Since this subsection on testing is the only one in which differences between HOr and RR can occur, the latter will be included in the following tables for this subsection only. Because of the very poor performance of OP-FE reported in the previous sections of results, it will be omitted from the following presentation.

Rejection Rates in $\mathfrak{S}_1$ The results for $\mathfrak{S}_1$ are considered first. In addition to the estimators under investigation in the previous sections, four variants for testing the mean effect size in the framework of the HS approach are included. The several variants correspond to four possibilities to compute the standard error of the mean effect size. The reader is referred to Section 5.3 for a recapitulation of the several forms of standard errors proposed in this approach. Furthermore, the DSL approach is also added to examine its performance in the homogeneous case. As a criterion for the evaluation of the approaches, whether they show *higher* rates than nominal α will be assessed. Values lower than α are interpreted as indicating good performance since the null hypothesis is true.

Table 8.7 shows the rejection rates of the tests aggregated over all combinations of k and n. Readers interested in the results for specific combinations of the design variables may consult Table C.1 in the appendix where detailed results for $\alpha = .05$ are provided.

The first line for each approach in Table 8.7 provides the results for tests at $\alpha = .05$ and the second line those for $\alpha = .01$. As can be seen, the approaches that perform best are DSL and HOT. Despite both approaches having slightly higher standard deviations in comparison to HOr, which more closely attains nominal α, they also show mean rejection rates below α in this situation. At least for DSL — a random effects approach — it is suspected that this more conservative behavior comes at the cost of a loss in power. The downward correction of the mean Fisher-z based effect size by HOT effectively leads to smaller rejection rates in comparison to HOr. Note that the same standard errors were applied for HOr and HOT. Hence, apparently small differences in bias between these approaches indeed transfer to differences in test results.

For the present purpose of testing the null hypothesis, there are small procedural differences between HOr and RR, which were omitted until now. The only difference between RR and HOr lies in the weights employed where RR uses degrees of freedom instead of standard error based weights. This ob-

Table 8.7   Rejection Rates for Testing the Mean Effect Size in $\mathfrak{S}_1$, $\mu_\rho = 0$

	Statistic				
Approach	Max.	Mean	Median	Min.	SD
HO*r*	.0547	.0501	.0504	.0437	.0022
	.0119	.0100	.0099	.0077	.0009
HOT	.0535	.0458	.0472	.0313	.0054
	.0110	.0086	.0090	.0044	.0017
HO*d*	.0702	.0554	.0530	.0476	.0059
	.0190	.0119	.0111	.0078	.0025
RR	.0688	.0543	.0523	.0475	.0052
	.0170	.0114	.0110	.0078	.0020
HS1	.0695	.0519	.0511	.0460	.0041
	.0250	.0111	.0104	.0077	.0027
HS2	.0866	.0591	.0547	.0480	.0104
	.0316	.0141	.0120	.0078	.0054
HS3	.1291	.0705	.0577	.0475	.0257
	.0741	.0247	.0140	.0096	.0205
HS4	.1256	.0645	.0539	.0330	.0261
	.0701	.0219	.0123	.0050	.0196
OP	.0853	.0560	.0531	.0475	.0079
	.0341	.0129	.0115	.0078	.0046
OP-RE	.2224	.0849	.0582	.0433	.0491
	.1392	.0320	.0139	.0066	.0347
DSL	.0503	.0430	.0434	.0356	.0036
	.0101	.0079	.0080	.0057	.0011

Note. The total number of values described by these statistics is 42. Proportion for tests at $\alpha = .05$ are given in the first row of each approach and for tests at $\alpha = .01$ in the second row.

viously leads to slightly higher rejection rates in comparison to the nominal α-level.

Amongst the HS variants two groups can be identified: HS1 and HS2 versus HS3 and HS4. This corresponds to standard errors proposed for homogeneous (HS1 and HS2) and heterogeneous (HS3 and HS4) situations. Since HS3 is assumed to be adequate both for homogeneous and heterogeneous situations (Osburn & Callender, 1992), special attention may be paid to the results of this particular variant. The results in Table 8.7 show that, for the group of HS-variants proposed for homogeneous situations such as the present one, HS1 is closest on the α-levels whereas HS2 overshoots. Usage of the tests from the second group leads to rejection rates being too high overall. This predominantly occurs in cases where a low number of studies are aggregated.

OP performs as well (or bad) as RR and HO*d* whereas the random effects approaches behave quite differently. DSL performs as expected from theory,

Table 8.8   Rejection Rates for Testing the Mean Effect Size in $\mathfrak{S}_1, \mu_\rho \neq 0, \alpha = .05$

Approach	μ_ρ								
	.10	.20	.30	.40	.50	.60	.70	.80	.90
HOr	.7856	.9228	.9690	.9875	.9958	.9990	.9999	1	1
HOT	.7761	.9162	.9650	.9852	.9946	.9986	.9998	1	1
HOd	.7965	.9300	.9732	.9897	.9966	.9992	.9999	1	1
RR	.7945	.9287	.9724	.9894	.9965	.9992	.9999	1	1
HS1	.7907	.9275	.9724	.9895	.9966	.9992	.9999	1	1
HS2	.8035	.9348	.9762	.9913	.9974	.9995	1	1	1
HS3	.8094	.9357	.9753	.9901	.9965	.9989	.9998	1	1
HS4	.7978	.9291	.9718	.9884	.9958	.9987	.9997	.9999	1
OP	.7985	.9325	.9751	.9908	.9972	.9994	.9999	1	1
OP-RE	.8162	.9385	.9765	.9904	.9965	.9989	.9997	.9999	1
DSL	.7680	.9122	.9625	.9836	.9937	.9980	.9996	.9999	1

Note. The total number of values described by these statistics is 42 for each μ_ρ.

showing rejection rates below the nominal α due to overestimates of random effects variance in this situation (see also Section 8.5). OP-RE in contrast, shows very high rejection rates, a fact that would not be expected for random effects approaches. The reason for this finding is the bad performance of OP-RE in cases of $n < 64$. A combination of small n and *high k* exacerbate this malperformance. Again, bad results from estimation of the mean effect size transfer to bad results in significance testing.

The case of $\mu_\rho \neq 0$ can be considered to enable an examination of the test results with regard to their power.[3] That is, rejection rates for the null hypothesis are presented when it is actually false. Hence, they should be interpreted as rate estimates of correctly rejecting the null hypothesis. Table 8.8 provides an overview of the results for increasing μ_ρ and $\alpha = .05$.

As can be seen in the table, all the tests seem to rapidly attain satisfactory[4] levels of .80 when aggregated across k and n. Of course, approaches showing higher rejection rates when the null hypothesis is true generally perform better in this context. Results for the rejection rates when $\alpha = .01$ are not presented. They show a similar performance for the approaches as compared to those in the presented case.

As would be expected from theory, rejection rates are larger for higher levels of *n and k*. Satisfactory power levels are rapidly reached even for modest values of $k = 32$, for example. The general trends are illustrated in Figure 8.12.

---

[3]This term is used somewhat loosely in the present context because no alternative hypotheses are explicitly considered. The values to be presented for the rejection rates may nevertheless be regarded as some approximation to the power function of the tests (cf. Barnett, 1981).
[4]According to Cohen (1988, 1992).

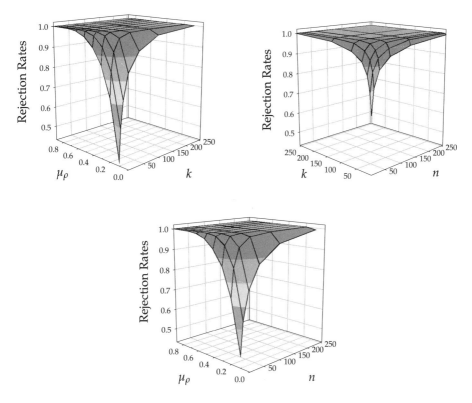

Figure 8.12 Rejection rates for testing the mean effect size in $\mathfrak{S}_1$, $\mu_\rho \neq 0$, $\alpha = .05$, HOr approach.

Here, the results for only one approach (HOr) are depicted since the trends are the same for all approaches and the surfaces would not be discriminable. In general, differences between approaches are not very large in testing the null hypothesis in $\mathfrak{S}_1$. HOr exhibits a performance closest to nominal α-levels when the null hypothesis is true and all approaches reach satisfactory levels for power rather quickly.

Nonetheless, the three panels in Figure 8.12 also point to cases for which power might not be satisfactorily high. An additional table is provided in the appendix (Table C.2) which is especially informative to qualify the results in Table 8.8 with respect to k and n. It shows rejection rates for selected levels of design variables supposed to be of highest interest with respect to regions in the figure where power is not very high. The results basically underscore the general impression gained from the figure. Power can be low for small effect sizes in the universe ($\rho = .10$), especially when n and k are very low. Even when n is at a level presumably considered as moderate or sufficient by many researchers ($n = 126$) and which can be observed quite often in correlational studies in the behavioral sciences, detection of a small universe effect size can be conducted without reaching satisfactorily high levels of power. For exam-

Table 8.9 Rejection Rates for Testing the Mean Effect Size in $\mathfrak{S}_2$ for Selected $\mu_\rho \neq 0, \alpha = .05$

Approach	μ_ρ							
	.05	.10	.15	.20	.30	.40	.50	.60
HOr	.5815	.7889	.8787	.9270	.9730	.9915	.9978	.9995
HOT	.5703	.7792	.8707	.9205	.9691	.9896	.9971	.9993
HOd	.5936	.7976	.8856	.9313	.9739	.9900	.9961	.9990
RR	.5910	.7957	.8840	.9301	.9736	.9908	.9973	.9994
HS1	.5847	.7917	.8818	.9290	.9735	.9910	.9974	.9994
HS2	.6025	.8066	.8930	.9381	.9790	.9939	.9986	.9997
HS3	.5875	.7669	.8679	.9083	.9563	.9768	.9914	.9978
HS4	.5725	.7544	.8582	.9004	.9512	.9738	.9899	.9974
OP	.5944	.7995	.8879	.9335	.9758	.9918	.9976	.9995
OP-RE	.6145	.7891	.8792	.9165	.9542	.9609	.9817	.9963
DSL	.5444	.7309	.8366	.8822	.9385	.9653	.9872	.9966

Note. The total number of values described by these statistics varies between 42 and 168 for each μ_ρ due to some differences occurring more often than others for the combination of design variable levels. For the omitted values of $\mu_\rho \geq .70$ all values are practically equal to 1.

ple, power is lower than .80 for all approaches in cases where $k = 4$, $n = 128$, and $\rho = .10$. Overall, the approaches do not vary greatly in behavior with respect to power in $\mathfrak{S}_1$. Although some approaches (e.g., DSL) show lower rejections rates than others (e.g., OP), differences are small in comparison.

Rejection Rates in $\mathfrak{S}_2$ Next, we turn to the test results in $\mathfrak{S}_2$. The null hypothesis μ_ρ is always false in $\mathfrak{S}_2$ because at least one $\rho \neq 0$. Accordingly, the results of the Monte Carlo study only reflect the power of the tests. In Table 8.9 the mean rejection rates are presented for varying values of μ_ρ.

Once more, rejection rates show only small differences between approaches. The overall trends as presented in Table 8.9 are similar in comparison to the results in $\mathfrak{S}_1$. As far as general trends across the design variables are concerned, only a selection of figures is presented here to illustrate the largest differences between the approaches.

The series of graphs in Figure 8.13 depict the dependencies of rejection rates on the design variables n, k, and μ_ρ for the approaches HOr and DSL. All other approaches show a performance "in between" the ones presented. As can be seen by comparison of the left and right panels, the random effects approach leads to more conservative test results especially for small k and intermediate μ_ρ. This is due to incorporation of heterogeneity variances in the standard errors of the tests making them more conservative than fixed effects approaches. This difference occurs for DSL and also OP-RE not shown in the figure. In comparison to the homogeneous situation $\mathfrak{S}_1$ the tests are not as powerful

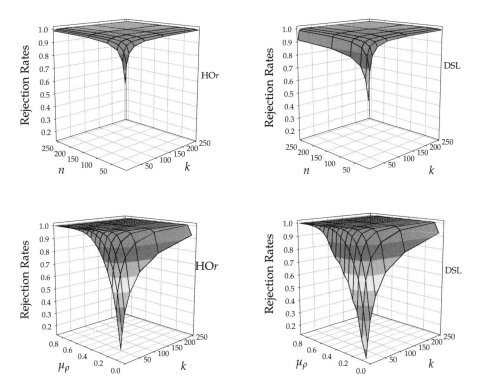

Figure 8.13   Rejection rates for testing for the mean effect size in $\mathfrak{S}_2$, $\mu_\rho \neq 0$, $\alpha = .05$, HO*r* and DSL approach.

for small effects (e.g., $\rho = .10$). The lower panels in Figure 8.13 in particular point to the result of inadequate power for the approaches for the boundary regions of the design. The interested reader might wish to consult Tables C.3 and C.4 where detailed results for these boundary regions are presented. In short, even when the study sample size seems reasonable for the aggregated studies in a meta-analysis ($n = 128$) and a number of studies — rather typical for some meta-analyses and considered by some as "large" — of $k = 32$ is available, small effects of $\mu_\rho = .05$ are not detectable with a power of .80 by any of the approaches. However, the power raises very quickly for all approaches for higher effects in the universe of studies. In sum, performance of the approaches in testing the generally adopted null hypothesis $\mu_\rho = 0$ in $\mathfrak{S}_2$ is very similar. In cases where power problems seem to prevail, none of the approaches seem to offer a considerable advantage over the others.

Rejection Rates in $\mathfrak{S}_3$ The last part of results for significance tests is presented for $\mathfrak{S}_3$, where two cases are distinguished. As in $\mathfrak{S}_1$, results for $\mu_\rho = 0$ will first be given followed by the results for $\mu_\rho \neq 0$. Table 8.10 provides a condensed overview of the results for the case when the null hypothesis is true.

Table 8.10   Rejection Rates for Testing the Mean Effect Size in $\mathfrak{S}_3$, $\mu_\rho = 0$

| | Statistic | | | | |
Approach	Max.	Mean	Median	Min.	SD
HOr	.3599	.1410	.1026	.0472	.0880
	.3046	.0775	.0364	.0089	.0795
HOT	.3596	.1360	.0994	.0338	.0912
	.3044	.0749	.0349	.0054	.0806
HOd	.3539	.1427	.1043	.0576	.0828
	.2946	.0769	.0369	.0127	.0754
RR	.3519	.1408	.1013	.0562	.0828
	.2928	.0753	.0359	.0119	.0751
HS1	.3518	.1381	.1003	.0485	.0845
	.2926	.0747	.0358	.0095	.0754
HS2	.3603	.1510	.1145	.0595	.0821
	.3043	.0837	.0449	.0144	.0766
HS3	.1347	.0698	.0583	.0465	.0250
	.0760	.0246	.0144	.0079	.0201
HS4	.1289	.0639	.0541	.0318	.0255
	.0743	.0220	.0131	.0040	.0195
OP	.3519	.1425	.1041	.0566	.0818
	.2928	.0773	.0391	.0129	.0743
OP-RE	.2139	.0906	.0814	.0499	.0335
	.1336	.0351	.0260	.0094	.0236
DSL	.1005	.0551	.0527	.0349	.0111
	.0494	.0143	.0114	.0055	.0079

Note. The total number of values described by these statistics is 210. Proportion for tests at $\alpha = .05$ are given in the first row of each approach and for tests at $\alpha = .01$ in the second row.

As can be seen from the results in Table 8.10, the performance of the approaches can roughly be categorized in two groups. On the one hand, fixed effects approaches like HOr, HOd, HS1, and OP, for example, show relatively large inflated mean Type I error rates. These approaches show adequate rejection rates only in minimum and also have relatively high standard deviations. On the other hand, random effects approaches like OP-RE and especially DSL perform adequately overall in this situation. The HS variants HS3 and HS4 perform like the random effects approaches though not as well as DSL, for example. Hence, the violation of basic assumptions of the fixed effects approach in $\mathfrak{S}_3$ leads to differences in rejection rates. This was not as clear in $\mathfrak{S}_2$, though this is a heterogeneous situation too.

Apart from the overall performance, it should be mentioned that the results markedly differ across levels of the design variables. The results for varying levels of these variables are therefore presented next. In Figure 8.14, a selection

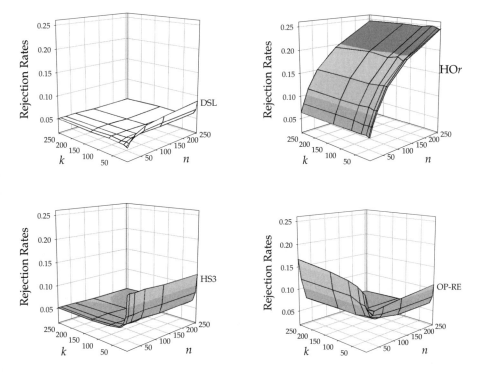

Figure 8.14   Rejection rates for testing the mean effects size in $\mathfrak{S}_3$ by n and k, $\mu_\rho = 0$, $\alpha = .05$.

of approaches is depicted that represents prototypical trends of the results for rejection rates in $\mathfrak{S}_3$ when the null hypothesis is true.

The upper left panel shows that the DSL approach leads to rejection rates corresponding to the nominal α for most of the values of k and n, the only exception is a slight elevation of rejection rates for k less than 16. Nonetheless, the rejection rates for DSL are not very high in any region of the n and k combinations under investigation. The lower left panel shows that HS3 (and HS4 which performs equally well) yields inflated rejection rates for small k invariably across values of n. Notwithstanding these elevated Type I errors, the overall performance of this approach seems acceptable here. OP-RE in the lower right panel shows too high rejection rates for a small number of studies and also for values of small k. Although this approach suffers from inadequate performance in estimating the mean effect size, the rejection rates in this situation do not seem unacceptable for moderate values of n and k.

In marked contrast to these results, *all* other other approaches (HOr, HOT, HOd, RR, HS1, HS2, and OP), for which HOr is depicted in the upper right panel as a representative, show a totally different trend across values of n. The rejection rates steadily increase with higher values of n but show no variation across values of k. In effect, the performance of these tests in $\mathfrak{S}_3$ becomes worse the higher the n of the studies. This demonstrates that the standard errors of

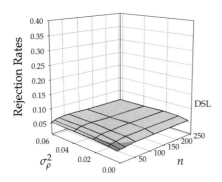 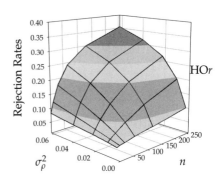

Figure 8.15   Rejection rates for testing the mean effects size in $\mathfrak{S}_3$ by n and σ_ρ^2, $\mu_\rho = 0$, $\alpha = .05$.

these approaches are too small in this heterogeneous situation, not reflecting variation with respect to σ_ρ^2.

In addition to the rejection rates getting higher with n, Figure 8.15 shows that rejection rates are also higher for larger values of σ_ρ^2 — at least for HOr and the other fixed effects approaches. The variation of the rejection rates across values of n and σ_ρ^2 is depicted in Figure 8.15.

For comparison, the rejection rates for the DSL approach are shown in the left panel and the results for the fixed effects approaches as represented by HOr in the right panel. Evidently, the rejection rates of the HOr approach quickly become far too large even for moderate values of n and σ_ρ^2. Because this approach did not show remarkable bias across levels of the design variables, this can be interpreted as an effect of the standard error estimates. In marked contrast, DSL shows a very good performance across values of σ_ρ^2. There are no elevations of the rejection rate surface in the left panel of Figure 8.15. Taking further into account that DSL also showed rejection rates close to nominal α, apart from in cases of very low n, it is certainly the best approach of those under consideration for testing the mean effect size in $\mathfrak{S}_3$-type situations.

Next, the results for the case $\mu_\rho \neq 0$ will be presented to assess the power of the approaches in $\mathfrak{S}_3$. The main findings are illustrated in an array of graphs in Figure 8.16.

In this figure, only two approaches are depicted that illustrate the different results for fixed versus random effects approaches. The shaded surface in the three panels portrays the slightly more powerful rejection rates for the fixed effects approaches (e.g., HOr). However, the differences to the random effects approach (e.g., DSL) — shown as a white surface lying underneath but close to the one of the FE approaches — are quite small across all design dimensions. Altogether, the figures show only minor differences in power *between* the approaches. With regard to the levels of the design variables, it is noteworthy that different variances in the universe of studies σ_ρ^2 do not have a strong effect on testing the mean effect size. Although there is indeed a drop in rejection rates in the upper right panel of Figure 8.16, the effect is not strong for both types of

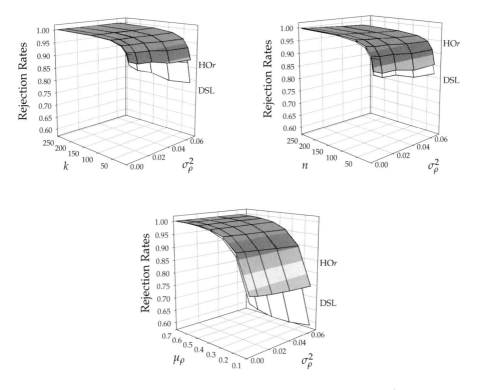

Figure 8.16   Rejection rates for testing the mean effect size in $\mathfrak{S}_3$, $\mu_\rho \neq 0$, $\alpha = .05$.

approaches. In contrast, low levels of k, n and small effects are predictors for low levels of power in $\mathfrak{S}_3$ as well.

With reference to the absolute values shown in the figures, it must again be emphasized that the results shown are always aggregates across the other design dimensions. For example, the DSL approach does not always attain a rejection rate of at least .65 as the array of graphics may suggest at first glance. In a worst-case-scenario of $n = 8$, $k = 4$, $\mu_\rho = .10$, and $\sigma_\rho^2 = .0625$ the estimator only shows a minimum rejection rate for the levels of the design variables of .1353, thereby highlighting the point that the figures are intended for comparison of approaches only, as outlined in the introduction of this chapter.

In sum, the results of the tests for the approaches are best when their basic model assumptions with respect to the fixed versus random effects model of meta-analysis are met (see also Hedges & Vevea, 1998). Differences in $\mathfrak{S}_1$ and $\mathfrak{S}_2$ do not seem to be very large between the approaches, but in $\mathfrak{S}_3$ — when μ_ρ is zero — there are tremendous differences in rejection rates. Hence, in a state of ignorance about the true situation, the potential loss in power caused by applying a random effects approach seems to be justifiable. In light of the errors potentially committed by applying fixed effects models in $\mathfrak{S}_3$ it seems advisable to accept slightly lower power levels.

8.4   CONFIDENCE INTERVALS

Confidence intervals for the approaches will be evaluated with respect to the rate to which they cover the universe parameter the estimators are supposed to estimate. These rates will be labeled as *coverage rates* in the following. They are often considered as a rather important aspect of the quality of meta-analytical approaches. This is evidenced, for example, by the fact that Brockwell and Gordon (2001) based their empirical comparison of approaches (fixed-effects method for log odds ratios, DSL, and a conditionally random effects procedure) almost exclusively on the results for coverage rates and interval widths. Since high coverage rates may be achieved by unduly large confidence interval widths, the mean interval widths will also be presented along with the coverage rates to establish a better foundation for evaluation. The coverage rates were computed as proportions over 10,000 iterations. The confidence limits are also aggregates over iterations so that they need not be exactly symmetrical about the mean effect sizes. Information given for the widths of intervals was computed from these confidence limits. In all cases, only 95%-confidence limits were investigated.

Coverage Rates and Interval Widths in $\mathfrak{S}_1$ Overall statistics for the coverage rates and 95%-confidence interval widths in $\mathfrak{S}_1$ are presented in Table 8.11. They will again be complemented by some graphical representations of the approaches' performance across levels of design variables, after a short discussion of the overall findings.

Of all the approaches, HOT reaches the highest coverage rates for a 95%-confidence interval. All other approaches show coverage rates lower than the standard of .95. In comparison to the overall interval widths of the other approaches, however, HOT also shows larger values. Hence, the high coverage rates may be obtained by virtue of larger interval widths. A second approach with rather good performance is OP. In this case however, relatively good coverage rates are not coupled with high interval widths.

The overall coverage rates for HS3, HS4, and OP-RE, for example, shown in Table 8.11 are too low to be acceptable. Interval widths are not simultaneously very small and minimum coverages show that these approaches show unacceptable performance at least in same regions of the design.

There are several determinants of the coverage rates of the approaches, so that differences between approaches are not easily interpretable. One possible reason for coverage rates being lower than expected is the bias of the estimators. For example, HOr and HOT are subject to exactly the same procedures for construction of the intervals, the only difference between these estimators is the correction of the estimator proposed by Hotelling (1953). This makes it possible to trace the reason for the lower coverage rates of HOr back to the bias in the estimator because the corrected version HOT shows appropriate rates. An analogous comparison is also possible for HS1 and OP. The standard errors are computed for OP the same way as for HS1 (compare Equations 5.7

Table 8.11   Coverage Rates and Confidence Interval Widths in $\mathfrak{S}_1$

	Statistic				
Approach	Max.	Mean	Median	Min.	SD
HO*r*	.9552	.9225	.9467	.1714	.0820
	.8244	.1208	.0702	.0029	.1383
HOT	.9715	.9548	.9530	.9449	.0059
	.8244	.1228	.0726	.0029	.1404
HO*d*	.9534	.8911	.9276	.0187	.1118
	.6830	.1070	.0617	.0023	.1182
HS1	.9545	.9202	.9446	.1877	.0801
	.7136	.1142	.0700	.0029	.1242
HS2	.9549	.9174	.9407	.2892	.0732
	.6436	.1105	.0707	.0029	.1159
HS3	.9521	.8941	.9214	.3035	.0713
	.6005	.1056	.0689	.0029	.1086
HS4	.9706	.8946	.9227	.1961	.0799
	.6657	.1090	.0677	.0029	.1166
OP	.9539	.9360	.9438	.8363	.0198
	.7095	.1125	.0667	.0029	.1223
OP-RE	.9584	.6525	.7786	.0001	.3113
	.8574	.1270	.0766	.0030	.1440
DSL	.9674	.9317	.9550	.1742	.0823
	.9098	.1301	.0729	.0030	.1523

Note. The total number of values described by these statistics is 420. Statistics for coverage rates are given in the first row of each approach and statistics for the widths of the confidence intervals in the second row.

and 5.11) but estimators differ. Hence, the benefit of an estimator's small bias is recognizable in the given context too.

In addition to the potential bias of an estimator, differences in standard error computations also contribute to the differences in rates and widths of the intervals. However, standard errors are not readily comparable between all estimators, except for the case of HS1 to HS4. Here, the mean effect size is exactly the same for all variants but standard errors differ. Amongst the HS variants, HS1 and HS2 show better performance than HS3 and HS4 in $\mathfrak{S}_1$. Recall again that HS3 was proposed to show good performance both in homogeneous and heterogeneous situations. The comparison between HOT and DSL shows that smaller interval widths do not necessarily lead to lower coverage rates, though this is a strong tendency in the results. The reason for better performance of HOT on both accounts is its smaller bias. This fact again underscores the importance of small bias in estimators, even when differences in accuracy between estimators appeared to be relatively small. The consideration of the minima of coverage rates also strongly emphasizes the importance

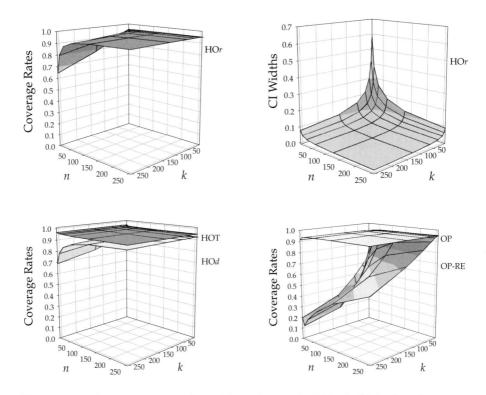

Figure 8.17 Coverage rates and confidence interval widths in $\mathfrak{S}_1$ by k and n.

of small biases. Remarkably, the estimators having shown the smallest bias exhibit, even in minimum across *all* situations considered in the design, very good (HOT) or fairly good (OP) coverage rates.

To illustrate the constellations of levels of design variables leading to poor performance of some approaches, a series of graphs is presented in Figure 8.17. They depict the dependencies of coverages and interval widths on n and k.

The first set of graphs in Figure 8.17 (upper left and both lower panels) shows the coverage rates for a selection of approaches and a separate graph for the interval widths (upper right panel). As in the figures presented in previous sections, approaches are omitted that show very similar surfaces in comparison to the ones depicted and might not be discriminated even when included in the graphs. The selection of approaches is chosen to illustrate the main trends: HO*r* also represents HS1 to HS4, RR, and DSL. HOT, HO*d*, OP, and OP-RE are depicted separately. Although HS3 and HS4 show smaller coverage rates as shown in Table 8.11, they can also be subsumed under HO*r* because of their similarity in trends. For the confidence interval widths only one graph is shown because all approaches nearly have the same surfaces. Interestingly, interval widths do not depend differently on levels of n and k for all approaches. Interval widths grow large for all approaches only in cases of both small sample sizes and a small number of studies. The shrinkage in widths seems to be

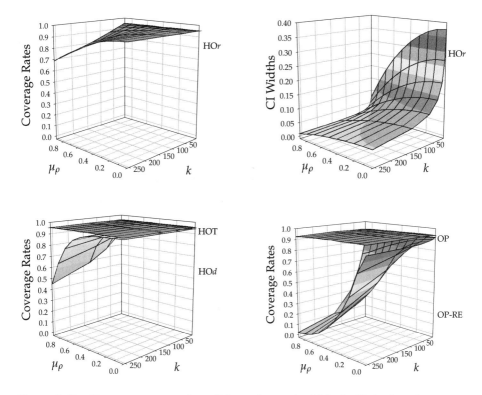

Figure 8.18 Coverage rates and confidence interval widths in $\mathfrak{S}_1$ by k and μ_ρ.

approximately the same when holding n constant and focusing on a growing number of studies and vice versa.

As is evident from Figure 8.17, small n in combination with large k leads to diminishing coverage rates for all approaches except OP and HOT. This again suggest that biases are the cause for poor performance because standard errors are smallest for large k — as is also evidenced by the smaller interval widths — and biases are largest with small n (see Section 8.2.1.1). Cautions are raised by this finding against the use confidence intervals of most procedures to construct confidence intervals in $\mathfrak{S}_1$ when n is small and k is large. Nevertheless, the excellent coverage rates for HOT and OP as evidenced by their flat surface in Figure 8.17 makes them first choice in $\mathfrak{S}_1$ not only for the purpose of estimating the mean effect size but also for the construction of confidence intervals.

For further insight into the dependencies of coverage rates and interval widths on levels of design variables, Figure 8.18 provides the results for levels of k and μ_ρ. It can again be expected that the results of the coverage rates mirror performance of the estimators' bias.

As before, interval widths as shown in the upper right panel in Figure 8.18 do not markedly differ between approaches. Hence, one graph seems to suffice to portray all relevant information for a comparison of approaches. The gradient of the confidence interval width surface is again in agreement with expectations from statistical theory. Intervals are smaller for large k and — for the case of correlation coefficients as effect sizes — widths become smaller with larger μ_ρ. It might be surprising that this should also be the case for Fisher-z based approaches because it was highlighted in several sections that the standard errors of the mean effect size estimators for these approaches do *not* depend on the parameter itself (see, e.g., Equation 5.2 on page 58). This is true, however, in z-space and the results depicted in the figures are all in r-space. A certain interval width of .09 in z-space — which approximately results for the case $n = 32$ and $k = 16$ — corresponds to an interval width of approximately .04 at a mean effect size level of .90 and to a width of .12 at the level of .60. Hence, the change of spaces from z to r in the present case makes the shape of the surface appear reasonable also for Fisher-z based approaches.

The upper left and lower panels in Figure 8.18 depict the coverage rates for the approaches. As can be seen for most approaches, lower coverage rates result for combinations of vary large μ_ρ and *high k*. For OP-RE this phenomenon is certainly due to its large bias but for HOr and HOd biases were shown to be quite small. Especially for HOd rather low coverage rates are shown in the critical design region.

The performance of OP and HOT again stands in marked contrast to those of other approaches. The coverage rates of both approaches is again depicted as a surface at the level of approximately .95. Almost the same picture emerges in the final set of graphs in Figure 8.19. As in the previous figures, the coverage rates and interval widths are shown for combinations of n and μ_ρ in three panels and the upper right one shows the interval widths.

The interval widths basically show the same trends for all approaches and a surface is shown in Figure 8.19 which very much resembles that in the previous figure, only shown from a different angle of view. The widths of confidence intervals are largest for all approaches in combinations of small n and small μ_ρ, as would be expected. The coverage rates decline for combinations of very large μ_ρ and rather small n. This shows again the deleterious effect of small interval widths and large biases.

Coverage Rates and Interval Widths in $\mathfrak{S}_2$ Next, the heterogeneous situation with two different values in the universe of studies is treated. First of all, it should again be noted that the coverages are evaluated with respect to the parameters the estimators are supposed to estimate, just as in Section 8.2.1.2. This is important for a comparative evaluation of approaches in this context. That is, the universe values to be covered by the confidence limits are *different* for the Fisher-z based and r-based approaches with differences in universe parameters (μ_ρ vs. $\mu_{\rho z}$) being larger, the higher the difference is between the two universe values of ρ (i.e., $\Delta\rho$). Furthermore, as in Section 8.2.1.2, the coverage rates for HOd in $\mathfrak{S}_2$ were evaluated with respect to μ_ρ and not to $\mu_{\rho d}$. For an explanation as to why this is the case, see Section 5.5.

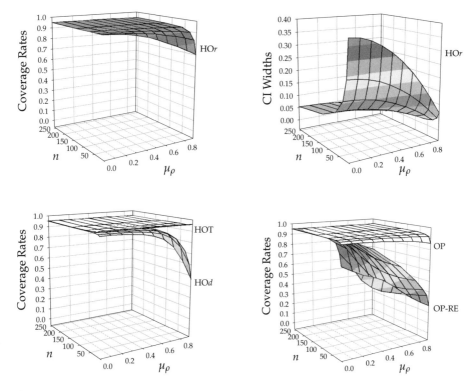

Figure 8.19 Coverage rates and confidence interval widths in $\mathfrak{S}_1$ by n and μ_ρ.

The overall results on coverage rates and confidence interval widths for 95%-Intervals are first presented. Table 8.12 shows descriptive statistics for a comparative evaluation of the approaches.

The values presented in Table 8.12 suggest that the interval widths are considerably larger for all approaches, not only random effects approaches. Nevertheless, for the latter the intervals are approximately twice as wide as for the fixed effects approaches. In the extreme, this leads to intervals larger than one and to coverage rates of up to one in maximum (e.g., DSL).

The results shown in Table 8.12 again demonstrate that OP and particularly HOT approximately attain the desired coverage rates without having excessively large interval widths. Additionally, even the minimum values for the coverage rates indicate a very good performance of the approaches in all cases under investigation. In contrast, the minimum values for all other approaches suggest that there are situations in which they perform very poorly. Other fixed effects approaches like HS1 and HS2, however, also attain good mean overall coverage rates without excessively large interval widths, but the minima for these approaches indicate bad performance at least in some cases under consideration. The highest mean coverages are shown for DSL, but this

Table 8.12   Coverage Rates and Confidence Interval Widths in $\mathfrak{S}_2$

Approach	Statistic				
	Max.	Mean	Median	Min.	SD
HOr	.9559	.9266	.9464	.2237	.0639
	.8223	.1219	.0760	.0041	.1321
HOT	.9714	.9544	.9529	.9247	.0057
	.8226	.1244	.0776	.0041	.1353
HOd	.9751	.8883	.9311	.0000	.1385
	.6508	.1160	.0764	.0035	.1170
HS1	.9751	.9345	.9470	.2595	.0514
	.7130	.1213	.0790	.0043	.1229
HS2	.9555	.9238	.9410	.3468	.0510
	.6415	.1144	.0758	.0044	.1120
HS3	1	.9718	.9958	.4515	.0486
	.9494	.2060	.1500	.0131	.1690
HS4	1	.9738	.9961	.3653	.0479
	.9993	.2104	.1514	.0130	.1745
OP	.9743	.9407	.9457	.8303	.0200
	.7088	.1198	.0785	.0043	.1209
OP-RE	1	.8627	.9714	.0012	.2249
	1.2930	.2538	.1780	.0149	.2219
DSL	1	.9784	.9971	.2611	.0516
	1.1109	.2280	.1556	.0127	.2034

Note. The total number of values described by these statistics is 1890. Statistics for 95% confidence intervals are given in the first row of each approach and statistics for the width of the confidence intervals in the second row.

is easily explained by the fact that the interval widths are unduly large and should therefore not lead to an overly positive evaluation.

The set of graphs provided in Figure 8.20 illustrates the trends of the coverages and interval widths in $\mathfrak{S}_2$. Again, only a small selection of approaches is depicted to show overall trends in cases where some classes of approaches do not differ markedly in performance. As representatives, DSL and HOr are given. DSL stands for the random effects approaches as well as HS3 and HS4, whereas HOr roughly represents all other approaches except for OP and HOT. The latter two both show flat surfaces at a height of approximately .95 across all levels of design variables for the coverage rates and interval width surfaces similar to those of HOr shown in Figure 8.20. Hence, these two approaches perform uniformly best in all cases but, again, it should be noted that HOT does so with respect to $\mu_{\rho z}$ and OP with respect to μ_ρ. Taking this into account, OP seems to be the approach of choice in the present context.

The upper panels in Figure 8.20 show coverage rates and interval widths by n and k. As expected, DSL shows larger widths of intervals than HOr and also

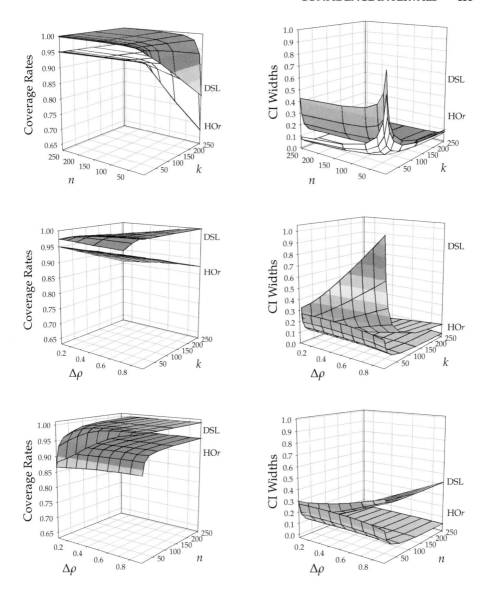

Figure 8.20   Coverage rates and confidence interval widths in $\mathfrak{S}_2$.

higher coverage rates. The coverage rates for DSL actually approach a value of one even for small values of n and k. Thus, they are higher than can be expected for the construction of 95% confidence intervals. This also stands in contrast to the coverages of HOr attaining a value of .95 in limit. However, the effect of bias emerges again in extreme combinations of high k and small n for both approaches. As can be seen in the mid- and lower panels, DSL does react to different values of $\Delta\rho$ in contrast to HOr which performs almost equally

Table 8.13   Coverage Rates and Confidence Interval Widths in $\mathfrak{S}_3$

Approach	Max.	Mean	Median	Min.	SD
HO*d*	.9418	.7014	.7628	.0320	.2039
	.6942	.1179	.0773	.0024	.1223
HS1	.9507	.7215	.7842	.1897	.1944
	.7140	.1235	.0805	.0029	.1272
HS2	.9361	.7106	.7731	.1992	.1876
	.6429	.1174	.0783	.0032	.1166
HS3	.9532	.9044	.9262	.4588	.0542
	.6863	.1700	.1299	.0127	.1280
HS4	.9707	.9082	.9322	.4002	.0566
	.7573	.1747	.1327	.0126	.1355
OP	.9425	.7246	.7915	.1913	.1922
	.7100	.1221	.0800	.0029	.1254
OP-RE	.9970	.8059	.8696	.0024	.1953
	.9283	.2041	.1522	.0150	.1637

Note. The total number of values described by these statistics is 1848. Statistics for coverage rates are given in the first row of each approach and statistics for the widths of the confidence intervals in the second row.

across all levels of $\Delta\rho$. As a fixed effects approach, HO*r* therefore does not reflect the additional variability introduced by larger universe parameter differences. However, the results also suggest that DSL does overreact on these differences in the sense of overestimating the heterogeneity variance. An examination of this impression will not be presented here but postponed to an in-depth assessment of the estimators of heterogeneity variance in Section 8.6.

Coverage Rates and Interval Widths in $\mathfrak{S}_3$ For a full evaluation of all approaches in $\mathfrak{S}_3$ it would have been necessary to implement expected values of the beta distribution in *z*-space (i.e., μ_ζ) as a standard for comparison for the approaches that use the Fisher-*z* transformation. As already noted, this was considered not to be feasible. Accordingly, the following presentation has to be restricted to approaches for which μ_ρ can be used as a standard for comparison. As before, a table of overall results is presented for a comparison of the performance of the approaches. Table 8.13 gives descriptive results for the available approaches in this situation.

First, it is noted that none of the approaches yields the desired coverage rate of .95 in mean or median. Somewhat surprisingly, HS3 and HS4 stand out here with best performance amongst the approaches under consideration. Although these approaches also show higher interval widths in relation to the fixed effects approaches, they attain better coverage rates than OP-RE with smaller mean confidence intervals. In contrast to the previous situations, OP does *not* show acceptable performance. Mean and median coverage rates are

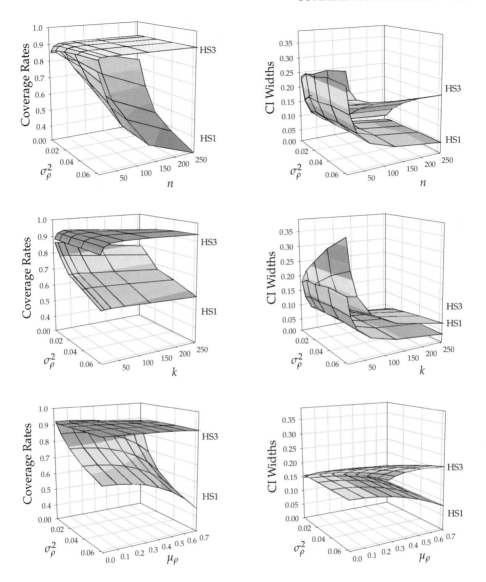

Figure 8.21 Coverage rates and confidence interval widths in $\mathfrak{S}_3$.

too small and the minimum coverage rate also shows that there are cases of very bad performance for this approach. This is astonishing given the estimator's brilliant performance with respect to mean effect size estimation. Hence, the additional variability in the universe of effect sizes is not adequately reflected in the computation of the standard errors in this FE approach, leading to unacceptable performance in the construction of confidence intervals.

The information presented in Table 8.13 shows that there are conditions for all approaches in which they perform rather poorly. The series of graphs in Figure 8.21 shows the results for some combinations of the design variables.

It can be gathered from the graphs in Figure 8.21 that HS3 generally retains its coverage rates across the levels of the design variables whereas the results for HS1 vary strongly. Here, HS3 also represents the results for HS4, and HS1 is depicted to stand for all other approaches available. The reason for this finding lies in the adjustment of interval widths in HS3 for high values of σ_ρ^2. As can be seen in the lower right panel, for example, interval widths are becoming larger the higher the heterogeneity variance (σ_ρ^2) is. This adequately reflects additional uncertainty in estimating the limits of an interval which covers the parameter of interest with a probability of .95. In contrast, HS1 (and all other FE approaches) evidences much more stable confidence interval widths for all values of σ_ρ^2. The minimum values for coverage rates of about .40 are only attained by HS3 and HS4 in very extreme cases of $n = 8$, $k = 256$ and large μ_ρ in combination with large σ_ρ^2. The coverage rates rapidly increase with growing n in this case and already show a value of .75 for $n = 16$ in the same case.

In summing up the results on coverage rates and interval widths, it can be stated that in situations $\mathfrak{S}_1$, $\mathfrak{S}_2$, and $\mathfrak{S}_3$ both HOT and OP showed very good performance in absolute terms and in comparison to other approaches. Since HOT is a Fisher-z based approach, OP should be preferred at least in situations of type $\mathfrak{S}_2$. The picture of results is different in $\mathfrak{S}_3$. Although HOT is not available for a comparative evaluation, as an FE approach it is not suspected to show good performance, especially not when furthermore taking the use of the Fisher-z transformation in this approach into account. OP showed disappointing performance in $\mathfrak{S}_3$. The only well performing approaches emerged to be HS3 and HS4. Although they did not reach coverage rates as prescribed by the $1 - \alpha$ level of the confidence intervals, they appeared to be best amongst the approaches under consideration. Hence, for different situations varying recommendations can be given for the purpose of constructing confidence intervals.

8.5   HOMOGENEITY TESTS

Tests of the homogeneity of effect sizes play a central role in meta-analysis and are conducted for various purposes (see Chapter 4). The present section is devoted to an evaluation of these tests in the three situations of the Monte Carlo study. Note that not all approaches and refinements provide distinct tests so that only tests based on the Q-statistic as described in Chapter 5 are available. The subsections are divided into standard methods, that is, the Q-test for the various approaches on the one hand, and the HS methods on the other. Since Hunter and Schmidt (1990; Hunter et al., 1982) also provide a standard Q-test in addition to the tests unique to their approach, HS appears in both sections. The special tests that Hunter and Schmidt provide are only widespread in I/O psychology and have a completely different statistical rationale than the Q-

Table 8.14   Rejection Rates for the Q-Test in $\mathfrak{S}_1$

Approach	Statistic				
	Max.	Mean	Median	Min.	SD
HOr	.0623	.0492	.0499	.0095	.0058
	.0175	.0105	.0104	.0011	.0019
HOd	1	.3572	.2191	.0512	.3162
	1	.2357	.0808	.0098	.3080
HS	.9412	.0878	.0535	.0190	.1105
	.8853	.0337	.0115	.0011	.0873
OP-FE	1	.2018	.0859	.0005	.2524
	1	.1319	.0266	.0001	.2430

Note. The total number of values described by these statistics is 420. Proportion for tests at $\alpha = .05$ are given in the first row of each approach and for tests at $\alpha = .01$ in the second row.

test. For this reason and for greater focus on the peculiarities of results for these distinct procedures they will be separated from the Q-tests.

8.5.1   Homogeneity Tests Based on the Q-Statistic

For the results on the homogeneity tests, situations $\mathfrak{S}_1$ versus $\mathfrak{S}_2$ and $\mathfrak{S}_3$ provide the two most relevant classes of situations. $\mathfrak{S}_1$ is the homogeneous case and $\mathfrak{S}_2$ as well as $\mathfrak{S}_3$ both represent different heterogeneous cases. The following subsections are structured in correspondence with this distinction, where $\mathfrak{S}_1$ is used to investigate Type I error rates and the heterogeneous situations are relevant to examine the power of the tests based on the Q-statistic.

8.5.1.1   *Homogeneous Situation $\mathfrak{S}_1$: Type I Errors*   The first examination of results is concerned with overall performance of the proposed tests. The results for tests both on a significance level $\alpha = .05$ as well as $\alpha = .01$ are presented in Table 8.14.

As is shown in Table 8.14, only HOr and with strong reservations also HS approximately reach the desired significance levels. All other approaches show unacceptably large Type I error rates. Although HS performs better than HOd and OP-FE, the minima, maxima, and standard deviations indicate very large variability of test results in comparison to the Fisher-z-based approach HOr. To investigate this variability, the rejection rates are depicted in the following series of graphs by combinations of design variables. Figure 8.22 permits an inspection of the different surfaces across all the dimensions of the design.

Approaches are again clustered for better visibility of the surfaces. OP-FE is omitted for its general poor performance. The upper left panel illustrates that excessive rejection rates occur for combinations of large k and small n for HOd. HS also shows its largest values in this case. In marked contrast to these findings, the upper right panel with a rescaled vertical axis indicates that HOr

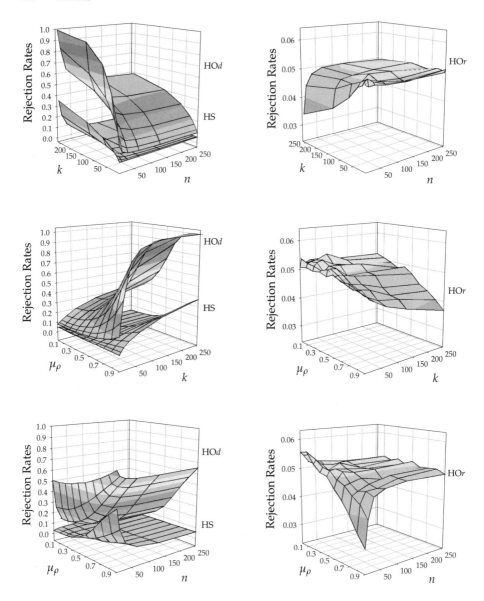

Figure 8.22   Rejection rates for the Q-test in $\mathfrak{S}_1$, $\alpha = .05$.

performs very well in $\mathfrak{S}_1$. Although HOr deviates from the nominal α in the same cases where HOd and HS perform worst, it actually shows *low* rejection rates indicating good performance when the null hypothesis is true as is the case in $\mathfrak{S}_1$.

The mid-panels in Figure 8.22 show a similar picture. Excessive rejection rates for HOd occur for large k and μ_ρ. HS also performs poorly in such cases, but HOr performs adequately in most situations. The same relative performance is observed in the lower panels for the three approaches depicted. A worst-case scenario is given in the lower left panel for a combination of low sample sizes coupled with a high value for the universe parameter. Hence, it becomes clear that HOd performs most poorly overall for high values of μ_ρ when results are aggregated across values of k, small n seems to even exacerbate this problem.

The question arises how the distinct results of the approaches can be explained. In a Monte Carlo study based comparison of the HS and HOr approach, Alexander et al. (1989) showed similar differences between these approaches. They actually used a slightly different HS-estimator for μ_ρ in computing the Q-statistic that is equivalent to the one used in the present context with constant n for all studies. As an aside, in contrast to the present study they used different n for each study simulated. The fact that the results presented here agree with those reported by Alexander et al. lends support to the claim that a constant n for all studies does not lead to limitations in interpretation in the given context. The same is true in comparison to Field's study (2001), which also used varying n within studies and reported similar results. With reference to Snedecor and Cochran (1967), Alexander et al. (1989) attributed the observed differences to the nonnormal distribution of the correlation coefficients. Applying this explanation to the present results can explain the high rates of HS for large values of μ_ρ, but does not readily explain the values reported for HOd being even more deviant from the nominal α-level. As pointed out in Sections 3.3 and 5.5, it is the transformation of r to d that may be the cause for intensification of the variability of the d values about the estimated mean effect size. Additionally, the weights used to compute Q also vary with d. They are smaller for higher d and thereby also introduce a further component that amplifies variability in values to be summed to the Q-statistic. All in all, the transformation of r to d results in homogeneity tests not suitable for application.

8.5.1.2   Heterogeneous Situations $\mathfrak{S}_2$ and $\mathfrak{S}_3$: Power   The first heterogeneous situation in which rejection rates of the homogeneity tests will be examined is $\mathfrak{S}_2$. Results for the rejection rates by values of k and selected $\Delta\rho$ are presented in Table 8.15.

The results in Table 8.15 show relatively low rejection rates when $\Delta\rho$ is small for all approaches. As expected, rejection rates rise for higher values of k and $\Delta\rho$. From the findings in the previous subsection, it is expected that HOd will also show higher rejection rates in $\mathfrak{S}_2$. This is indeed the case but the high Type I error rates in $\mathfrak{S}_1$ should be kept in mind when evaluating the performance of HOd. A notable result shown in Table 8.15 is the relatively low power to detect small differences between ρ_1 and ρ_2. Even in a meta-analysis of 256 studies, the power to detect such effects is not impressively high. Moderate differences between universe effect sizes of .30 are also only detected with an appreciable number of studies (more than 16) for approaches with acceptable Type I error rates in the homogeneous situation. In a situation with a very small number of studies — potentially occurring in a meta-analysis when subgroups of studies

Table 8.15   Rejection Rates for the Q-Test by k and $\Delta\rho$ in $\mathfrak{S}_2$

k	$\Delta\rho$	HOr	HOd	HS	OP-FE
	.1	.2112	.2972	.2089	.2242
	.3	.5964	.6738	.5897	.6068
4	.5	.7858	.8539	.7766	.7911
	.7	.8994	.9485	.8890	.8910
	.9	.9736	.9930	.9628	.9442
	.1	.2560	.3781	.2606	.3021
	.3	.6667	.7655	.6655	.7141
8	.5	.8451	.9193	.8402	.8779
	.7	.9445	.9832	.9389	.9517
	.9	.9949	.9999	.9920	.9841
	.1	.3190	.4878	.3337	.4133
	.3	.7372	.8566	.7427	.8279
16	.5	.8999	.9695	.8993	.9505
	.7	.9775	.9978	.9766	.9897
	.9	.9999	1	.9997	.9992
	.1	.3922	.6167	.4199	.5473
	.3	.8025	.9335	.8136	.9230
32	.5	.9436	.9940	.9459	.9897
	.7	.9950	1	.9953	.9996
	.9	1	1	1	1
	.1	.4685	.7491	.5134	.6882
	.3	.8591	.9824	.8742	.9788
64	.5	.9743	.9998	.9775	.9996
	.7	.9998	1	.9999	1
	.9	1	1	1	1
	.1	.5426	.8639	.6055	.8239
	.3	.9055	.9984	.9227	.9973
128	.5	.9935	1	.9952	1
	.7	1	1	1	1
	.9	1	1	1	1
	.1	.6096	.9425	.6910	.9293
	.3	.9424	1	.9587	1
256	.5	.9995	1	.9998	1
	.7	1	1	1	1
	.9	1	1	1	1

Note. Proportion for tests at $\alpha = .05$.

are examined — the power is only acceptable for large differences between the universe parameters. This is the case for all of the approaches in Table 8.15. Nevertheless, the results shown in this table indicate a very similar overall performance of the approaches in $\mathfrak{S}_2$.

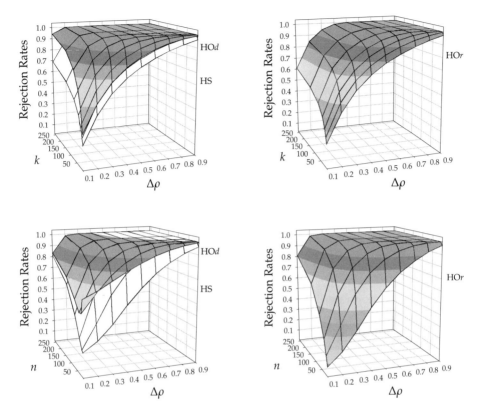

Figure 8.23   Rejection rates for the Q-test in $\mathfrak{S}_2$, $\alpha = .05$.

These results have to be qualified, however, by including the additional design variable n. The lower panels in Figure 8.23 show rejection rates across different values of n. The upper panels depict the results of Table 8.15 but values omitted from the table are added to the graphs. The lower panels indicate that rejection rates also depend on n. In general, the shapes of the surfaces are again quite similar, not favoring any of the approaches in particular. The results in $\mathfrak{S}_2$ show that medium effects sensu Cohen (1988, 1992) of .30 are only detected with acceptable power when n and k are at least 32. Whereas this may be considered a customary condition for n in most fields of correlational research, this is not the case for k. Small effects (.10) are hardly detected by the Q-test unless n and/or k are quite large.

In sum, for some constellations of the design variables' levels the probability to detect differences between universe parameters can be quite low. Although including many studies in a meta-analysis raises power, even a large number does not guarantee sufficient power. The present case can be interpreted as a situation arising from an unobserved dichotomous explanatory variable. Since it is not always the case that such variables can be observed, indications of their existence are of great interest to the meta-analyst. Because the use of explanatory models is sometimes conditioned upon the results of homogeneity tests, the results point to cases in which such conditional procedures are problematic. Of course, the present examination is restricted to a two-point distribution in the universe of studies, and different results may emerge for more unobserved classes. The more general case of the homogeneity test performance with a continuous mixing distribution is therefore also of interest.

The rejection rates for the approaches in $\mathfrak{S}_3$ are shown in Table 8.16 for varying values of k and σ_ρ^2, and also in an array of graphs in Figure 8.24.

As was the case in $\mathfrak{S}_2$, rejection rates generally rise for higher values of k and σ_ρ^2. In contrast to $\mathfrak{S}_2$, a continuous distribution is given in the universe of studies and homogeneity tests are supposed to indicate variances of this distribution different from zero. As the results in Table 8.16 show, this universe variance in effect sizes is detected by the approaches only with acceptable rates when k is at least 16 and variances are large. Small variances are likely to go unrecognized even in meta-analyses with large k. Though HOd shows the highest power among the approaches under investigation, this comes at the cost of excessive rejection rates in $\mathfrak{S}_1$. Figure 8.24 provides an overview of changes in rejection rates for varying values of σ_ρ^2, n, and k.

The upper panels in 8.24 show that for k and σ_ρ^2 the rejection rates are only satisfactory when both values are relatively high. The mid-panels also indicate decreasing rejection rates for very small n and the lower panels show that these trends do not strongly depend on values of μ_ρ. Hence, almost irrespective of the size of μ_ρ in the universe of studies, an appreciable number of studies is needed to detect even moderate heterogeneity at a power level conventionally considered as acceptable. In sum, all tests show somewhat unsatisfactory rejection rates in $\mathfrak{S}_3$ and cannot safely be taken as indicants of heterogeneity under all configurations of the design variables.

Again, this result is quite important if the Q-test is considered as a decision-making device for the choice between fixed and random effects models as in the so-called conditional random effects model. The results of the Q-test may lead researchers to an unwarranted application of the random effects model in $\mathfrak{S}_1$ especially when using HOd. As a consequence, a loss of power for significance testing would result. Alternatively, the application of the Q-test may lead to the application of fixed effects models in heterogeneous situations like $\mathfrak{S}_2$ and $\mathfrak{S}_3$. In the latter case, tests and confidence intervals would result in unduly small widths for intervals and overpowered tests for most approaches.

8.5.2 The Hunter-Schmidt Approach to the Test of Homogeneity: The 75%- and 90%-rule

In Section 5.3, the 75%-rule by Hunter and Schmidt (1990) was introduced. In short form, it states that if 75% of the observed variance of effect sizes can be explained by artifacts — especially sampling error of the estimator — then the rest of the variance in observed effect sizes can be attributed to unobserved artifacts and homogeneity is therefore given. As the indicant of homogeneity

Table 8.16 Rejection Rates for the Q-Test by k and σ_ρ^2 in $\mathfrak{S}_3$

k	σ_ρ^2	HOr	HOd	HS	OP-FE
	.0025	.1873	.2720	.1844	.1988
	.01	.3220	.3988	.3162	.3416
4	.0225	.4712	.5452	.4614	.4888
	.04	.5528	.6214	.5421	.5818
	.0625	.6473	.7120	.6331	.6720
	.0025	.2515	.3709	.2547	.2960
	.01	.4409	.5462	.4378	.5031
8	.0225	.6087	.7008	.5999	.6690
	.04	.6949	.7794	.6828	.7684
	.0625	.7824	.8552	.7661	.8458
	.0025	.3221	.4846	.3348	.4153
	.01	.5483	.6839	.5513	.6652
16	.0225	.7111	.8210	.7064	.8189
	.04	.7916	.8884	.7812	.9016
	.0625	.8675	.9406	.8534	.9510
	.0025	.4002	.6132	.4253	.5535
	.01	.6361	.8063	.6478	.8091
32	.0225	.7885	.9143	.7887	.9292
	.04	.8628	.9603	.8556	.9755
	.0625	.9264	.9859	.9160	.9933
	.0025	.4806	.7441	.5198	.6969
	.01	.7119	.9084	.7327	.9200
64	.0225	.8501	.9745	.8550	.9848
	.04	.9164	.9936	.9123	.9977
	.0625	.9650	.9989	.9584	.9998
	.0025	.5548	.8574	.6095	.8297
	.01	.7782	.9736	.8051	.9810
128	.0225	.8997	.9973	.9067	.9988
	.04	.9555	.9998	.9536	1
	.0625	.9892	1	.9857	1
	.0025	.6228	.9389	.6927	.9341
	.01	.8327	.9970	.8639	.9980
256	.0225	.9382	1	.9457	1
	.04	.9831	1	.9817	1
	.0625	.9989	1	.9983	1

Note. Proportion for tests at $\alpha = .05$.

in this procedure, the ratio of the estimated sampling error over the observed variance of effect sizes is considered. The ratios are compared to a value of .75 for the 75%-rule and to .90 for the 90%-rule, respectively. The 90%-rule is usually considered to be more suitable for Monte Carlo studies like the present one, where no artifacts are part of the design (see Cornwell & Ladd, 1993; Sack-

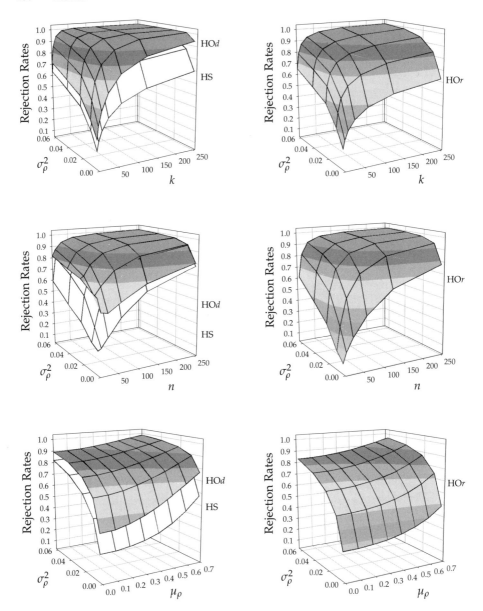

Figure 8.24   Rejection rates for the Q-test in $\mathfrak{S}_3$, $\alpha = .05$.

ett et al., 1986), and for this reason is also included in the results. If the ratios are larger than or equal to the mentioned values, homogeneity is assumed to prevail. In analogy to the hypothesis tests for homogeneity already presented, the rates of rejecting the hypothesis of homogeneity by using these rules are assessed. Since no artifacts are present in the Monte Carlo study, the situations correspond to cases in which all possible artifacts have been corrected for.

Table 8.17   Rejection Rates for 75%- and 90%-Rule in $\mathfrak{S}_1$

	Statistic				
	Max.	Mean	Median	Min.	SD
HS-75%	.7339	.1035	.1101	0	0.0916
HS-90%	.9637	.2687	.2622	.0660	0.1194
HS-ratio	6.0165	1.5040	1.0859	.6759	0.9538

Note. The total number of values described by these statistics is 420. HS-75% = Proportion of meta-analyses indicating heterogeneity according to 75%-rule, HS-90% = Proportion of meta-analyses indicating heterogeneity according to 90%-rule, HS-ratio = Ratio of estimated variance due to sampling error ($\hat{\sigma}_e^2$) over observed variance of effect sizes ($\hat{\sigma}_r^2$).

The rejection rates in $\mathfrak{S}_1$ for applying both rules along with descriptive statistics for the values of the ratio are provided in Table 8.17.

Since the 75%- and 90%-rule are not tests in a formal statistical sense it is not clear what the standards of comparison are. Adopting the procedures applied in previous Monte Carlo studies on the subject (e.g., Cornwell & Ladd, 1993; Sackett et al., 1986; Sagie & Koslowsky, 1993), the tests are expected to falsely indicate heterogeneity only in 5% of the cases in analogy to standard statistical tests. By applying this criterion to the results in $\mathfrak{S}_1$ in Table 8.17 it is recognized that neither of the rules attains a value of 5% and both rules indicate heterogeneity in a homogeneous situation far too often. Although the mean value of the HS-ratio is clearly larger than one, this does not necessarily mean that only a small portion of the ratios reaches values smaller than the criteria. As is evident from the standard deviation, there is also high variability among the ratios leading to the relatively high rejection rates. Results not shown here indicate that the minima reported in Table 8.17 only occur in cases of maximum k and n (both 256). Because the value in the denominator of the ratio is simply the observed variance of the effect sizes and this variance actually *is* sampling error in $\mathfrak{S}_1$, the results point to underestimates of the sampling error variance by the term in the numerator.

Additional information on the changes in the rejection rates across values of n and μ_ρ in $\mathfrak{S}_1$ can be seen in Figure 8.25. Both rules are depicted in this graph and represented by different surfaces.

The tendency for very large rejection rates to occur for large effects and small n is clearly visible. Moreover, both surfaces maintain a height that indicates rejection rates generally too high for both rules, though the 75%-rule performs better in $\mathfrak{S}_1$, — a fact that is trivial — it does not perform satisfactorily. This is rather surprising at first glance since an assumption that about 75% of observed variance can simply be ignored and attributed to some unobserved causes of data turbulences seems quite liberal and favoring homogeneity. Ironically then, the seemingly liberal rules lead to a false rejection of the hypothesis of homogeneity far too often.

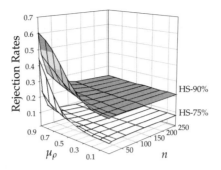

Figure 8.25   Rejection rates for the 75%- and 90%-rule in $\mathfrak{S}_1$ by n and μ_ρ.

Table 8.18   **Rejection Rates for 75%- and 90%-Rule in $\mathfrak{S}_2$**

	Max.	Mean	Median	Min.	SD
			Statistic		
HS-75%	1	.7814	.9995	0	.3219
HS-90%	1	.8635	1	.0838	.2284
HS-ratio	6.9055	.5447	.3944	.0122	.5962

Note. The total number of values described by these statistics is 1890. HS-75% = Proportion of meta-analyses indicating heterogeneity according to 75%-rule, HS-90% = Proportion of meta-analyses indicating heterogeneity according to 90%-rule, HS-ratio = Ratio of estimated variance due to sampling error ($\hat{\sigma}_e^2$) to observed variance of effect sizes ($\hat{\sigma}_r^2$).

None of the rules therefore seems to represent a viable alternative to the Q-test in $\mathfrak{S}_1$. A trivial consequence of the high rejection rates in $\mathfrak{S}_1$ is a better performance in heterogeneous situations. Hence, it should again be kept in mind that these "tests" do not perform well in $\mathfrak{S}_1$ when inspecting the results for other cases.

The results for the next two situations, $\mathfrak{S}_2$ and $\mathfrak{S}_3$ are shown in Tables 8.18 and 8.19, respectively. The results for $\mathfrak{S}_2$ shown in Table 8.18 indicate a smaller mean ratio and high rates of rejecting the assumption of homogeneity, as would be expected in a heterogeneous situation and by the high baseline of rejection rates in $\mathfrak{S}_1$.

If the conventional level of 80% rejection rates is considered satisfactory for such a "test" and applied to evaluate the results, both rules approximately reach this criterion overall. The results for $\mathfrak{S}_3$ in Table 8.19 lead to the same conclusion based on the mean values of rejection rates.

However, minimum values and standard deviations also indicate that there are considerable differences across levels of the design variables. In contrast to $\mathfrak{S}_1$, the ratios increase for larger values of n, k, and μ_ρ, reaching their maximum when all design variables take on their highest values. Examples for the

Table 8.19   Rejection Rates for 75%- and 90%-Rule in $\mathfrak{S}_3$

	Statistic				
	Max.	Mean	Median	Min.	SD
HS-75%	1	.7076	.9035	0	.3391
HS-90%	1	.8130	.9719	.0795	.2479
HS-ratio	5.0551	.6991	.5736	.0163	.6650

Note. The total number of values described by these statistics is 1848. HS-75% = Proportion of meta-analyses indicating heterogeneity according to 75%-rule, HS-90% = Proportion of meta-analyses indicating heterogeneity according to 90%-rule, HS-ratio = Ratio of estimated variance due to sampling error ($\hat{\sigma}_e^2$) to observed variance of effect sizes ($\hat{\sigma}_r^2$).

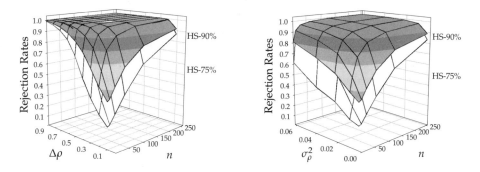

Figure 8.26   Rejection rates for the 75%- and 90%-rule in $\mathfrak{S}_2$ and $\mathfrak{S}_3$.

change in rejection rates for both rules as they occur across levels of the design variables are presented in Figure 8.26.

The general trends look similar to those reported for significance tests in previous sections with smaller rejection rates for lower n, $\Delta\rho$, and σ_ρ^2, respectively. The graphs in Figure 8.26 support the notion of some deficiencies for both rules when the levels of design variables are not at least of medium value.

In sum, the 75%- and 90%-rule of Hunter and Schmidt do not perform much better in all three situations in comparison to homogeneity tests presented in preceding subsections. Results not provided here show that, in general, power to detect heterogeneity can become quite low for combinations of low n, $\Delta\rho$, and σ_ρ^2, respectively. Due to the very high rejection rates in $\mathfrak{S}_1$ and low power in many conditions in heterogeneous situations, the rules should be used with caution. Especially when n and the assumed heterogeneity variance are rather small, decisions about the application of random effects approaches or explanatory models and conclusions concerning the generalizability of an effect should not be solely based on the results of the 75%- or 90%-rule.

8.6   ESTIMATION OF HETEROGENEITY VARIANCE

The estimation of the variance of effect sizes in the universe of studies is an important part of random effects models and also of the HS-type meta-analysis. It is a parameter of interest in itself, like the expected value in the universe of studies. It may, however, also be used in further computations in meta-analysis. For example, heterogeneity variance is used to construct so-called *credibility intervals* as proposed by Hunter and Schmidt (1990). Credibility intervals are constructed analogously to confidence intervals but use the standard deviation of the heterogeneity variance instead of the standard error of the estimator to arrive at estimates for the interval limits. Credibility intervals are not part of the Monte Carlo study and are therefore not considered here.

The most prominent estimators of heterogeneity variance in applications of meta-analysis in psychology, DSL and HS, will be evaluated in this section. In addition, the estimator OP-RE presented in Subsection 5.4.2 will also be evaluated to assess its performance in relation to the standard approaches.

As was the case in the context of estimating μ_ρ, the estimated parameter in the various situations will first be considered. In $\mathfrak{S}_1$, there simply is no variance to be estimated, that is, it is zero. The behavior of the estimators will be examined in two versions. First, the results for the truncated variance estimator will be reported, and second, the results for the non-truncated version thereafter. Recall from Section 5.4.1 that the truncated variance estimator in the DSL approach is $\hat{\sigma}^2_{\zeta+} = \max\{0, \hat{\sigma}^2_\zeta\}$. That is, negative variance estimates which may arise in practice are set to zero for the truncated estimator. The non-truncated version does not set negative estimates to zero. Of course, an analogue procedure is applied in r-space when HS and OP-RE are considered: $\hat{\sigma}^2_{\rho+} = \max\{0, \hat{\sigma}^2_\rho\}$.

Since the DSL estimator of heterogeneity variance is based on Fisher-z transformed correlation coefficients, the corresponding parameter is also in z-space. This is mainly of importance for situations $\mathfrak{S}_2$ and $\mathfrak{S}_3$, where the universe variances have to be computed in order to assess biases. In $\mathfrak{S}_2$, the variance of the universe effect sizes is computed as follows:

$$\sigma^2_\zeta = \frac{\left(\zeta_1 - \mu_\zeta\right)^2 + \left(\zeta_2 - \mu_\zeta\right)^2}{2}.$$

For $\mathfrak{S}_3$, no simple form to compute the variance in z-space resulting from a beta distributed variable P is available. Thus, variances have to be determined via

$$\sigma^2_\zeta = \int_{-1}^{1} \left(\tanh^{-1} r\right)^2 f(r)dr - \mu^2_\zeta,$$

where $f(r)$ denotes the beta probability density function. μ_ζ and σ^2_ζ are in z-space. Note that μ_ζ is given by $\mu_\zeta = \int_{-1}^{1} \tanh^{-1}(r)f(r)dr$. The various values as used in the Monte Carlo study can be found in Tables A.1 and A.2 in the appendix.

Table 8.20   Bias of $\hat{\sigma}_\rho^2$ (HS & OP-RE) and $\hat{\sigma}_\zeta^2$ (DSL) in $\mathfrak{S}_1$

	Statistic				
	Max.	Mean	Median	Min.	SD
HS-nt	.0110	.0014	.0001	−.0001	.0027
HS	.0433	.0042	.0013	0	.0068
OP-RE-nt	.1289	.0099	.0001	−.0144	.0249
OP-RE	.1289	.0130	.0015	0	.0264
DSL-nt	.0009	−.0013	−.0001	−.0164	.0031
DSL	.0622	.0070	.0024	.0001	.0116

Note. The total number of values described by these statistics is 420. -nt designates non-truncated estimators.

8.6.1   Homogeneous Situation $\mathfrak{S}_1$

In the homogeneous situation, the estimators presented in Chapter 5 generally overestimate the heterogeneity variance. This is due to the truncation of the resulting estimates at a value of zero when values less than zero are encountered. To assess whether the non-truncated versions actually estimate the universe parameter precisely and how far off the truncated versions are from zero, both versions are provided in the following presentation. The truncated versions therefore correspond to the estimators used in practice and the non-truncated versions are only given for comparison. The non-truncated estimators are labeled by the additional suffix -*nt*.

In Table 8.20 results for the biases of the estimators in $\mathfrak{S}_1$ are presented. The values are computed in analogy to the biases of the estimators of μ_ρ (see Section 8.2.1).

Unfortunately, the biases of variances in Table 8.20 and also those presented in the following are not directly comparable because the values for HS and OP-RE are given in *r*-space and those of DSL in the space of *z*. Nevertheless, in the given situation one would expect the biases of DSL to be uniformly larger to a certain degree than the variances of HS and OP-RE due to the characteristics of the different spaces. Recall from Section 3.1 that the Fisher-*z* transformation stretches the values of *r* particularly in the boundary regions (see also Figure 3.1) and therefore leads to larger variances in *z*-space as compared to *r*-space. Trivially, the truncated values are always at least as large as their non-truncated counterparts.

As evidenced by the minimum values in Table 8.20, some remarkable negative estimates indeed emerge in some cases. Interestingly, the maxima of both versions for the estimators do not always agree. This is due to rare cases in which very large variances occur for the estimates and a large portion of variance estimates is less than zero. The values reported in Table 8.20 indicate some deficiencies associated with OP-RE in relation to DSL and HS. The OP-RE estimator shows maximum values far too large to be acceptable. The mean

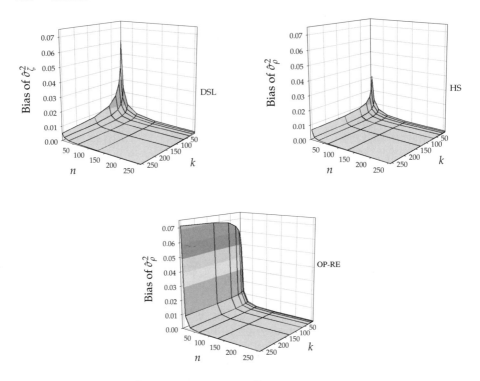

Figure 8.27   Bias of $\hat{\sigma}_\rho^2$ (HS & OP-RE) and $\hat{\sigma}_\zeta^2$ (DSL) in $\mathfrak{S}_1$ by k and n.

and median values shown, however, indicate rather good performance of the approaches overall.

To elucidate under which constellations of the design variables the estimators perform better or worse, a series of graphs is presented in Figure 8.27. Again, an array of graphs shows the estimators' performance across combinations of the design variable levels of k and n.

The estimators' biases shown in Figure 8.27 are only given for the truncated versions to focus on findings relevant for the application of the methods in practice. In general, all panels indicate good performance of the estimators for large values of the design variables. However, DSL obviously overestimates σ_ζ^2 when n and k are very small and also retains a positive bias for all values of k when n is very small. This is due to the truncation of the variances. The same shape of surface emerges for HS in the upper right panel but the biases for combinations of a small number of studies and very small sample sizes appear smaller than those of DSL. Since these two estimators operate in different spaces (r vs. z), it is not perfectly clear which estimator actually shows larger bias in comparison. The lower panel gives the results for OP-RE and indicates a very poor performance of the estimator for small values of n across all values of k. Only when n grows larger and reaches a value of approximately 64 does the estimator show acceptable performance.

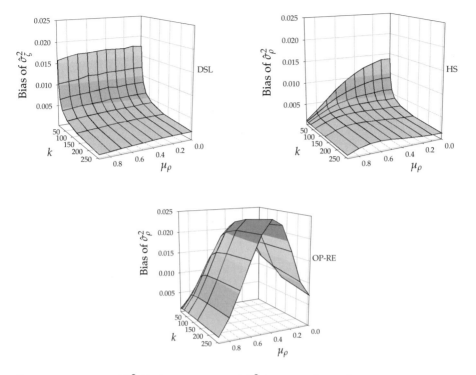

Figure 8.28   Bias of $\hat{\sigma}_\rho^2$ ((HS & OP-RE) and $\hat{\sigma}_\zeta^2$ (DSL) in $\mathfrak{S}_1$ by k and μ_ρ.

It is, of course, also of interest whether biases of the estimators vary across values of the universe effect size. Figure 8.28 provides graphs for the design dimensions k and μ_ρ.

For DSL and HS, both upper panels in Figure 8.28 show an improved performance for larger values of k. DSL shows a relatively stable performance across all values of μ_ρ, but it is acknowledge that the slope of the surface indicates slightly better performance for larger values of μ_ρ. The results depicted in the figure suggest that at least a modest number of studies (approximately 32) have to be available when using this approach for a sufficiently precise estimation of the heterogeneity variance (i.e., very close to zero). HS, in contrast, performs best when μ_ρ is large. This tendency is most obvious for a small number of studies. Unfortunately, for values of ρ suspected to occur often in practice (around .40) the bias still seems non-negligible. Although the absolute values seem small on the vertical axis, it should be remembered that a value of .01 corresponds to a standard deviation of .10. Hence, there seems to be nontrivial bias for the HS estimator for small values of k and moderate to low μ_ρ in the universe of studies. As is the case for DSL, when the number of studies is 32 or larger, the bias seems negligible for HS.

Unlike these first two approaches, OP-RE strongly varies in biases across levels of μ_ρ, notwithstanding how many studies are aggregated, with a max-

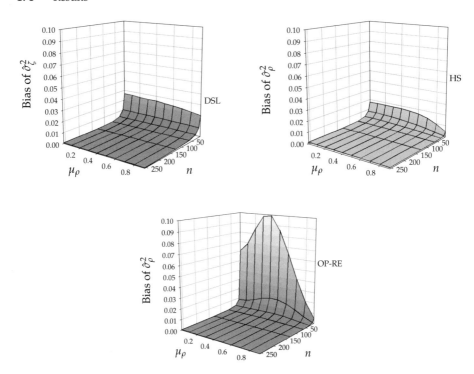

Figure 8.29   Bias of $\hat{\sigma}_\rho^2$ (HS & OP-RE) and $\hat{\sigma}_\zeta^2$ (DSL) in $\mathfrak{S}_1$ by n and μ_ρ.

imum bias at a value of approximately $\mu_\rho = .40$. It is again suspected that this phenomenon is caused by the weighting scheme of OP-RE. The region of maximum bias falls near the point of $\mu_\rho = .347$ where the biggest *change* in the variance of G occurs (see Section 3.1). A big change in variance transfers to big differences in weights since the variance estimates are used in the weighting scheme of the OP-RE approach. If this were true, then the bias should diminish for larger sample sizes. This is indeed the case as the lower panel in Figure 8.29 shows. This figure completes the results for the biases of $\hat{\sigma}_\rho^2$ and $\hat{\sigma}_\zeta^2$ in $\mathfrak{S}_1$.

Again, it can clearly be seen that for very low values of n none of the estimators shows acceptable performance but performance quickly gets better and reaches acceptable levels for sample sizes supposed to be encountered most often in practice (32 or larger). Poor performance for the approaches only occurs for very small n. Though DSL in the upper left panel does not seem to reach small biases for growing n as fast as HS, the reader is again cautioned against such a comparative interpretation because of the different spaces in which DSL and the other approaches operate. Overall, at least the estimators HS and DSL seem to show acceptable performance in $\mathfrak{S}_1$ when n and k are not very small.

Table 8.21   Bias of $\hat{\sigma}_\rho^2$ (HS & OP-RE) and $\hat{\sigma}_\zeta^2$ (DSL) in $\mathfrak{S}_2$

	Statistic				
	Max.	Mean	Median	Min.	SD
HS-nt	.0665	.0034	.0009	−.0253	.0087
HS	.0665	.0044	.0014	−.0253	.0096
OP-RE-nt	.2739	.0440	.0184	−.0130	.0560
OP-RE	.2739	.0452	.0189	−.0018	.0559
DSL-nt	.2559	.0121	.0030	−.0115	.0254
DSL	.2566	.0150	.0051	−.0099	.0262

Note. The total number of values described by these statistics is 1890. -nt designates non-truncated estimators.

8.6.2   Heterogeneous Situations $\mathfrak{S}_2$ and $\mathfrak{S}_3$

The heterogeneity variance estimators become especially important in cases where $\sigma_\rho^2 \neq 0$. In such cases, it can be evaluated whether the truncated versions of the estimators still provide overestimates, as is the case for some combinations of levels of design variables in $\mathfrak{S}_1$. Additionally, the two situations $\mathfrak{S}_2$ and $\mathfrak{S}_3$ enable an evaluation of the estimators for a discrete distribution in the universe of studies and for a continuous distribution. For the latter, it should be kept in mind that the beta distribution strongly deviates from normality the larger μ_ρ is. This is considered to be more adequate for r-space in comparison to a truncated or otherwise distorted normal distribution, for example, as was used in other Monte Carlo studies (e.g., Overton, 1998; and probably also Field, 2001).

Table 8.21 provides overall results of the three estimators in both versions available. As can be seen, differences between the truncated and non-truncated versions of the estimators do not differ substantially. The focus will therefore be exclusively laid on the truncated estimators.

All three approaches differ in biases. HS is close to the variances to be estimated amongst the approaches under consideration. Mean and median values indicate a good overall performance but minima and maxima also show that there are conditions under which the estimator over- or underestimates the universe variance of effect sizes. OP-RE, in contrast, generally overestimates variances, in some cases to a very large degree. DSL shows a slight tendency for overestimation as indicated by the values in the table but clearly not as strong as OP-RE. The measures of central tendency for DSL close to zero suggest a performance similar to HS. Yet, the maximum values for DSL also suggest that the tendency for overestimation can be strong in some cases. Unfortunately, this is no unequivocal indicator for strong overestimation because it is the bias computed in z-space. To elucidate conditions under which the estimators do not perform very well, a series of graphs is provided once more.

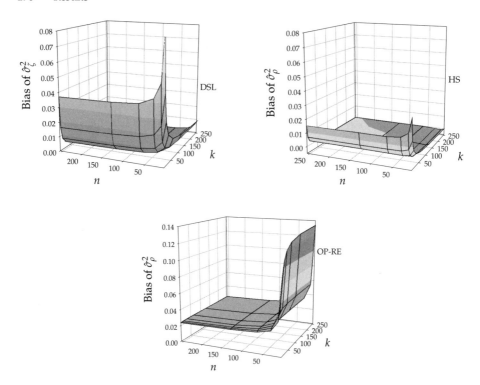

Figure 8.30   Bias of $\hat{\sigma}_\rho^2$ (HS & OP-RE) and $\hat{\sigma}_\zeta^2$ (DSL) in $\mathfrak{S}_2$ by n and k.

The conditions for largest biases of DSL and HS, indicated by the upper panels in Figure 8.30, are again cases of low n and especially k. The combination of both low n and k represents the worst case in terms of bias. Unlike the results presented for $\mathfrak{S}_1$, the biases for these approaches are generally high for k less than 16, irrespective of n. Absolute values for biases are also different for each of these estimators in comparison to the results in $\mathfrak{S}_1$.

A very different shape of surface emerges again for the bias of OP-RE. Results for this estimator indicate a poor performance for low n whereas biases decline for larger n, irrespective of k. The surfaces of DSL and OP-RE do not approximate a value of zero bias for larger k and n, respectively. Note that this is actually the case for HS, which can be regarded as performing best in this respect. The biases of DSL and OP-RE instead converge to some nonzero positive value. This is due to the fact that for both estimators biases also very strongly vary for different values of $\Delta\rho$. This is illustrated in Figure 8.31 where the estimators operating in r-space are shown in one panel. The upper panels provide biases for $\Delta\rho$ by n and the lower two for $\Delta\rho$ by k.

Both panels illustrate the rising bias both for DSL and OP-RE for larger values of $\Delta\rho$. The results explain why the values to which these approaches converge (as shown in Figure 8.30) are larger than zero. The larger the difference between universe values in $\mathfrak{S}_2$, the larger are the biases of DSL and OP-RE.

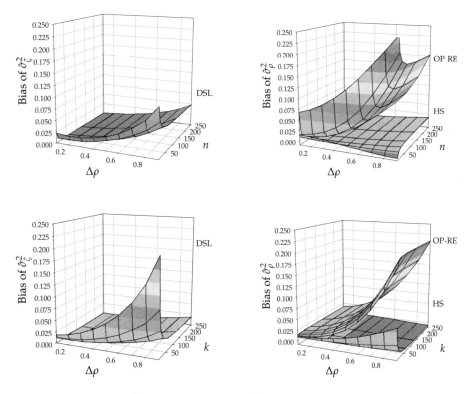

Figure 8.31   Bias of $\hat{\sigma}_\rho^2$ (HS & OP-RE) and $\hat{\sigma}_\zeta^2$ (DSL) in $\mathfrak{S}_2$ by n and $\Delta\rho$ as well as k and $\Delta\rho$.

In the case of OP-RE this is suspected to be caused by the weighting scheme, whereas in the case of DSL — though biases are not directly comparable in absolute terms — this is proposed to be a result of transformation into z-space. In contrast to the performance of these two approaches, HS shows a very good performance in $\mathfrak{S}_2$ and seems to be the approach of choice amongst the ones available in this situation. Cautions against the use of the HS estimator appear reasonable in cases of small k (i.e., $k < 16$), especially when large differences between effect sizes in the universe if studies are suspected.

Finally, the results for biases in $\mathfrak{S}_3$ are presented, the situation with a continuous distribution in the universe of studies. Table 8.22 provides overall results first.

The results in Table 8.22 seem to indicate a much better overall performance of DSL as compared to the previous situation. However, due to difficulties in directly comparing variances in situations of type $\mathfrak{S}_2$ and $\mathfrak{S}_3$ as well as complications arising from interpreting absolute values for biases in z-space, the indication of a better performance are not strong. HS shows very small mean bias whereas OP-RE again strongly overestimates universe variances of effects sizes. Again, maximum and minimum values indicate varying performance of

Table 8.22   Bias of $\hat{\sigma}_\rho^2$ (HS & OP-RE) and $\hat{\sigma}_\zeta^2$ (DSL) in $\mathfrak{S}_3$

	Statistic				
	Max.	Mean	Median	Min.	SD
HS-nt	.0121	−.0001	−.0001	−.0193	.0036
HS	.0433	.0014	0	−.0193	.0059
OP-RE-nt	.2161	.0237	.0062	−.0162	.0373
OP-RE	.2161	.0255	.0074	−.0147	.0376
DSL-nt	.0243	.0008	.0003	−.0154	.0029
DSL	.0648	.0047	.0010	−.0129	.0099

Note. Valid values for all entries are 1848. -nt designates non-truncated estimators.

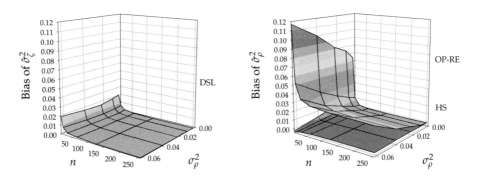

Figure 8.32   Bias of $\hat{\sigma}_\rho^2$ (HS & OP-RE) and $\hat{\sigma}_\zeta^2$ (DSL) in $\mathfrak{S}_3$ by n and σ_ρ^2.

the approaches across levels of the design variables. Interestingly, the maxima for the truncated versions of the HS and DSL estimators occur in cases similar to $\mathfrak{S}_1$, that is, for smallest values of k, n, and σ_ρ^2. In all other cases both approaches show smaller biases.

Graphs are finally presented to assess the performance of the approaches in various design regions. Figure 8.32 illustrates the results for n and σ_ρ^2.

The left panel in this figure shows that overestimation is larger for DSL only for very small n. With sample sizes larger than 16, the bias seems negligible. In the right panel of Figure 8.32, both HS and OP-RE are depicted. The high biases of OP-RE for small n are clearly visible. Since OP-RE is r-based and does not use the Fisher-z transformation, the absolute values for biases can be deemed extremely large. Furthermore, biases strongly raise for OP-RE with increasing values of σ_ρ^2. This is neither true for DSL nor HS. The results for HS indicate that biases are only elevated for small n and small σ_ρ^2, a case that approaches homogeneity. This is however, not visible in the right panel of Figure 8.32 since the surface of OP-RE covers this region. As was highlighted in the context of presenting the results in $\mathfrak{S}_1$, the biases for HS can be considered as non-negligible in some extreme cases in this design region. Nevertheless,

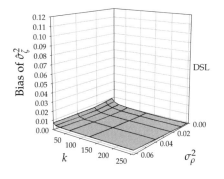
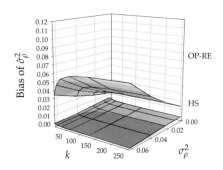

Figure 8.33   Bias of $\hat{\sigma}_\rho^2$ (HS & OP-RE) and $\hat{\sigma}_\zeta^2$ (DSL) in $\mathfrak{S}_3$ by k and σ_ρ^2.

biases are generally relatively small for the HS approach in $\mathfrak{S}_3$. Although DSL also shows a rather good performance in $\mathfrak{S}_3$, HS appears as the most recommendable approach of the three approaches under examination for this situation, since it shows the smallest biases and provides estimates in the space of r.

The next two panels in Figure 8.33 give a very similar impression of the relative performance of the approaches across values of k and σ_ρ^2. For high universe variances, biases of DSL and OP-RE are rather large. On the other hand, HS shows small biases in most cases, albeit the values evidently also vary across levels of k and σ_ρ^2. The trend of larger biases across values of σ_ρ^2 is the opposite as compared to the other two approaches. High variances seem to be estimated with appreciable precisions whereas low variances are over-estimated. This is due to the truncation in the HS estimator. Results for the non-truncated version, not shown here, indicate almost zero bias in all regions of the design, in particular also those for which values are slightly elevated in Figure 8.33.

The last graphs provided to assess biases are given in Figure 8.34. They underscore the generally good performance of HS, as is evident in the upper right panel. Although biases are not zero across all levels of the design variables, the absolute values are very small. DSL is depicted in the upper left panel and does not show a clear trend of bias across levels of σ_ρ^2 and μ_ρ. Nevertheless, absolute biases are also small in absolute value for this approach. OP-RE again shows some variation in biases across levels of the design variables with largest biases occurring for combinations of large μ_ρ and large σ_ρ^2. Due to the large biases shown in all design level combinations in $\mathfrak{S}_3$, it is certainly no interesting alternative to the other two estimators.

In sum, despite small overestimation of the truncated version of the HS estimator in $\mathfrak{S}_1$, it seems to provide the best estimator of heterogeneity variance amongst the three approaches examined. The cases where HS shows overestimation of heterogeneity variance are not likely to be encountered often in practice, but are of interest to find the boundary values for levels of design variables in order to caution against potential problems in estimation. The bias

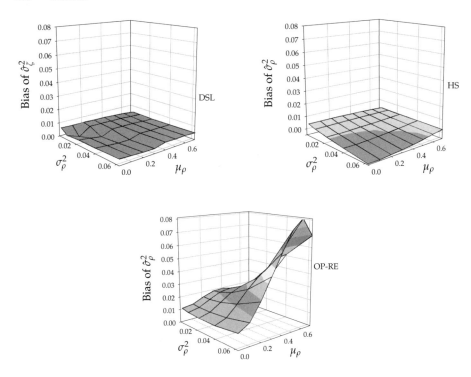

Figure 8.34   Bias of $\hat{\sigma}_{\rho}^2$ (HS & OP-RE) and $\hat{\sigma}_{\zeta}^2$ (DSL) in $\mathfrak{S}_3$ by μ_{ρ} and σ_{ρ}^2.

of DSL was only examined in z-space, so some reservations with respect to a negative evaluation are in order. The performance of this estimator nonetheless showed variation in the Monte Carlo study that does not let it appear as a promising alternative in comparison to the simple HS estimator. Furthermore, there is no option available to date to transform the results of the DSL estimator into r-space. Hence, variance estimates are in z-space and hard to interpret. This is another limitation of this approach which makes its use in practical applications of meta-analysis unattractive.

Part IV

Putting It All Together

9

Synopsis of Statistical Methods and Monte Carlo Study Results

The statistical methods for meta-analysis of correlations were outlined in this book and classified with respect to a series of characteristics. The main relevant characteristics for the comparison of approaches were identified to be a) the effect size measure used, b) the weighting scheme used, and c) the underlying statistical model. Although these classificatory aspects are not mutually exclusive, they are nevertheless useful to differentiate between approaches with reference to characteristics that cause differences in results.

Effect Size Used in the Approaches   The coefficients under examination were

- the untransformed correlation coefficient r,
- the Fisher-z transformed correlation z,
- a bias-corrected mean Fisher-z transformed correlation $\bar{z}_{Hot}$,
- a bias-corrected untransformed correlation coefficient G, and
- the r-to-d transformed d.

For the untransformed correlation r it was shown that it is biased with respect to ρ and that the variance of the estimator depends on ρ. Fisher-z transformed correlations are biased as well but they have the desirable property that their variance only depends on the sample size and not on the population parameter. Hotelling (1953) has analyzed the bias both of r and z and proposed several corrections which were presented in Part II. Of these corrections, a bias-correction for mean z was considered to be especially attractive for use in meta-analysis and was incorporated as an independent approach in the subsequent comparison of approaches. The UMVU estimator presented by Olkin and Pratt (1958) was also considered and it was shown that its variance does also depends on the population parameter. Finally, the transformation of r to d was also included because of its high relevance for practical applications meta-analysis. This offered the opportunity to examine whether the transformation leads to different meta-analytic results when computations are based on the transformed d instead of r or z. Some of these effect sizes are used in well-known and often applied meta-analytic approaches (r, z, and d) whereas others (bias-corrected $\bar{z}_{Hot}$ and G) — interestingly those with desirable properties with respect to bias — are not widely known and used.

Many of these effect sizes involve what can be called a "change of space". That is, there is a change from r-space to z-space by application of the Fisher-z transformation and a change from r-space to d-space by the corresponding conversion formula. In more mathematical parlance, this is called change of variable. The initial motivation for the former change of space was to circumvent problems with the rather untractable probability density function of R. The motivation for the latter is simply the need to bring available research findings into a common space to carry out the meta-analytic computations of an approach. Hence, both kinds of transformations are justified in the meta-analytic context. The change of space, basically designating the use of a non-linear transformation of the correlation coefficient r to either z or d, was hypothesized to be a cause for differences in results between approaches. When meta-analytic computations are carried out in the "transformed space" (z or d) and computational results are transformed back into r-space subsequently, then differences to results from computations based on r can be expected.

Weighting Schemes   The weighting scheme used in aggregating effect sizes of k studies was pointed out to be another important characteristic. There are basically two variants of weights in meta-analysis of (transformed) correlations: sample size and reciprocals of the estimator's variance. The former has the rather simple rationale of giving those studies higher weight that provide "more evidence". Of course, larger studies are simultaneously also thought to provide more precise estimates of the parameter in question (assuming consistency). Weighting by the reciprocals of the estimator's variance has a clearer statistical rationale as these weights are optimal in the sense that they provide a pooled estimator with minimum variance. Furthermore, it can be shown that under certain assumptions these weights are also those of the maximum likelihood estimator for the universe parameter in a fixed effects situation (for a proof, see Böhning, 2000, pp. 101–102). Hence, weighting by the reciprocal of the estimator's variance has very desirable statistical properties.

However, it was repeatedly argued in this book that under certain circumstances the optimal weights become suboptimal. The first reason leading to bias in the pooled estimator in the present context is lack of knowledge about the variance, and hence the need to plug in estimates in the weights. The above mentioned dependency of some estimators' variance on the universe parameter and small sample sizes making the individual estimates highly variable exacerbate the problem. This already points to the second cause for bias, namely, the dependency of the variance on the universe parameter. These two causes together produce the undesirable effect of bias in some estimators. It becomes particularly problematic when the fixed effects model is used instead of the random effects model (see below) in a situation where the latter is appropriate. In this case, this dependency leads to bias even when n grows large.

Meta-Analytic Models   The presented models were the fixed effects model, the random effects model, mixture models, and hierarchical linear models. The two models of highest relevance for the classification of approaches are the FE and RE model. The difference between the FE and RE model is the conceptualization of the universe of studies as characterized either by a single constant parameter (ρ; FE; homogeneous case) or by a random variable (P; RE; heterogeneous case). In the RE model, the variance of P (heterogeneity variance) is always some positive value, whereas in the FE model it is zero by definition. Hence, approaches categorized as using the FE model do not include estimators for heterogeneity variance whereas in approaches using the RE model they are an integral part. In addition to estimating the heterogeneity variance, it is also used in the weights in approaches using the RE model.

As examples of more general models for meta-analysis, mixture models and HLM were introduced. In the latter case, it was shown that the FE and RE model are special cases, thereby revealing in what respect these two models are special or limited. In contrast to HLM, mixture models include latent variables as causes for heterogeneity of effects. These models were used to conceptualize three situations to which the approaches under examination may be applied.

Situations   The first situation ($\mathfrak{S}_1$) represented the homogeneous case for which FE model approaches are appropriate. The second situation ($\mathfrak{S}_2$) was a heterogeneous situation characterized by a discrete distribution in the universe of studies. The examination in this book was limited to a dichotomous latent variable where categories have equal weights, hence a two-point uniform distribution. The third situation ($\mathfrak{S}_3$) was characterized by a continuous latent variable, thus also qualifying as a heterogeneous case, and the subsequent presentation focused on the beta distribution. For both $\mathfrak{S}_2$ and $\mathfrak{S}_3$, RE model approaches are appropriate.

Approaches   The specific approaches for meta-analysis of correlations in common use in the social sciences were outlined in Part II and details on the computational procedures were given. In addition, refinements were also presented that have not yet been widely applied. A concise overview of the approaches that provides their classification according to the above mentioned characteristics and also specifies the homogeneity test and whether heterogeneity variance is estimated, is given in Table 9.1.

There are several things to note with regard to the entries in Table 9.1. Firstly, although HOT is characterized by the effect size z, the defining characteristic of this approach is actually a correction of the mean z resulting from aggregation as done in the HOr approach. Secondly, the weights are given as used in the approaches but it can be easily identified which of them are solely based on

Table 9.1   Overview of Approaches

Approach	Effect Size	Weight	Model	Homog. Test	Heterog. Variance
HOr	z	$n-3$	FE	Q	No
HOT	z	$n-3$	FE	–	No
HOd	d	$\hat{\sigma}_D^{-2}$	FE	Q	No
RR	z	n	FE	–	No
HS	r	n	RE?	75% & Q	Yes
DSL	z	$\left(\frac{1}{n-3}+\hat{\sigma}_\zeta^2\right)^{-1}$	RE	–	Yes
OP	G	n	FE	–	No
OP-FE	G	$\hat{\sigma}_G^{-2}$	FE	Q	No
OP-RE	G	$\left(\hat{\sigma}_G^2+\hat{\sigma}_\rho^2\right)^{-1}$	RE	–	Yes

Note. – = redundant to other approaches or not included in Monte Carlo study.

n and which incorporate estimated variances. Thirdly, although the weights of the HOr approach, for example, are only based on n, these are the optimal weights in the above mentioned sense. This is due to the fact that in the case of Fisher-z transformed correlations the variances are $(n-3)^{-1}$. Hence, such approaches use the optimal weights but do not suffer from the above mentioned problems. Fourthly, apart from a minor difference in testing procedures, RR is basically identical to HOr. The weight as given in Table 9.1 for the RR approach could have also been the same as for HOr according to the proponents of the RR approach. Fifthly, the classification of the HS approach as belonging to the RE model class is not entirely clear. This is indicated by a question mark but it is also recognized that the HS approach is mostly an RE approach in conceptualization. Lastly, for some of the approaches there is no entry in the column labeled "Homog. Test" because first, the test would be identical to others (e.g., HOr, HOT, RR), second, a plausible test is not included in the subsequent Monte Carlo study (OP), or such a test would simply make no sense (DSL, OP-RE).

Estimated Parameters in the Universe of Studies   It was shown that differences between approaches in the effect size used are very important with respect to the estimated universe parameter. Whereas μ_ρ, the first moment of the distribution of universe effect sizes, is the estimated parameter for r- or G-based approaches (HS, OP, OP-FE, OP-RE), the parameters are different for Fisher-z-based ($\mu_{\rho z}$) and d-based ($\mu_{\rho d}$) approaches in heterogeneous situations. For the latter approach, however, it was shown that the weighting scheme leads to results for estimates of mean effect sizes to be closer to μ_ρ than $\mu_{\rho d}$. Hence, μ_ρ was considered to be the more sensible standard of comparison in the Monte Carlo study for HOd. Since μ_ρ is considered to be the parameter of interest for most meta-analysts when pooling correlation coefficients, cautions were raised about the use of approaches that do not use r in heterogeneous situations.

Monte Carlo Study   In addition to the theoretical analyses of the second part, the results of a comprehensive Monte Carlo study were presented. This was done to comparatively evaluate the outcomes of the various approaches — including those not well-known and examined in previous Monte Carlo studies — in several situations ($\mathfrak{S}_1$ to $\mathfrak{S}_3$). The design was specified to include levels of several design variables (n, k, μ_ρ, σ_ρ^2) likely to arise in practice as well as levels (small n and k) to study and evaluate the performance of the approaches at boundary values. This seemed reasonable as properties of the estimators and tests are known theoretically only in approximation (for n and/or k approaching infinity).

For the design and conducting of the Monte Carlo study, several candidates for the simulation procedures were considered for generating the database of correlation coefficients. The candidates under consideration were a series of approximations to the distribution of R that were examined and evaluated in comparison to the exact density of R. None of the approximations were considered sufficiently good as to be used to generate correlation coefficients in a simulation study. The simulation procedures used in the Monte Carlo study were therefore specified in a computationally rather expensive form. Several predictions for the performance of the approaches mainly based on the previously mentioned differences between approaches (e.g., consequences of different effect sizes used) were explicated and largely confirmed.

An overview of results is presented in Table 9.2. The table provides the results in the form of recommendations for applications of meta-analysis to correlational data. The recommendations in Table 9.2 only apply to applications of the approaches to correlation coefficients and may not be used for other effect size data. Of course, some of the cut-off values listed in the recommendations might seem arbitrarily chosen as it is naturally the case with most cut-off values in the methodological context. Nevertheless, the values have been chosen to reflect the results of the present study as closely as possible.

The table is structured according to the tasks to be performed in a meta-analysis and the situation given. Of course, the situation is something a meta-analyst does ordinarily not know in advance. The statements in the tables have thus to be interpreted as summaries of the performance of the various approaches in the Monte Carlo study and to give an indication which procedure is recommended when a certain situation is given.

As can be seen in the table, there is no single approach performing best for all tasks under all conditions. Instead, approaches seem to perform best overall when their basic model assumptions are met. For some of the tasks in meta-analysis specified in the table nearly all, and for some others none, of the approaches performs at an acceptable level according to conventional criteria. This indicates tasks and conditions for which the approaches evaluated here do not provide adequate statistical tools. This is the case, for example, for the homogeneity test Q in heterogeneous situations.

Table 9.2 Recommendations for Meta-Analysis of Correlational Data

Task	$\mathfrak{S}$	Recommendation
Estimation of μ_ρ	$\mathfrak{S}_1$	All estimators, except OP-FE and OP-RE, are usable when $n > 16$. However, OP shows *no* bias notwithstanding which n, k, or μ_ρ is given. OP is therefore recommended. HOT performs almost as well as OP and is more efficient when μ_ρ is small ($\mu_\rho < .10$). It can thus be considered as a good alternative in this situation.
	$\mathfrak{S}_2$	Only good r-based estimators should be used (OP and HS) to provide estimates of μ_ρ. Among these estimators OP shows *no* bias notwithstanding which n, k, or μ_ρ is given. OP-FE and OP-RE are not good choices. HS seems to be a good alternative to OP when $n > 32$. The estimate of μ_ρ should, however, be interpreted with caution when vastly different universe effect sizes are suspected. To determine whether this may be the case, a homogeneity test might be considered.
	$\mathfrak{S}_3$	Only good r-based estimators should be used (OP and HS) to provide estimates of μ_ρ. All estimators, except OP-FE and OP-RE are usable when $n > 32$. OP is preferable to all other estimators.
Significance tests for $\mu_\rho = 0$	$\mathfrak{S}_1$	DSL and HOT perform best by showing mean rejection rates below α. HOr shows rejection rates closest to α when the null hypothesis is true. Except for HS3, HS4 and OP-RE, all rejection rates are quite close to α, so the choice of test does not make a big difference. When the null hypothesis is false, all tests reach satisfactory power levels very quickly. The choice of a test does not make a substantial difference here as well.
	$\mathfrak{S}_2$	No substantial differences in power between approaches prevail. Random effects approaches are generally more conservative, though differences are marginal.
	$\mathfrak{S}_3$	When the null hypothesis is true, only random effects approaches (especially DSL) perform adequately. All other approaches show rejection rates far too high, even for moderate n (64) and σ_ρ^2 (.01), and should not be used here. When the null hypothesis is false, there are only small disadvantages in power by using random effects approaches. Thus, DSL is recommended, deliberately accepting a disadvantage in power.

table continues

continued table

Task	$\mathfrak{S}$	Results and Recommendations
Confidence intervals for μ_ρ	$\mathfrak{S}_1$	HOT and OP reach the desired coverage rates most closely, and show a very stable performance across all levels of the design variables. Thus, both are recommended though with some reservations because of much larger interval widths when n and k are very small (i.e., less than 16). All other approaches, except OP-RE, HOd, HS3, and HS4 also show mean coverage values of about .93 for 95% confidence intervals and may also be useful when bearing this in mind.
	$\mathfrak{S}_2$	HOT and OP reach the desired coverage rates most closely and show a very stable performance across all levels of the design variables. Since only OP estimates μ_ρ, it is recommended.
	$\mathfrak{S}_3$	All approaches show at least some deficiencies and none can be recommended without reservations (note that only r-based estimators were evaluated). Amongst the evaluated approaches, HS3 and HS4 performed best.
Homogeneity test: Q	$\mathfrak{S}_1$	HOr and, with some reservations when $n < 32$, also HS are usable. The transformation of r to d leads to excessive rejection rates which strongly cautions against the use of the HOd approach here.
	$\mathfrak{S}_2$	All approaches show deficiencies in detecting small to medium effects, especially when n or k are small. Thus, reliance on the Q-test for a decision on the conduct of HLM-type procedures or for the choice of model (FE vs. RE) can be a risky business.
	$\mathfrak{S}_3$	None of the approaches show satisfactory power in detecting small to medium variances (.0025 to .0225), especially when n or k are small. Unless $k > 32$, tests are not reliable indicators of heterogeneity.
Homogeneity test: 75%- and 90%-rule	$\mathfrak{S}_1$	Both the 75%- and 90%-rule are not viable alternatives to the Q-test (see above). Rejection rates are generally too high in this situation.
	$\mathfrak{S}_2$	Both the 75%- and 90%-rule are not viable alternatives to the Q-test (see above). Rejection rates are too low unless $n > 64$ and heterogeneity variance is at least medium.

table continues

Task	$\mathfrak{S}$	Results and Recommendations
		continued table
	$\mathfrak{S}_3$	Basically the same results as in $\mathfrak{S}_2$ emerged. Hence the same recommendations also apply here.
Estimation of σ_ρ^2	$\mathfrak{S}_1$	For very low k and n below 32 all estimators show strong overestimation. OP-RE is unusable for $n < 16$ in all cases. All estimators provide acceptable estimates for $n > 32$ and k not less than 32.
	$\mathfrak{S}_2$	For very low k and n below 32 DSL and OP-RE show high biases. For even modest $\Delta\rho$ both OP-RE and DSL should not be used. In general, HS performs best in $\mathfrak{S}_2$ though it should be used with some caution when $k < 16$.
	$\mathfrak{S}_3$	OP-RE performs generally poorly and should not be used in this situation. HS and DSL both perform well, but HS performs best.

Note. $\mathfrak{S}_1$ to $\mathfrak{S}_3$ = Assumed situation in meta-analysis.

Overall, the good performance of OP in various situations and for various purposes is remarkable. For estimating the mean effect size, for example, it can be recommended without reservations. However, Table 9.2 also indicates when it should used with strong reservations at best (construction of confidence intervals in $\mathfrak{S}_3$).

For the tasks of testing $\mu_\rho = 0$ and homogeneity tests, approaches do not differ markedly. In the former case they show equally good performance and in the latter they all perform equally badly. For homogeneity tests, the procedures unique to the HS approach are not interesting alternatives. For the purpose of estimating the heterogeneity variance, however, HS emerged as the best approach, though it should be added that DSL is hard to compare because computations and results are in z-space.

Finally, a caveat seems indicated. Note that it is *not* recommended in general to employ any of the methods in $\mathfrak{S}_2$ and to abstain from using HLM procedures. Since appropriate predictors are not always available to the meta-analyst, the methods of meta-analysis as described in this book are the only available option. Hence, an evaluation of their performance as provided here is of vital importance.

10
Discussion and Conclusions

Reviews of meta-analytical methods have generally been very positive, at least in the social sciences (e.g., Kavale, 1995). The ongoing debate about its usefulness as a scientific research tool (cf. Hunter & Schmidt, 1996; Feinstein, 1995) has not hampered its growth in the literature or the willingness to adopt it as a useful tool by researchers. Most critics argue not on purely statistical grounds but attack the application of meta-analytical methods for reasons founded in the philosophy of science or on conceptual grounds from the specific field of application. Some of these lines of criticism seem legitimate, indeed, and meta-analysis is certainly not free of conceptual problems and ambiguities in application. For example, it was pointed out in the introductory chapter that meta-analysis is not a strictly standardized technique for which clearly articulated rules of conduct are available at *any* step of the whole process. Reviews have shown that meta-analyses on the same issue do not provide nearly identical results but are quite different and variable (e.g., Steiner, Lane, Dobbins, Schnur, & McDonnell, 1991). Moreover, doubts have been raised regarding the reliability of implementing meta-analysis in practice (Zakzanis, 1998). As was pointed out by Wanous, Sullivan, and Malinak (1989), judgement calls are important and seem to influence the results and conclusions drawn in meta-analyses on the same topic. Thus, problems pertaining to the application of meta-analysis seem to mainly result because meta-analysis is more than just estimating parameters (see, e.g., Bailar, 1995).

The present examination focused on the *statistical* methods most common for meta-analysis of correlations, that is, the analysis step. This step is probably viewed by many as the immune core of meta-analysis, hence regarded as the step with the least problems or potential for subjective influences. A result of this may be the seemingly generally adopted assumption that it makes no difference which of the available sets of statistical procedures is used. The choice of an approach seems more a question of the field of research in which the methods are applied rather than a question of the statistical model assumed for a research situation. However, it was shown that there are many important implications for the results and therefore potentially also for the conclusions drawn from a meta-analysis due to the choice of one of the available approaches.

Interestingly, it is not an easy task to clearly answer the question of what approaches are actually available, because ambiguities arise in exactly specifying the available ones. One possibility to do this would be to focus only on major presentations of meta-analytic methods for correlations in the literature. This basically leads to three approaches (Hedges & Olkin, 1985; Hunter & Schmidt, 1990; Rosenthal, 1991). In this book, these three major approaches were complemented by further approaches which are partly already included in the treatment by Hedges and Olkin (1985) or represent sometimes minor but consequential differences in statistical procedures. It seems legitimate to call into question such a concept of approaches or the meaningfulness of the very concept of approaches. A good example for not classifying approaches according to author groups or major treatments in the literature is given by comparison of HOr and RR.

The reason to classify RR differently in comparison to HOr is, in fact, a minor one at best, concentrated on a single aspect of significance testing for the mean effect size (compare procedures on page 60 and page 62). This is not regarded as a compelling reason to differentiate between HOr and RR. With the same reasoning it might be argued that HOT, for example, is also not an independent approach but represents only a minor change in the HOr procedures. Indeed, this is true. However, this argument extends to other approaches as well. It is argued that criteria to differentiate or classify *statistical approaches* in meta-analysis should better be based more on classes of statistical models and effect size measures, for example, rather than authors, books, or any other historical and seemingly arbitrary reason. This was done in the present book. A slightly extended list of classification aspects includes:

- effect size measure used,
- weighting scheme used,
- FE versus RE models, including conditional RE approaches,
- explanatory (e.g., HLM) versus non-explanatory models, and
- use of observed and/or latent variables (HLM vs. mixture analysis).

These aspects may even be extended by some models not presented in this book, for example, (empirical) Bayes models (see, e.g., Raudenbush & Bryk, 2002). Although such classification aspects are partly overlapping, they enable a distinction between meta-analytic procedures more in line with common statistical distinctions. These aspects also show that there is a wealth of models and procedures for the meta-analysis of correlations that let statements like "...there is only one dominant approach for conducting meta-analysis of correlation research and that is the Hunter and Schmidt (1990) approach" (Huffcutt, 2002, p. 209) appear untenable. In retrospect then, the use of *approaches* in this book is only a vehicle to differentiate between statistical procedures and does not necessarily designate fundamentally different routes to meta-analysis of correlations.

Of the classification aspects listed above, the choice of effect size measure seems to be one accompanied by more fundamental consequences than previously thought. As has been pointed out, r-based approaches do not in principle suffer from changes in estimated parameters in heterogeneous situations. The change in spaces by the Fisher-z or r to d transformation of the original correlation has manifest consequences for interpretation many users of meta-analysis may not be aware of. It was shown that the use of the Fisher-z transformation leads to higher absolute estimates of $\mu_{\rho z}$ as compared to μ_ρ in heterogeneous situations. Interpreting estimates of $\mu_{\rho z}$ as estimates of μ_ρ would simply be a misinterpretation in heterogeneous situations.

It is difficult to assess the severity of this problem in previous practical applications of meta-analysis at least for two reasons. First, the difference between the universe parameters μ_ρ and $\mu_{\rho z}$ estimated in the approaches based on the Fisher-z transformation versus r-based approaches depends on the unknown heterogeneity in the universe of studies. To quantify the difference it would be necessary to know exactly the categorical or continuous distribution in the universe. Such knowledge is, of course, not available and it would be interesting to reanalyze existing meta-analytic databases to examine the differences arising in practice. Second, even if the difference could be quantified, severity is a very subjective aspect. For example, in a situation with a beta distributed random variable with $\mu_\rho = .60$ and $\sigma_\rho^2 = .0625$ in the universe of studies, a corresponding $\mu_{\rho z} \approx .67$ is given. The difference of .07 would certainly be judged by some researchers for a certain research question — for example in the personnel selection context — as substantial and in the context of other research questions it might not change interpretation of results and therefore be inconsequential.

Hence, doubts are raised as to whether the Fisher-z transformation should be applied to correlation coefficients in meta-analysis. Arguments put forward in favor of its use often rest on highlighting the bias of r (e.g., Silver & Dunlap, 1987). As was shown in the current book, differences in bias favor r over z but are minuscule in absolute value, anyway. Moreover, in light of the fact that an UMVU estimator G is available, easily computed, and shows excellent performance in terms of bias as reported in the Monte Carlo study, arguments in favor of Fisher-z which are based on the bias of r are not convincing.

Another line of argument against the use of r draws on the dependency of the variance of the estimators on the universe parameter (e.g., James et al., 1986). This is indeed a serious issue not only for r but also for other estimators in meta-analysis and therefore represents a *general* problem for pooled estimators. The optimal weights require the correct variances of the estimators. Since only estimates of these variances are available in practice and these estimates are plugged in the weights in aggregation, a dependency of the variance on the universe parameters, or more precisely on the estimator when estimates are plugged in, induces a bias in the pooled estimator, especially when n is small. This was most clearly evident in the Monte Carlo study for OP-FE and OP-RE, the UMVU estimator weighted by the inverse of its (estimated) variances. Note that the problem not only pertains to these estimators. Since this problem does not arise with suboptimal weights that depend only on n, the use of G weighted by the sample sizes of the studies is recommended here when precise estimation of the universe parameter is of vital interest, as is nearly always the case in meta-analysis of correlations. As may be noted, the approach proposed by Hunter and Schmidt (1990) is also an r-based approach with the sample sizes as weights. The usage of this approach is thus also encouraged. Nevertheless, a better choice than r is to use the UMVU estimator. The recommended approach based on the UMVU estimator is not without problems. There are also certain tasks in meta-analysis for which the approach — as it was specified — does not perform satisfactorily, for example, for testing $\mu_\rho = 0$ in $\mathfrak{S}_3$. In consequence, there is no single best approach amongst the set of examined approaches. Such an approach has yet to be developed. However, taking into account the many possible situations, many tasks, and many boundary conditions (e.g., with respect to n and k) in meta-analysis, it seems unlikely that such a single approach will ever become available.

Problems in interpreting a mean effect size estimate in meta-analysis not only arise in the context of transformations of the correlation coefficient. Interpretation also depends on whether heterogeneity in universe effect sizes is present at all, detected, and modeled. In general, mean effect sizes have an undisputable interpretation in homogeneous situations but not in heterogeneous situations. This does not mean, however, that they are not interpretable in heterogeneous situations. As has been argued, the mean effect size generally has to be interpreted like the grand mean in ANOVA-type analyses. Of course, if heterogeneity is suspected or detected by any of the available tests, then models to explain heterogeneity (e.g., HLM) are certainly indicated to go beyond grand mean interpretations.

In any case, the interpretation of results in meta-analysis has to be done within the framework of a chosen model, another characteristic to differentiate between approaches. Unfortunately, the choice of a model is often done in practice just en passant. As has also been shown with other methods as those used in this book (Hedges & Vevea, 1998) and in different contexts (Overton, 1998), methods generally perform best when their model assumptions are met. This conclusion seems trivial at first glance, but in light of the fact that many of the statistical derivations of procedures used in meta-analysis rest on large-sample theory, it is important to test by simulation methods whether the properties of estimators, for example, also hold for constellations of design characteristics likely to arise in practice. Unfortunately, this information is not of great help for the meta-analyst, who wants to decide which model to adopt, though it is certainly reassuring. A theoretically founded line of reasoning may lead researchers to the choice of a model. Questions about the intended inference, theoretically expected heterogeneity, or simply the number and origin of available studies help in deciding which model to adopt.

Another possibility is to condition the choice of the model on the result of the Q-test. As was shown in the Monte Carlo study as well as in the literature (e.g., Harwell, 1997), the Q-test to detect heterogeneity is not satisfactorily powerful in many situations and heterogeneity may therefore remain undetected. This test is thus not a very good guide for a model decision because it leads to many wrong decisions. Hence, statements like "if the chi square is not significant, this is strong evidence that there is no true variation across studies, but if it is significant, the variation may still be negligible in magnitude" (Hunter & Schmidt, 1990, p. 112) are questionable (see also Harwell, 1997). Proposed alternatives to this test, like the 75%- or 90%-rule do not represent viable alternatives to the Q-test (see also Sánchez-Meca & Marín-Martínez, 1997). Interestingly, the 75%-rule seems to be in widespread use, at least in I/O psychology. Cortina (2003) reviewed 59 quantitative reviews containing not less than 1,647 meta-analyses, of which all appeared in one of the most prestigious journals of I/O psychology, the Journal of Applied Psychology. He found that as many as 57% of the meta-analyses used the 75%-rule as a homogeneity test and only 19% the Q-statistic. Thus, further theoretical developments as well as their empirical evaluation to establish procedures that perform better for this task of meta-analysis are needed. Hartung and Knapp (2003), for example, recently proposed such an alternative test procedure for meta-analysis.

Yet another option would be to explore heterogeneity by application of mixture models (Böhning, 2000; Schlattmann et al., 2003). These models provide a statistically well-founded framework for meta-analysis that is not widely used yet. Though early presentations of these techniques have been given in the psychological literature (Thomas, 1989b; Thompson, 1989; Thomas, 1990b), they have not been adopted very often. The reasons for this fact may lie in unfamiliarity with these models or in perceived technical difficulties. Since easy-to-use software for the application of these models has recently become available (Böhning et al., 1992; Schlattmann et al., 2003), their use is encouraged because they address one of the central questions of meta-analysis quite elegantly, the modeling of heterogeneity.

Apart from suggesting to condition the use of a model on the outcome of a homogeneity test — a so-called conditional random effects procedure — Hedges and Vevea (1998) have proposed to make a choice between the FE and RE model on the basis of the intended inference. The intended inference is a question about properties of the universe of studies to which results are generalized to. These properties may be restricted to characteristics like those of the observed studies (FE model) or more general (RE model). The question of intended inference is not always an easy question to answer since generalization not only depends on the desire of a researcher as Hunter and Schmidt (2000) suggest, but also on a series of other aspects, like those Matt (2003) has described, for example. The shift from applications of FE models to RE models that is strongly encouraged in the literature (e.g., Erez et al., 1996) is not without problems, as the presented Monte Carlo study results suggest. Especially when the number of studies is small ($k < 32$), the most important aspect of RE models, the heterogeneity variance, can not be estimated with acceptable precision. Note that a number of 32 studies is far from unusual in practice and even in some Monte Carlo studies considered to be large (e.g., Field, 2001).

Another aspect addressed in the present Monte Carlo study with potentially far-reaching implications is the conversion of correlations to standardized mean differences d. Transformations of effect sizes are necessary in most applications because of different designs and analysis methods used in the primary studies to address the same research question. The implicit assumption of applying the transformation is that computations based on the transformed effect size (e.g., d from r) lead to equivalent results in comparison to computations based on the untransformed effect size (e.g., r). In other words, the transformation does not introduce any bias or distortion of results. If the equivalence were given, then it would not matter whether meta-analytic computations were carried out with r or d as an effect size, the results would be the same. However, the r to d transformation leads to changes in results in meta-analysis as reported in the Monte Carlo study. This clearly challenges the assumption of an inconsequential application of this transformation. Since the influences of weights that depend on the universe parameter are also involved in explanations of results, the origin of the deviant results by using d is not entirely clear. The derivation of the transformation formula, however, rests on assumptions that seem questionable. Of course, as has repeatedly been highlighted, there would be no need to apply the transformation to a database consisting only of r in practice. Instead, this would be ordinarily necessary only for a subset of studies. The results presented in this book suggest that it is wise to at least conduct a sensitivity analysis to assess the effect of the transformed effect sizes on the results.

To conclude, the choice of an approach to meta-analytically synthesize correlation coefficients as presented in this book does make a difference. Some approaches are better than others for various tasks but a single best set of procedures has yet to be established. The present book has nevertheless pointed out some procedures that should be used with caution and others that seem under-utilized and deserve more attention in methodological developments and applications.

Nomenclature

B	Complete Beta function, page 21
c	Number of components in mixture analysis, page 43
d	Standardized mean difference, page 29
δ	Population standardized mean difference, page 28
$\Delta\rho$	Difference between ρ_1 and ρ_2 in $\mathfrak{S}_2$, page 125
DSL	Approach proposed by DerSimonian and Laird (1986), page 71
$_2F_1$	Gaussian hypergeometric function, page 21
FE	Fixed effects (model), page 35
G	Unique minimum variance unbiased estimator of ρ, page 26
g	Standard normal deviate, page 58
g_α	Critical value for a prespecified α-level from a standard normal distribution to construct two-sided confidence intervals, page 37
Γ	Euler Gamma function, page 21
HLM	Hierarchical linear models, page 45
HOd	Approach proposed by Hedges and Olkin (1985) based on d as resulting from an r to d transformation, page 59
HOr	Approach proposed by Hedges and Olkin (1985) based on Fisher-z transformed correlations, page 57
HOT	Approach proposed by Hedges and Olkin (1985) based on a corrected average z as suggested by Hotelling (1953), page 58
HS	Approach proposed by Hunter and Schmidt (1990), page 62
HS1	HS approach employing version 1 of the estimator for the sampling variance of the mean effect size, page 65
HS2	HS approach employing version 2 of the estimator for the sampling variance of the mean effect size, page 65
HS3	HS approach employing version 3 of the estimator for the sampling variance of the mean effect size, page 66
HS4	HS approach employing version 4 of the estimator for the standard error of the mean effect size, page 66
k	Number of studies, page 35
λ_j	Weight of the jth component in mixture analysis, page 43
MSE	Mean squared error, page 134
μ_ρ	Expected value of the distribution in the universe of studies (in the space of r), page 49

$\mu_{\rho d}$	Expected value of the distribution in the universe of studies (in the space of r) that results from the d to r transformation as given in Equation 3.11, page 79
$\mu_{\rho z}$	Expected value of the distribution in the universe of studies (in the space of r) that results from the inverse Fisher-z transformation $\mu_{\rho z} = \tanh \mu_\zeta$, page 76
μ_Θ	Expected value of the random variable Θ, page 39
μ_ζ	Expected value of the distribution in the universe of studies (in the space of z), page 130
N	$N = \sum_{i=1}^k n_i$, page 58
n	Number of observations per study, page 9
ν_i	Variance of the effect size estimate T_i, page 36
$\nu_{\hat{\Theta}}$	Variance of $\hat{\Theta}$, page 40
OP	Approach based on the UMVU estimator proposed by Olkin and Pratt (1958) with n as weights, page 73
OP-FE	Approach based on the UMVU estimator proposed by Olkin and Pratt (1958) with FE model weights, page 73
OP-RE	Approach based on the UMVU estimator proposed by Olkin and Pratt (1958) with RE model weights, page 74
$\mathcal{P}$	Probability, page 43
PDF	Probability density function, page 21
Q	Q-statistic, used in homogeneity tests, page 37
r	Correlation coefficient, page 20
RE	Random effects (model), page 39
P	Correlation coefficient as a random variable in the universe of studies, page 43
ρ	Population correlation coefficient, page 21
RR	Approach proposed by Rosenthal and Rubin (1979), page 61
$\mathfrak{S}_1$	Class of discrete distributions in the universe of studies: one single ρ with probability mass one, page 49
$\mathfrak{S}_2$	Class of discrete distributions in the universe of studies: $\rho_1 \neq \rho_2$ both with equal probability mass, page 50
$\mathfrak{S}_3$	Class of continuous distributions in the universe of studies: Almost exclusively considered to be the family of beta distributions in this book, page 53
σ_R^2	Variance of R, page 26
σ_ρ^2	Variance of the distribution in the universe of studies (in the space of r), also called heterogeneity variance, page 49
σ_Θ^2	Variance of Θ, also called heterogeneity variance, page 39
σ_Z^2	Variance of Z (Fisher-z transformed correlation), page 23
σ_ζ^2	Variance of the distribution in the universe of studies (in the space of z), also called heterogeneity variance, page 71

Θ	Random variable Θ used in the RE model to designate the effect size of interest in the universe of studies, page 39
θ	Effect size in the universe of studies, page 35
$\hat{\Theta}$	Mean effect size estimate in the RE model, page 39
$\hat{\theta}$	Mean effect size estimate in the FE model, page 36
T_i	Effect size measure of the ith study, page 35
UMVU	Unique minimum variance unbiased, page 26
w_i	Weights applied to the ith study in the FE model, page 36
w_i^*	Weights applied to the ith study in the RE model, page 39
z	Fisher-z transformed correlation coefficient, page 22
ζ	Fisher-z transformed population correlation coefficient, page 22

References

Aaron, B., Kromrey, J. D., & Ferron, J. (1998, November). *Equating r-based and d-based effect size indices: Problems with a commonly recommended formula.* Paper presented at the annual meeting of the Florida Educational Research Association, Orlando, FL. (ERIC Document Reproduction Service No. ED 433353).

Aguinis, H., & Whitehead, R. (1997). Sampling variance in the correlation coefficient under indirect range restriction: Implications for validity generalization. *Journal of Applied Psychology, 82,* 528–538.

Alexander, R. A., Hanges, P. J., & Alliger, G. M. (1985). An empirical examination of two transformations of sample correlations. *Educational and Psychological Measurement, 45,* 797–801.

Alexander, R. A., Scozarro, M. J., & Borodkin, L. J. (1989). Statistical and empirical examination of the chi-square test for homogeneity of correlations in meta-analysis. *Psychological Bulletin, 106,* 329–331.

American Psychological Association. (2001). *Publication manual of the American Psychological Association* (5th ed.). Washington, DC: Author.

Andersson, G. (1999). The role of meta-analysis in the significance test controversy. *European Psychologist, 4,* 75–82.

Bailar, J. C., III. (1995). The practice of meta-analysis. *Journal of Clinical Epidemiology, 48,* 149–157.

Bangert-Drowns, R. L. (1986). Review of developments in meta-analytic method. *Psychological Bulletin, 99,* 388–399.

Barnett, V. (1981). *Comparative statistical inference* (2nd ed.). New York: Wiley.

Barrick, M. R., & Mount, M. K. (2003). Impact of meta-analysis methods on understanding personality–performance relations. In K. R. Murphy (Ed.), *Validity generalization: A critical review* (pp. 197–221). Mahwah, NJ: Lawrence Erlbaum.

Beaman, A. L. (1991). An empirical comparison of meta-analytic and traditional reviews. *Personality and Social Psychology Bulletin, 17,* 252–257.

Beelmann, A., & Bliesener, T. (1994). Aktuelle Probleme und Strategien der Metaanalyse [Current problems and strategies in meta-analysis]. *Psychologische Rundschau, 45,* 211–233.

Begg, C. B. (1994). Publication bias. In H. M. Cooper & L. V. Hedges (Eds.), *The handbook of research synthesis* (pp. 399–409). New York: Russell Sage Foundation.

Biggerstaff, B. J., & Tweedie, R. L. (1997). Incorporating variability in estimates of heterogeneity in the random effects model in meta-analysis. *Statistics in Medicine, 16,* 753–768.

Bobko, P., & Stone-Romero, E. F. (1998). Meta-analysis may be another useful research tool, but it is not a panacea. *Research in Personnel and Human Resources Management, 16,* 359–397.

Böhning, D. (2000). *Computer-assisted analysis of mixtures and applications: Meta-analysis, disease mapping and others.* Boca Raton, FL: Chapman & Hall/CRC.

Böhning, D., Malzahn, U., Dietz, E., Schlattmann, P., Viwatwongkasem, C., & Biggeri, A. (2002). Some general points in estimating heterogeneity variance with the DerSimonian-Laird estimator. *Biostatistics, 3,* 445-457.

Böhning, D., Schlattmann, P., & Lindzey, B. G. (1992). Computer assisted analysis of mixtures (C.A.MAN): Statistical algorithms. *Biometrics, 48,* 283–303.

Boorsbom, D., & Mellenbergh, G. J. (2002). True scores, latent variables, and constructs: A comment on Schmidt and Hunter. *Intelligence, 30,* 505–514.

Brockwell, S. E., & Gordon, I. R. (2001). A comparison of statistical methods for meta-analysis. *Statistics in Medicine, 20,* 825–840.

Burke, M. J. (1984). Validity generalization: A review and critique of the correlation model. *Personnel Psychology, 37,* 93–115.

Callender, J. C., & Osburn, H. G. (1980). Development and test of a new model for validity generalization. *Journal of Applied Psychology, 65,* 543–558.

Callender, J. C., & Osburn, H. G. (1988). Unbiased estimation of sampling variance of correlations. *Journal of Applied Psychology, 73,* 312–315.

Callender, J. C., Osburn, H. G., Greener, J. M., & Ashworth, S. (1982). Multiplicative validity generalization model: Accuracy of estimates as a function of sample size, mean, variance, and shape of the distribution of true validities. *Journal of Applied Psychology, 67,* 859–867.

Chalmers, T. C., Smith, H., Jr., Blackburn, B., Silverman, B., Schroeder, B., Reitman, D., & Ambroz, A. (1981). A method for assessing the quality of a randomized control trial. *Controlled Clinical Trials, 2,* 31–49.

Chow, S. L. (1988). Significance test or effect size? *Psychological Bulletin, 103,* 105–110.

Chow, S. L. (1996). *Statistical significance.* Thousand Oaks, CA: Sage.

Cohen, J. (1988). *Statistical power analysis for the behavioral sciences* (2nd ed.). Hillsdale, NJ: Lawrence Erlbaum.

Cohen, J. (1992). A power primer. *Psychological Bulletin, 112,* 155–159.

Cohn, L. D., & Becker, B. J. (2003). How meta-analysis increases statistical power. *Psychological Methods, 8,* 243–253.

Cook, D. J., Sackett, D. L., & Spitzer, W. O. (1995). Methodologic guidelines for systematic reviews of randomized control trials in health care from the Potsdam consultation on meta-analysis. *Journal of Clinical Epidemiology, 48,* 167–171.

Cook, T. D., & Leviton, L. C. (1980). Reviewing the literature: A comparison of traditional methods with meta-analysis. *Journal of Personality, 48,* 449–472.

Cooper, H. M. (1982). Scientific guidelines for conducting integrative research reviews. *Review of Educational Research, 52,* 291–302.

Cooper, H. M., & Hedges, L. V. (1994a). Research synthesis as a scientific enterprise. In H. M. Cooper & L. V. Hedges (Eds.), *The handbook of research synthesis* (pp. 3–14). New York: Russell Sage Foundation.

Cooper, H. M., & Hedges, L. V. (Eds.). (1994b). *The handbook of research synthesis.* New York: Russell Sage Foundation.

Cooper, H. M., & Lindsay, J. L. (1998). Research synthesis and meta-analysis. In L. Bickman & D. J. Rog (Eds.), *Handbook of applied social research methods* (pp. 315–337). Thousand Oaks, CA: Sage.

Corey, D. M., Dunlap, W. P., & Burke, M. J. (1998). Averaging correlations: Expected values and bias in combined Pearson rs and Fisher's z transformations. *The Journal of General Psychology, 125,* 245–261.

Cornwell, J. M. (1988, August). *Content analysis of meta-analytic studies from I/O psychology.* Paper presented at the 96th annual meeting of the American Psychological Association, Atlanta, GA. (ERIC Document Reproduction Service No. ED 304469).

Cornwell, J. M. (1993). Monte Carlo comparisons of three tests for homogeneity of independent correlations. *Educational and Psychological Measurement, 53,* 605–618.

Cornwell, J. M., & Ladd, R. T. (1993). Power and accuracy of the Schmidt and Hunter meta-analytic procedures. *Educational and Psychological Measurement, 53,* 877–895.

Cortina, J. M. (2003). Apples and oranges (and pears, oh my!): The search for moderators in meta-analysis. *Organizational Research Methods, 6,* 415–439.

Cronbach, L. J., Gleser, G. C., Nanda, H., & Rajaratnam, N. (1972). *The dependability of behavioral measurements.* New York: Wiley.

Czienskowski, U. (2003). Meta-analysis — not just research synthesis. In R. Schulze, H. Holling, & D. Böhning (Eds.), *Meta-analysis: New developments and applications in medical and social sciences* (pp. 141–152). Seattle, WA: Hogrefe & Huber.

DerSimonian, R., & Laird, N. M. (1983). Evaluating the effect of coaching on SAT scores: A meta-analysis. *Harvard Educational Review, 53,* 1–15.

DerSimonian, R., & Laird, N. M. (1986). Meta-analysis in clinical trials. *Controlled Clinical Trials, 7,* 177–188.

Dickersin, K., & Berlin, J. A. (1992). Meta-analysis: State-of-the-science. *Epidemiologic Reviews, 14,* 154–176.

Donner, A., & Rosner, B. (1980). On inferences concerning a common correlation coefficient. *Applied Statistics, 29,* 69–76.

Duan, B., & Dunlap, W. P. (1997). The accuracy of different methods for estimating the standard error of correlations corrected for range restriction. *Educational and Psychological Measurement, 57,* 254–265.

Dunlap, W. P., Cortina, J. M., Vaslow, J. B., & Burke, M. J. (1996). Meta-analysis of experiments with matched groups or repeated measures designs. *Psychological Methods, 1,* 170–177.

Durlak, J. A. (2003). Basic principles of meta-analysis. In M. Roberts & S. S. Ilardi (Eds.), *Handbook of research methods in clinical psychology* (pp. 196–209). Malden, MA: Blackwell.

Eckes, T., & Six, B. (1994). Fakten und Fiktionen in der Einstellungs–Verhaltens-Forschung: Eine Meta-Analyse [Facts and fiction in attitude–behavior research: A meta-analysis]. *Zeitschrift für Sozialpsychologie, 25,* 253–271.

Erez, A., Bloom, M. C., & Wells, M. T. (1996). Using random rather than fixed effects models in meta-analysis: Implications for situational specificity and validity generalization. *Personnel Psychology, 49,* 275–306.

Eysenck, H.-J. (1978). An exercise in mega-silliness. *American Psychologist, 33,* 517.

Farley, J. U., Lehmann, D. R., & Ryan, M. J. (1981). Generalizing from "imperfect" replication. *Journal of Business, 54,* 597–610.

Farrell, S., & Hakstian, A. R. (2001). Improving salesforce performance: A meta-analytic investigation of the effectiveness and utility of personnel selection procedures and training interventions. *Psychology & Marketing, 18,* 281–316.

Feinstein, A. R. (1995). Meta-analysis: Statistical alchemy for the 21st century. *Journal of Clinical Epidemiology, 48,* 71–79.

Field, A. P. (2001). Meta-analysis of correlation coefficients: A Monte Carlo comparison of fixed- and random-effects methods. *Psychological Methods, 6,* 161–180.

Fisher, R. A. (1915). Frequency distribution of the values of the correlation coefficient in samples from an indefinitely large population. *Biometrika, 10,* 507–521.

Fisher, R. A. (1921). On the "probable error" of a coefficient of correlation deduced from a small sample. *Metron, 1,* 1–32.

Frick, R. W. (1998). Interpreting statistical testing: Process and propensity, not population and random sampling. *Behavior Research Methods, Instruments, & Computers, 30,* 527–535.

Friedman, L. (2000). Estimators of random effects variance components in meta-analysis. *Journal of Educational and Behavioral Statistics, 25,* 1–12.

Fuller, J. B., & Hester, K. (1999). Comparing the sample-weighted and unweighted meta-analysis: An applied perspective. *Journal of Management, 25,* 803–828.

Gadenne, V. (1984). *Theorie und Erfahrung in der psychologischen Forschung [Theory and experience in psychological research].* Tübingen: J.C.B. Mohr.

Glass, G. V. (1976). Primary, secondary and metaanalysis research. *Educational Researcher, 5,* 3–8.

Glass, G. V., McGaw, B., & Smith, M. L. (1981). *Meta-analysis in social research.* Beverly Hills, CA: Sage.

Hall, J. A., Tickle-Degnen, L., Rosenthal, R., & Mosteller, F. (1994). Hypotheses and problems in research synthesis. In H. M. Cooper & L. V. Hedges (Eds.), *The handbook of research synthesis* (pp. 17–38). New York: Russell Sage Foundation.

Hall, S. M., & Brannick, M. T. (2002). Comparison of two random-effects methods of meta-analysis. *Journal of Applied Psychology, 87,* 377–389.

Halvorsen, K. T. (1994). The reporting format. In H. M. Cooper & L. V. Hedges (Eds.), *The handbook of research synthesis* (pp. 425–437). New York: Russell Sage Foundation.

Hardy, R. J., & Thompson, S. G. (1998). Detecting and describing heterogeneity in meta-analysis. *Statistics in Medicine, 17,* 841–856.

Harley, B. I. (1957). Relation between the distributions of non-central *t* and of a transformed correlation coefficient. *Biometrika, 44,* 219–224.

Harlow, L. L., Mulaik, S. A., & Steiger, J. H. (Eds.). (1997). *What if there were no significance tests?* Mahwah, NJ: Lawrence Erlbaum.

Harris, R. J. (1997). Reforming significance testing via three-valued logic. In L. L. Harlow, S. A. Mulaik, & J. H. Steiger (Eds.), *What if there were no significance tests?* (pp. 145–174). Mahwah, NJ: Lawrence Erlbaum.

Hartung, J., Argaç, D., & Makambi, K. (2003). Homogeneity tests in meta-analysis. In R. Schulze, H. Holling, & D. Böhning (Eds.), *Meta-analysis: New developments and applications in medical and social sciences* (pp. 3–20). Seattle, WA: Hogrefe & Huber.

Hartung, J., & Knapp, G. (2003). An alternative test procedure for meta-analysis. In R. Schulze, H. Holling, & D. Böhning (Eds.), *Meta-analysis: New developments and applications in medical and social sciences* (pp. 53–69). Seattle, WA: Hogrefe & Huber.

Harwell, M. (1997). An empirical study of Hedges's homogeneity test. *Psychological Methods, 2*, 219–231.

Hedges, L. V. (1981). Distribution theory for Glass's estimator of effect size and related estimators. *Journal of Educational Statistics, 6*, 107–128.

Hedges, L. V. (1982a). Estimation of effect size from a series of independent experiments. *Psychological Bulletin, 92*, 490–499.

Hedges, L. V. (1982b). Fitting categorical models to effect sizes from series of experiments. *Journal of Educational Statistics, 7*, 119–137.

Hedges, L. V. (1982c). Fitting continuous models to effect size data. *Journal of Educational Statistics, 7*, 245–270.

Hedges, L. V. (1983a). Combining independent estimators in research synthesis. *British Journal of Mathematical and Statistical Psychology, 36*, 123–131.

Hedges, L. V. (1983b). A random effects model for effect sizes. *Psychological Bulletin, 93*, 388–395.

Hedges, L. V. (1987). How hard is hard science, how soft is soft science? *American Psychologist, 42*, 443–455.

Hedges, L. V. (1988). The meta-analysis of test validity studies: Some new approaches. In H. Wainer & H. I. Braun (Eds.), *Test validity* (pp. 191–212). Hillsdale, NJ: Lawrence Erlbaum.

Hedges, L. V. (1989). An unbiased correction for sampling error. *Journal of Applied Psychology, 74*, 469–477.

Hedges, L. V. (1991). Methodological aspects of the synthesis of social prevention research. In G. Albrecht & H.-U. Otto (Eds.), *Social prevention and the social sciences: Theoretical controversies, research problems, and evaluation strategies* (pp. 353–380). Berlin: de Gruyter.

Hedges, L. V. (1994a). Fixed effects models. In H. M. Cooper & L. V. Hedges (Eds.), *The handbook of research synthesis* (pp. 285–299). New York: Russell Sage Foundation.

Hedges, L. V. (1994b). Statistical considerations. In H. M. Cooper & L. V. Hedges (Eds.), *The handbook of research synthesis* (pp. 29–38). New York: Russell Sage Foundation.

Hedges, L. V., & Olkin, I. (1985). *Statistical methods for meta-analysis*. London: Academic Press.

Hedges, L. V., & Pigott, T. D. (2001). The power of statistical tests in meta-analysis. *Psychological Methods, 6*, 203–217.

Hedges, L. V., & Vevea, J. L. (1996). Estimating effect size under publication bias: Small sample properties and robustness of a random effects selection model. *Journal of Educational and Behavioral Statistics, 21*, 299–332.

Hedges, L. V., & Vevea, J. L. (1998). Fixed- and random effects models in meta-analysis. *Psychological Methods, 3,* 486–504.

Hellekalek, P. (1998). Good random number generators are (not so) easy to find. *Mathematics and Computers in Simulation, 46,* 485–505.

Hermelin, E., & Robertson, I. T. (2001). A critique and standardization of meta-analytic validity coefficients in personnel selection. *Journal of Occupational and Organizational Psychology, 74,* 253–277.

Hite, P. A. (1987). An application of meta-analysis for bankruptcy prediction studies. *Organizational Behavior and Human Decision Processes, 39,* 155–161.

Holling, H., & Schulze, R. (in press). Statistische Modelle und Auswertungsverfahren in der Organisationspsychologie [Statistical methods and data analysis procedures in organizational psychology]. In H. Schuler (Ed.), *Enzyklopädie der Psychologie: Themenbereich D Praxisgebiete, Serie III Wirtschafts-, Organisations-, und Arbeitspsychologie, Band 3 Organisationspsychologie — Grundlagen und Personalpsychologie.* Göttingen: Hogrefe.

Hotelling, H. (1953). New light on the correlation coefficient and its transforms. *Journal of the Royal Statistical Society, Series B, 15,* 193–232.

Hox, J. J., & de Leeuw, E. D. (2003). Multilevel models for meta-analysis. In S. P. Reise & N. Duan (Eds.), *Multilevel modeling: Methodological advances, issues, and applications* (pp. 90–111). Mahwah, NJ: Lawrence Erlbaum.

Hubbard, R., Parsa, R. A., & Luthy, M. R. (1997). The spread of statistical significance testing in psychology. *Theory & Psychology, 7,* 545–554.

Huffcutt, A. I. (2002). Research perspectives on meta-analysis. In S. G. Rogelberg (Ed.), *Handbook of research methods in industrial and organizational psychology* (pp. 198–215). Oxford: Blackwell.

Hunt, M. (1997). *How science takes stock: The story of meta-analysis.* New York: Russell Sage Foundation.

Hunter, J. E., & Hirsh, H. R. (1987). Applications of meta-analysis. In C. L. Cooper & I. T. Robertson (Eds.), *International review of industrial and organizational psychology* (pp. 321–357). New York: Wiley.

Hunter, J. E., & Schmidt, F. L. (1990). *Methods of meta-analysis: Correcting error and bias in research findings.* Newbury Park, CA: Sage.

Hunter, J. E., & Schmidt, F. L. (1994a). Correcting for sources of artifactual variation across studies. In H. M. Cooper & L. V. Hedges (Eds.), *The handbook of research synthesis* (pp. 323–336). New York: Russell Sage Foundation.

Hunter, J. E., & Schmidt, F. L. (1994b). Estimation of sampling error variance in the meta-analysis of correlations: Use of average correlation in the homogeneous case. *Journal of Applied Psychology, 79,* 171–177.

Hunter, J. E., & Schmidt, F. L. (1996). Cumulative research knowledge and social policy formulation: The critical role of meta-analysis. *Psychology, Public Policy, and Law, 2,* 324–347.

Hunter, J. E., & Schmidt, F. L. (2000). Fixed effects vs. random effects meta-analysis models: Implications for cumulative research knowledge. *International Journal of Selection and Assessment, 8,* 275–292.

Hunter, J. E., Schmidt, F. L., & Jackson, G. B. (1982). *Meta-analysis: Cumulating research findings across studies.* Beverly Hills, CA: Sage.

Hunter, J. E., Schmidt, F. L., & Pearlman, K. (1982). History and accuracy of validity generalization equations: A response to the Callender and Osburn reply. *Journal of Applied Psychology, 67*, 853–858.

Iyengar, S., & Greenhouse, J. B. (1988). Selection models and the file drawer problem. *Statistical Science, 3*, 109– 135.

Jackson, G. B. (1980). Methods for integrative reviews. *Review of Educational Research, 50*, 438–460.

James, L. R., Demaree, R. G., & Mulaik, S. A. (1986). A note on validity generalization procedures. *Journal of Applied Psychology, 71*, 440–450.

James, L. R., Demaree, R. G., Mulaik, S. A., & Ladd, R. T. (1992). Validity generalization in the context of situational models. *Journal of Applied Psychology, 77*, 3–14.

Johnson, B. T., & Eagly, A. H. (2000). Quantitative synthesis of social psychological research. In H. T. Reis & C. M. Judd (Eds.), *Handbook of research methods in social and personality psychology* (pp. 496–528). Cambridge: Cambridge University Press.

Johnson, B. T., Mullen, B., & Salas, E. (1995). Comparison of three major meta-analytic approaches. *Journal of Applied Psychology, 80*, 94–106.

Johnson, N. L., Kotz, S., & Balakrishnan, N. (1995). *Continuous univariate distributions* (2nd ed., Vol. 2). New York: Wiley.

Kalaian, H. A., & Raudenbush, S. W. (1996). A multivariate mixed linear model for meta-analysis. *Psychological Methods, 3*, 227–235.

Kavale, K. A. (1995). Meta-analysis at 20. Retrospect and prospect. *Evaluation & The Health Professions, 18*, 349–369.

Konishi, S. (1978). An approximation to the distribution of the sample correlation coefficient. *Biometrika, 65*, 654–656.

Konishi, S. (1981). Normalizing transformations of some statistics in multivariate analysis. *Biometrika, 68*, 647–651.

Koslowsky, M., & Sagie, A. (1993). On the efficacy of credibility intervals as indicators of moderator effects in meta-analytic research. *Journal of Organizational Behavior, 14*, 695–699.

Kraemer, H. C. (1973). Improved approximation to the non-null distribution of the correlation coefficient. *Journal of the American Statistical Association, 68*, 1004–1008.

Kraemer, H. C. (1975). On estimation and hypothesis testing problems for correlation coefficients. *Psychometrika, 40*, 473–485.

Kraemer, H. C. (1983). Theory of estimation and testing of effect sizes: Use in meta-analysis. *Journal of Educational Statistics, 8*, 93–101.

Kraemer, H. C., & Paik, M. (1979). A central t approximation to the noncentral t distribution. *Technometrics, 21*, 357–360.

Landy, F. J. (2003). Validity generalization: Then and now. In K. R. Murphy (Ed.), *Validity generalization: A critical review* (pp. 155–195). Mahwah, NJ: Lawrence Erlbaum.

Lane, D. M., & Dunlap, W. P. (1978). Estimating effect size: Bias resulting from the significance criterion in editorial decisions. *British Journal of Mathematical and Statistical Psychology, 31*, 107–112.

Lau, J., Ioannidis, J. P. A., & Schmid, C. H. (1998). Summing up evidence: One answer is not always enough. *Lancet, 351,* 123–127.

Law, K. S. (1992). Estimation accuracy of Thomas's likelihood-based procedure of meta-analysis: A Monte Carlo simulation. *Journal of Applied Psychology, 77,* 986–995.

Law, K. S. (1995). The use of Fisher's z in Schmidt-Hunter-type meta-analyses. *Journal of Educational and Behavioral Statistics, 20,* 287–306.

Law, K. S., Schmidt, F. L., & Hunter, J. E. (1994). Nonlinearity of range corrections in meta-analysis: Test of an improved procedure. *Journal of Applied Psychology, 79,* 425–438.

Lent, R. H., Aurbach, H. A., & Levin, L. S. (1971). Research design and validity assessment. *Personnel Psychology, 24,* 247– 274.

Light, R. J., Singer, J., & Willet, J. B. (1994). The visual presentation and interpretation of meta-analyses. In H. M. Cooper & L. V. Hedges (Eds.), *The handbook of research synthesis* (pp. 439–453). New York: Russell Sage Foundation.

Light, R. J., & Smith, P. V. (1971). Accumulating evidence: Procedures for resolving contradictions among different studies. *Harvard Educational Review, 41,* 429–471.

Lipsey, M. W., & Wilson, D. B. (1993). The efficacy of psychological, educational, and behavioral treatment. *American Psychologist, 48,* 1181–1209.

Lipsey, M. W., & Wilson, D. B. (2001). *Practical meta-analysis.* Thousand Oaks, CA: Sage.

Lord, F. M., & Novick, M. R. (1968). *Statistical theories of mental test scores.* Reading, MA: Addison-Wesley.

Malzahn, U. (2003). Meta-analysis: A general principle for estimating heterogeneity variance in several models. In R. Schulze, H. Holling, & D. Böhning (Eds.), *Meta-analysis: New developments and applications in medical and social sciences* (pp. 41–52). Seattle, WA: Hogrefe & Huber.

Malzahn, U., Böhning, D., & Holling, H. (2000). Nonparametric estimation of heterogeneity variance for the standardized difference used in meta-analysis. *Biometrika, 87,* 619–632.

Martinussen, M., & Bjørnstad, J. F. (1999). Meta-analysis calculations based on independent and nonindependent cases. *Educational and Psychological Measurement, 59,* 928–950.

Matsumoto, M., & Nishimura, T. (1998). Mersenne Twister: A 623-dimensionally equidistributed uniform pseudorandom number generator. *ACM Transactions on Modeling and Computer Simulation, 8,* 3–30.

Matt, G. E. (1989). Decision rules for selecting effect sizes in meta-analysis: A review and reanalysis of psychotherapy outcome studies. *Psychological Bulletin, 105,* 106–115.

Matt, G. E. (2003). Will it work in Münster? Meta-analysis in the empirical generalization of causal relationships. In R. Schulze, H. Holling, & D. Böhning (Eds.), *Meta-analysis: New developments and applications in medical and social sciences* (pp. 113–139). Seattle, WA: Hogrefe & Huber.

Meehl, P. E. (1978). Theoretical risks and tabular asterisks: Sir Karl, Sir Ronald, and the slow progress of soft psychology. *Journal of Consulting and Clinical Psychology, 46,* 806–834.

Meehl, P. E. (1990). Why summaries of research on psychological theories are often uninterpretable. *Psychological Reports, 66,* 195–244.

Mi, J. (1990). Notes on the MLE of correlation coefficient in meta-analysis. *Communication in Statistics — Theory and Methods, 19,* 2035–2052.

Miller, N., & Pollock, V. E. (1995). Use of meta-analysis for testing theory. *Evaluation & The Health Professions, 18,* 370–392.

Morris, S. B., & DeShon, R. P. (1997). Correcting effect sizes computed from factorial analysis of variance for use in meta-analysis. *Psychological Methods, 2,* 192–199.

Mulaik, S. A., Raju, N. S., & Harshman, R. A. (1997). There is a time and place for significance testing. In L. L. Harlow, S. A. Mulaik, & J. H. Steiger (Eds.), *What if there were no significance tests?* (pp. 65–115). Mahwah, NJ: Lawrence Erlbaum.

Murphy, K. R. (2000). Impact of assessments of validity generalization and situational specificity on the science and practice of personnel selection. *International Journal of Selection and Assessment, 8,* 194–206.

Murphy, K. R. (Ed.). (2003). *Validity generalization.* Mahwah, NJ: Lawrence Erlbaum.

National Research Council. (1992). *Combining information: Statistical issues and opportunities for research.* Washington, DC: National Academy Press.

Normand, S.-L. T. (1999). Tutorial in biostatistics. Meta-analysis: Formulating, evaluating, combining, and reporting. *Statistics in Medicine, 18,* 321–359.

Olejnik, S., & Algina, J. (2000). Measures of effect size for comparative studies: Applications, interpretations, and limitations. *Contemporary Educational Psychology, 25,* 241–286.

Olkin, I. (1967). Correlations revisited [with discussion]. In J. Stanley (Ed.), *Improving experimental design and statistical analysis. Seventh annual phi delta kappa symposium on educational research* (pp. 102–128). Chicago, IL: Rand McNally.

Olkin, I. (1990). History and goals. In K. W. Wachter & M. L. Straf (Eds.), *The future of meta-analysis* (pp. 3–10). New York: Russell Sage Foundation.

Olkin, I., & Pratt, J. W. (1958). Unbiased estimation of certain correlation coefficients. *Annals of Mathematical Statistics, 29,* 201–211.

Osburn, H. G., & Callender, J. C. (1990). Bias in validity generalization variance estimates: A reply to Hoben Thomas. *Journal of Applied Psychology, 75,* 328–333.

Osburn, H. G., & Callender, J. C. (1992). A note on the sampling variance of the mean uncorrected correlation in meta-analysis and validity generalization. *Journal of Applied Psychology, 77,* 115–122.

Oswald, F. L., & Johnson, J. W. (1998). On the robustness, bias, and stability of statistics from meta-analysis of correlation coefficients: Some initial Monte Carlo findings. *Journal of Applied Psychology, 83,* 164–178.

Overton, R. C. (1998). A comparison of fixed-effects and mixed (random-effects) models for meta-analysis tests of moderator variable effects. *Psychological Methods, 3,* 354–379.

Paul, S. R. (1988). Estimation of and testing significance for a common correlation coefficient. *Communication in Statistics — Theory and Methods, 17,* 39–53.

Raju, N. S., Anselmi, T. V., Goodman, J. S., & Thomas, A. (1998). The effect of correlated artifacts and true validity on the accuracy of parameter estimation in validity generalization. *Personnel Psychology, 51,* 453–465.

Raju, N. S., Burke, M. J., Normand, J., & Langlois, G. M. (1991). A new meta-analytic approach. *Journal of Applied Psychology, 76,* 432–446.

Raudenbush, S. W. (1994). Random effects models. In H. M. Cooper & L. V. Hedges (Eds.), *The handbook of research synthesis* (pp. 301–321). New York: Russell Sage Foundation.

Raudenbush, S. W., & Bryk, A. S. (2002). *Hierarchical linear models: Applications and data analysis methods* (2nd ed.). Thousand Oaks, CA: Sage.

Ray, J. W., & Shadish, W. R., Jr. (1996). How interchangeable are different estimators of effect size? *Journal of Consulting and Clinical Psychology, 64,* 1316–1325.

Reed, J. G., & Baxter, P. M. (1994). Using reference databases. In H. M. Cooper & L. V. Hedges (Eds.), *The handbook of research synthesis* (pp. 57–70). New York: Russell Sage Foundation.

Rosenthal, R. (1978). Combining results of independent studies. *Psychological Bulletin, 85,* 185–193.

Rosenthal, R. (1979). The "file drawer problem" and tolerance for null results. *Psychological Bulletin, 86,* 638–641.

Rosenthal, R. (1991). *Meta-analytic procedures for social research* (Rev. ed.). Newbury Park, CA: Sage.

Rosenthal, R. (1993). Cumulating evidence. In K. Gideon & C. Lewis (Eds.), *A handbook for data analysis in the behavioral science: Methodological issues* (pp. 519–559). Hillsdale, NJ: Lawrence Erlbaum.

Rosenthal, R. (1994). Parametric measures of effect size. In H. M. Cooper & L. V. Hedges (Eds.), *The handbook of research synthesis* (pp. 231–244). New York: Russell Sage Foundation.

Rosenthal, R., & DiMatteo, M. R. (2001). Meta-analysis: Recent developments in quantitative methods for research reviews. *Annual Review of Psychology, 52,* 59–82.

Rosenthal, R., Rosnow, R. L., & Rubin, D. B. (2000). *Contrasts and effect sizes in behavioral research: A correlational approach.* Cambridge: Cambridge University Press.

Rosenthal, R., & Rubin, D. B. (1979). Comparing significance levels of independent studies. *Psychological Bulletin, 86,* 1165–1168.

Rosenthal, R., & Rubin, D. B. (1982). Comparing effect sizes of independent studies. *Psychological Bulletin, 92,* 500–504.

Rosnow, R. L., & Rosenthal, R. (1996). Computing contrasts, effect sizes, and counternulls on other people's published data: General procedures for research consumers. *Psychological Methods, 1,* 331–340.

Rossi, J. S. (1997). A case study in the failure of psychology as a cumulative science: The spontaneous recovery of verbal learning. In L. L. Harlow, S. A. Mulaik, & J. H. Steiger (Eds.), *What if there were no significance tests?* (pp. 175–197). Mahwah, NJ: Lawrence Erlbaum.

Ruben, H. (1966). Some new results on the distribution of the sample correlation coefficient. *Journal of the Royal Statistical Society, Series B, 28,* 513–525.

Rust, T., Lehmann, D. R., & Farley, J. U. (1990). Estimating publication bias in meta-analysis. *Journal of Marketing Research, 27,* 220–226.

Sackett, P. R., Harris, M. M., & Orr, J. M. (1986). On seeking moderator variables in the meta-analysis of correlational data: A Monte Carlo investigation of statistical power and resistance to Type I error. *Journal of Applied Psychology, 71,* 302–310.

Sagie, A., & Koslowsky, M. (1993). Detecting moderators with meta-analysis: An evaluation and comparison of techniques. *Personnel Psychology, 46*, 629–640.

Samiuddin, M. (1970). On a test for an assigned value of correlation in a bivariate normal distribution. *Biometrika, 57*, 461–464.

Sánchez-Meca, J., & Marín-Martínez, F. (1997). Homogeneity tests in meta-analysis: A Monte-Carlo comparison of statistical power and Type I error. *Quality & Quantity, 31*, 385–399.

Sánchez-Meca, J., & Marín-Martínez, F. (1998a). Testing continuous moderators in meta-analysis: A comparison of methods. *British Journal of Mathematical and Statistical Psychology, 51*, 311–326.

Sánchez-Meca, J., & Marín-Martínez, F. (1998b). Weighting by inverse variance or by sample size in meta-analysis: A simulation study. *Educational and Psychological Measurement, 58*, 211–220.

Sauerbrei, W., & Blettner, M. (2003). Issues of traditional reviews and meta-analyses of observational studies in medical research. In R. Schulze, H. Holling, & D. Böhning (Eds.), *Meta-analysis: New developments and applications in medical and social sciences* (pp. 79–98). Seattle, WA: Hogrefe & Huber.

Scheffé, H. (1999). *The analysis of variance.* New York: Wiley. (Original work published 1959)

Schlattmann, P., Malzahn, U., & Böhning, D. (2003). META — a software package for meta-analysis. In R. Schulze, H. Holling, & D. Böhning (Eds.), *Meta-analysis: New developments and applications in the biomedical and social sciences* (pp. 251–258). Seattle, WA: Hogrefe & Huber.

Schmidt, F. L. (1992). What do data really mean? *American Psychologist, 47*, 1173–1181.

Schmidt, F. L. (1996). Statistical significance testing and cumulative knowledge in psychology: Implications for training of researchers. *Psychological Methods, 1*, 115–129.

Schmidt, F. L., & Hunter, J. E. (1977). Development of a general solution to the problem of validity generalization. *Journal of Applied Psychology, 62*, 529–540.

Schmidt, F. L., & Hunter, J. E. (1995). The impact of data-analysis methods on cumulative research knowledge. *Evaluation & The Health Professions, 18*, 408–427.

Schmidt, F. L., & Hunter, J. E. (1996). Measurement error in psychological research: Lessons from 26 research scenarios. *Psychological Methods, 1*, 199–223.

Schmidt, F. L., & Hunter, J. E. (1997). Eight common but false objections to the discontinuation of significance testing in the analysis of research data. In L. L. Harlow, S. A. Mulaik, & J. H. Steiger (Eds.), *What if there were no significance tests?* (pp. 37–64). Mahwah, NJ: Lawrence Erlbaum.

Schmidt, F. L., & Hunter, J. E. (1998). The validity and utility of selection methods in personnel psychology: Practical and theoretical implications of 85 years of research findings. *Psychological Bulletin, 124*, 262–274.

Schmidt, F. L., & Hunter, J. E. (1999a). Comparison of three meta-analysis methods revisited: An analysis of Johnson, Mullen, and Salas (1995). *Journal of Applied Psychology, 84*, 144–148.

Schmidt, F. L., & Hunter, J. E. (1999b). Theory testing and measurement error. *Intelligence, 27*, 183–198.

Schmidt, F. L., Hunter, J. E., & Pearlman, K. (1982). Progress in validity generalization: Comments on Callender and Osburn and further developments. *Journal of Applied Psychology, 67*, 835–845.

Schmidt, F. L., Hunter, J. E., Pearlman, K., & Hirsh, H. R. (1985). Forty questions about validity generalization and meta-analysis. *Personnel Psychology, 38*, 697–801.

Schmidt, F. L., Hunter, J. E., & Raju, N. S. (1988). Validity generalization and situational specificity: A second look at the 75% rule and Fisher's z transformation. *Journal of Applied Psychology, 73*, 665–672.

Schmidt, F. L., Law, K. S., Hunter, J. E., Rothstein, H. R., Pearlman, K., & McDaniel, M. (1993). Refinements in validity generalization methods: Implications for the situational specifity hypothesis. *Journal of Applied Psychology, 78*, 3–12.

Schulze, R., Holling, H., & Böhning, D. (Eds.). (2003). *Meta-analysis: New developments and applications in medical and social sciences*. Seattle, WA: Hogrefe & Huber.

Schulze, R., & Wittmann, W. W. (2003). A meta-analysis of the theory of reasoned action and the theory of planned behavior: The principle of compatibility and multidimensionality of beliefs as moderators. In R. Schulze, H. Holling, & D. Böhning (Eds.), *Meta-analysis: New developments and applications in medical and social sciences* (pp. 219–250). Seattle, WA: Hogrefe & Huber.

Schwarzer, G., Antes, G., & Schumacher, M. (2003). Statistical tests for the detection of bias in meta-analysis. In R. Schulze, H. Holling, & D. Böhning (Eds.), *Meta-analysis: New developments and applications in medical and social sciences* (pp. 71–78). Seattle, WA: Hogrefe & Huber.

Seifert, T. L. (1991). Determining effect sizes in various experimental designs. *Educational and Psychological Measurement, 51*, 341–347.

Shadish, W. R., Jr., Cook, T. D., & Campbell, D. T. (2002). *Experimental and quasi-experimental designs for generalized causal inference*. Boston, MA: Houghton Mifflin.

Shadish, W. R., Jr., & Haddock, C. K. (1994). Combining estimates of effect size. In H. M. Cooper & L. V. Hedges (Eds.), *The handbook of research synthesis* (pp. 261–281). New York: Russell Sage Foundation.

Sharpe, D. (1997). Of apples and oranges, file drawers and garbage: Why validity issues in meta-analysis will not go away. *Clinical Psychology Review, 17*, 881–901.

Silver, N. C., & Dunlap, W. P. (1987). Averaging correlation coefficients: Should Fisher's z transformation be used? *Journal of Applied Psychology, 72*, 146–148.

Skrondal, A. (2000). Design and analysis of Monte Carlo experiments: Attacking the conventional wisdom. *Multivariate Behavioral Research, 35*, 137–167.

Smith, M. L., & Glass, G. V. (1977). Meta-analysis of psychotherapy outcome studies. *American Psychologist*, 752–760.

Snedecor, G. W., & Cochran, W. G. (1967). *Statistical methods* (6th ed.). Ames, IA: Iowa State University Press.

Sohn, D. (1995). Meta-analysis as a means of discovery. *American Psychologist, 50*, 108–110.

Sohn, D. (1997). Questions for meta-analysis. *Psychological Reports, 81*, 3–15.

Spector, P. E., & Levine, E. L. (1987). Meta-analysis for integrating study outcomes: A Monte Carlo study of its susceptibility to Type I and Type II errors. *Journal of Applied Psychology, 72*, 3–9.

Spivak, M. (1967). *Calculus*. New York: W. A. Benjamin.

Steiner, D., Lane, I. M., Dobbins, G. H., Schnur, A., & McDonnell, S. (1991). A review of meta-analyses in organizational behavior and human resources management: An empirical assessment. *Educational and Psychological Measurement, 51,* 609–626.

Stuart, A., & Ord, K. (1994). *Kendall's advanced theory of statistics* (6th ed., Vol. 1: Distribution theory). London: Arnold.

Stuart, A., Ord, K., & Arnold, S. (1999). *Kendall's advanced theory of statistics* (6th ed., Vol. 2A: Classical inference and the linear model). London: Arnold.

Sutton, A. J., Abrams, K. R., Jones, D. R., Sheldon, T. A., & Song, F. (2000). *Methods for meta-analysis in medical research*. New York: Wiley.

Tett, R. P., Meyer, J. P., & Roese, N. J. (1994). Applications of meta-analysis: 1987–1992. In C. L. Cooper & I. T. Robertson (Eds.), *International review of industrial and organizational psychology* (Vol. 9, pp. 71–112). Chichester: Wiley.

Thomas, H. (1989a). *Distributions of correlation coefficients*. New York: Springer.

Thomas, H. (1989b). A mixture model for distributions of correlation coefficients. *Psychometrika, 54,* 523–530.

Thomas, H. (1990a). What is the interpretation of the validity generalization estimate $s_\rho^2 = s_r^2 - s_e^2$? *Journal of Applied Psychology, 75,* 13–20.

Thomas, H. (1990b). A likelihood-based model for validity generalization. *Journal of Applied Psychology, 75,* 13–20.

Thompson, B. (1989). Meta-analysis of factor structure studies: A case study example with Bem's androgyny measure. *Journal of Experimental Education, 58,* 187–197.

Vacha-Haase, T., Nilsson, J. E., Reetz, D. R., Lance, T. S., & Thompson, B. (2000). Reporting practices and APA editorial policies regarding statistical significance and effect size. *Theory & Psychology, 10,* 413–425.

Van den Noortgate, W., & Onghena, P. (2003). Multilevel meta-analysis: A comparison with traditional meta-analytic procedures. *Educational and Psychological Measurement, 63,* 765–790.

Vevea, J. L., & Hedges, L. V. (1995). A general linear model for estimating effect size in the presence of publication bias. *Psychometrika, 60,* 419–435.

Viana, M. A. G. (1980). Statistical methods for summarizing independent correlational results. *Journal of Educational Statistics, 1,* 83–104.

Viana, M. A. G. (1982). Combined estimators for the correlation coefficient. *Communication in Statistics — Theory and Methods, 11,* 1483–1504.

Viswesvaran, C., & Ones, D. S. (1995). Theory testing: Combining psychometric meta-analysis and structural equations modeling. *Personnel Psychology, 48,* 865–885.

Wanous, J. P., Sullivan, S. E., & Malinak, J. (1989). The role of judgement calls in meta-analysis. *Journal of Applied Psychology, 74,* 259–264.

White, H. D. (1994). Scientific communication and literature retrieval. In H. M. Cooper & L. V. Hedges (Eds.), *The handbook of research synthesis* (pp. 41–55). New York: Russell Sage Foundation.

Whitener, E. M. (1990). Confusion of confidence intervals and credibility intervals in meta-analysis. *Journal of Applied Psychology, 75,* 315–321.

Wilkinson, L., & Task Force on Statistical Inference. (1999). Statistical methods in psychology journals: Guidelines and explanations. *American Psychologist, 54,* 594–604.

Wilson, D. B., & Lipsey, M. W. (2001). The role of method in treatment effectiveness research: Evidence from meta-analysis. *Psychological Methods, 4,* 413–429.

Wolf, F. M. (1986). *Meta-analysis: Quantitative methods for research synthesis.* Newbury Park, CA: Sage.

Wortman, P. M. (1994). Judging research quality. In H. M. Cooper & L. V. Hedges (Eds.), *The handbook of research synthesis* (pp. 97–109). New York: Russell Sage Foundation.

Zakzanis, K. K. (1998). The reliability of meta-analytic review. *Psychological Reports, 83,* 215–222.

Appendices

Beta Distributions in the Universe of Effect Sizes

The beta distribution was chosen in the Monte Carlo study as the distribution of effect sizes ρ in the universe in $\mathfrak{S}_3$. The following Tables A.1 and A.2 list all values for the parameters p and q of the standard beta distribution as used in the simulation study. For further details on the beta distribution the interested reader is referred to Johnson, Kotz, and Balakrishnan (1995) and Section 4.5. In addition to the parameters of the beta distribution, the expected values for the Fisher-z transformed universe parameters along with the variances are given. Note that the expected values μ_ζ are in z-space and have to be transformed by the inverse Fisher transformation to result in values in r-space. These values ($\mu_{\rho z}$) are given in the last column of Tables A.1 and A.2.

Moreover, a series of figures is presented that depict the resulting beta distributions for the given parameter values. Figures A.1 to A.5 illustrate how the distributions of the universe parameters in the Monte Carlo study look like. It can be seen in Figures A.2 to A.5 that large variances in combination with large values of μ_ρ tend to produce J-shaped distributions. These distribution forms can also easily be identified by consulting Tables A.1 and A.2. All beta distributions for which one of the parameters p or q is less than 1 show this type of distribution form (Johnson, Kotz, & Balakrishnan, 1995). Because the present study focuses on one half of the interval $[-1, 1]$ as far as the μ_ρ are concerned, values less than one only occur for q.

Table A.1   Parameter Values of the Beta-Distribution for μ_ρ From 0 to .40 and Different Variances σ_ρ^2 As Well As Corresponding Expected Values μ_ζ (and $\mu_{\rho z}$) and Variances σ_ζ^2

μ_ρ	σ_ρ^2	p	q	μ_ζ	σ_ζ^2	$\mu_{\rho z}$
.00	.0025	199.5	199.5	.00	.00251256	.00
.00	.01	49.5	49.5	.00	.01020370	.00
.00	.0225	21.7222	21.7222	.00	.02355590	.00
.00	.04	12.0	12.0	.00	.04345090	.00
.00	.0625	7.5	7.5	.00	.07130790	.00
.10	.0025	217.25	177.75	.100592	.00256383	.100254
.10	.01	53.9	44.1	.101373	.01041520	.101027
.10	.0225	23.65	19.35	.102721	.02405700	.102361
.10	.04	13.0625	10.6875	.104709	.04441030	.104328
.10	.0625	8.162	6.678	.107450	.07296110	.107038
.20	.0025	229.8	153.2	.203277	.00272746	.200523
.20	.01	57.0	38.0	.204942	.01109090	.202120
.20	.0225	25.0	16.6667	.207815	.02566160	.204874
.20	.04	13.8	9.2	.212064	.04749230	.208941
.20	.0625	8.616	5.774	.215095	.07802670	.211838
.30	.0025	235.95	127.05	.310430	.00303729	.300828
.30	.01	58.5	31.5	.313212	.01237410	.303356
.30	.0225	25.6389	13.8056	.318031	.02872370	.307725
.30	.04	14.1375	7.6125	.325186	.05341550	.314189
.30	.0625	8.814	4.746	.335138	.08864550	.323130
.40	.0025	234.5	100.5	.425074	.00356835	.401196
.40	.01	58.1	24.9	.429441	.01458460	.404854
.40	.0225	25.4333	10.9	.437040	.03404540	.411188
.40	.04	14.0	6.0	.448400	.06384080	.420583
.40	.0625	8.708	3.732	.464350	.10717400	.433623

Note. The parameters p and q of the beta distribution were computed as described in Section 4.5.

Table A.2   Parameter Values of the Beta-Distribution for μ_ρ From .50 to .90 and Different Variances σ_ρ^2 As Well As Corresponding Expected Values μ_ζ (and $\mu_{\rho z}$) and Variances σ_ζ^2

μ_ρ	σ_ρ^2	p	q	μ_ζ	σ_ζ^2	$\mu_{\rho z}$
.50	.0025	224.25	74.75	.551542	.00448427	.501675
.50	.01	55.5	18.5	.558423	.01843060	.506806
.50	.0225	24.25	8.0833	.570493	.04344450	.515721
.50	.04	13.3125	4.4375	.588735	.08266040	.528985
.50	.0625	8.25	2.75	.614742	.14160600	.547456
.60	.0025	204.0	51.0	.696839	.00617883	.602358
.60	.01	50.4	12.6	.708274	.02565930	.609593
.60	.0225	21.9556	5.4889	.728599	.06159560	.622207
.60	.04	12.0	3.0	.759939	.12045900	.641041
.60	.0625	7.392	1.848	.805730	.21436900	.667228
.70	.0025	172.55	30.45	.874105	.00979953	.703458
.70	.01	42.5	7.5	.895468	.04160610	.714084
.70	.0225	18.4167	3.25	.934436	.10389900	.732655
.70	.04	9.9875	1.7625	.996729	.21561100	.760217
.70	.0625	6.086	1.074	1.091630	.41545400	.797472
.80	.0025	128.7	14.3	1.114350	.02005810	.805595
.80	.01	31.5	3.5	1.165440	.09065330	.822805
.80	.0225	13.5	1.5	1.264350	.25292200	.852259
.80	.04	7.2	0.8	1.434020	.61211300	.892487
.80	.0625	4.284	0.476	1.710340	1.40785000	.936689
.90	.0025	71.25	3.75	1.538310	.07986850	.911836
.90	.01	17.1	0.9	1.782240	.49569100	.944936
.90	.0225	7.0722	0.3722	2.330410	2.10599000	.981260
.90	.04	3.5625	0.1875	3.380960	7.51357000	.997689
.90	.0625	1.938	0.102	5.303410	24.55440000	.999951

Note. The parameters p and q of the beta distribution were computed as described in Section 4.5.

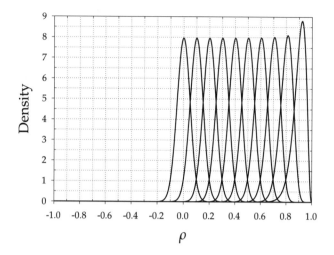

Figure A.1   Beta distributions with parameters chosen to correspond to $\mu_\rho = 0$ to $\mu_\rho = .90$ in increments of .01 and with constant $\sigma_\rho^2 = .0025$.

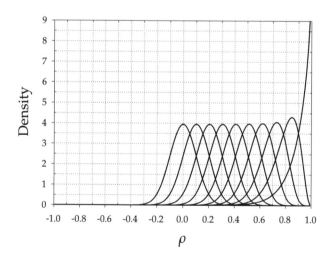

Figure A.2   Beta distributions with parameters chosen to correspond to $\mu_\rho = 0$ to $\mu_\rho = .90$ in increments of .01 and with constant $\sigma_\rho^2 = .01$.

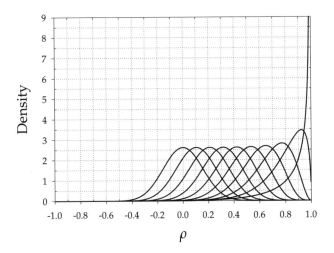

Figure A.3 Beta distributions with parameters chosen to correspond to $\mu_\rho = 0$ to $\mu_\rho = .90$ in increments of .01 and with constant $\sigma_\rho^2 = .0225$.

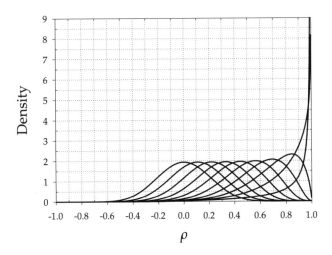

Figure A.4 Beta distributions with parameters chosen to correspond to $\mu_\rho = 0$ to $\mu_\rho = .90$ in increments of .01 and with constant $\sigma_\rho^2 = .04$.

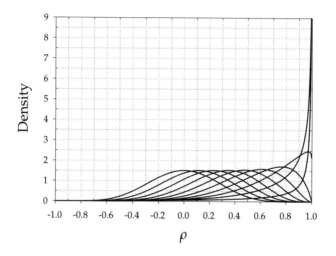

Figure A.5   Beta distributions with parameters chosen to correspond to $\mu_\rho = 0$ to $\mu_\rho = .90$ in increments of .01 and with constant $\sigma_\rho^2 = .0625$.

B

An Annotated MATHEMATICA Notebook for a Comparison of Approximations to the Exact Density of R

The following parts of code are annotated for better reproducibility of the results and potential adaptations where needed. The annotations are kept in roman font type and should not be confused with the actual code presented in `typewriter font`. The code reproduced is complete so that it can be transcribed to instantly work with MATHEMATICA Version 4 or later. The actual version used to produce the results reported in Section 7.5.2 was MATHEMATICA 4.0.1.0 on a windows platform but the code was also tested and works with Version 3.0. For better comprehension, the code is sectioned in a general part that comes first and then code pertaining to the single approximations.

General part. First, the degrees of freedom (as an example, 48 is used in the code) and the value of ρ (as an example, $\rho = .20$ is used) for the comparisons are fixed. Note that the degrees of freedom are df $= n - 2$ so that for a situation with 50 persons, for example, a value of 48 has to be inserted. Also, in some of the functions, the degrees of freedom appear as ν (or in `typewriterfont` as nu). Of course, this symbol should not be confused with the standard error of effect size estimators as introduced in the text.

As another preliminary step, the standard package for continuous statistical distributions is loaded and the density of the noncentral t distribution is defined in the following code.

```
df = 48
```

```
ActualRho = .2
```

```
<< Statistics'ContinuousDistributions'
```

```
DensityStudentT[x_, nu_] := PDF[StudentTDistribution[nu], x]
```

```
DensityNoncentralT[x_, nu_, delta_] :=
        PDF[NoncentralStudentTDistribution[nu,delta],x]
```

Hotelling's exact density.   First, the code to specify the density of *r* as given by Hotelling (1953) is presented (see also Equation 3.1).

```
TheoreticalRDensityHotelling[r_,nu_,rho_]:=
    nu/Sqrt[2 Pi]Beta[nu + 1, 1/2]/Gamma[1/2]
    (1 - rho^2)^(1/2(nu + 1))(1 - r^2)^(1/2  nu - 1)
    (1 - rho r)^(1/2 - (nu + 1))
    Hypergeometric2F1[1/2, 1/2,nu + 3/2, (1 + rho r)/2]
```

As can be seen, this is the exact density. It should be noted that the hypergeometric function is at some points numerically somewhat fragile, that is, it leads in the region of the singularity to unreliable values. For the present situations very high values for ρ (e.g., $\rho \geq .90$) in combination with large values for the degrees of freedom (e.g., df ≥ 250) may cause computational problems. Nevertheless, except for these borderline cases the specified function for the theoretical density given above works perfectly well. However, to avoid numerical problems the value of the hypergeometric function can be approximated to a very high and estimable degree. First, the approximation is computed as a truncation of the Taylor series expansion at the seventh term

```
Normal[Series[Hypergeometric2F1[a, b, c, x], {x, 0, 7}]]
```

The result is very large in expression and is subsequently defined as

```
Hgf[a_, b_, c_, x_] := 1 + (abx)/c +
                    (a(1 + a)b(1 + b)x^2)/(2 c (1 + c)) + ...
```

which is truncated as given, indicated by "...". The rest of the result from the step before has to be inserted instead of "...". One may now wish to estimate the error caused by this truncation. The error caused by truncating the series at any stage is less than $2/(1 - \rho r)$ times the last term used (Hotelling, 1953, p. 200). For the proposed truncation the error can therefore be estimated by

```
LastTerm[a_, b_, c_, x_] := (a (1 + a) (2 + a) (3 + a) (4 + a) (5 + a)
    (6 + a) b (1 + b) (2 + b) (3 + b) (4 + b) (5 + b) (6 + b) x^7)/
    (5040 c (1 + c) (2 + c) (3 + c) (4 + c) (5 + c) (6 + c))
```

```
UpperBoundForErrorCausedByTruncation[r_, nu_, rho_] :=
            2/(1 - rho r) LastTerm[1/2, 1/2, nu + 3/2, (1 + rho r)/2]
```

In the present case this error is approximately 1.4151^{-11} for a value of $r = 1$ which is also the maximum of error. This can be easily seen by inspecting a plot of the error for varying r, which produces for the present case Figure B.1.

```
Plot[UpperBoundForErrorCausedByTruncation[x, df, ActualRho],
     {x, -1, 1}, PlotRange -> All, AxesOrigin -> {-1.01, 0}]
```

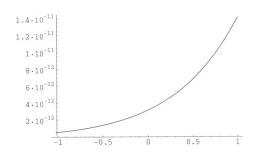

Figure B.1   Upper bounds of truncation error for the hypergeometric series used in the computation of the exact density for varying r, df$= 48$, and $\rho = .20$.

The error is obviously very small for all values of r and has its maximum on the interval $[-1, 1]$ at 1 which is still very small in value. The truncation can therefore safely be used. The modified density of r can now be defined as

```
RDensityHotelling[r_, nu_, rho_]  :=
      1/(Pi Sqrt[2])(1 - r^2)^((nu/2) - 1) nu
      (1 - r rho)^(-nu - (1/2)) (1 - rho^2)^(1/2(nu + 1))
      Beta[nu + 1, 1/2] Hgf[1/2, 1/2,nu + 3/2, (r rho + 1)/2]
```

where only the hypergeometric function is substituted by the truncated version. Using this form for the density of r the expected values and variances that are used as criteria values for all the following approximations are computed by

```
ExpectationOfHotellingsR[nu_, rho_]  :=
    NIntegrate[x RDensityHotelling[x, nu, rho], {x, -0.99999, 0.99999}]

ExpectationOfHotellingsR[df, ActualRho]

SecondMomentOfHotellingsR[nu_, rho_]  :=
    NIntegrate[x^2 RDensityHotelling[x, nu, rho],
    {x, -0.99999, 0.99999}]

VarOfHotellingsR[nu_, rho_]  :=
        SecondMomentOfHotellingsR[nu, rho] -
        (ExpectationOfHotellingsR[nu, rho])^2

VarOfHotellingsR[df, ActualRho]
```

resulting in values of 0.198047 for the expected value and 0.0188894 for the variance. Again, the density can be plotted for inspection by

```
P2 = Plot[RDensityHotelling[x, df, ActualRho], {x, -1, 1},
     PlotRange -> All, AxesOrigin -> {0, 0},
     PlotStyle -> {RGBColor[0, 0, 0]}]
```

resulting in Figure B.2.

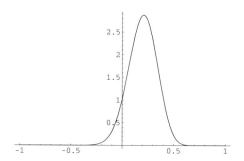

Figure B.2 Density given by Hotelling for values of $r = .40$ and df $= 48$.

The Fisher approximation.   Here and in the following parts the code begins with the definition of the relationship between r and its transformation. In the present case it is simply the Fisher-z transformation

```
FisherZFromR[r_] := 1/2Log[(1 + r)/(1 - r)]
```

Next, the derivative of Z with respect to r is computed with an additional simplification of the expression for convenience. This step is presented here for completeness and will be left out for the other approaches. The step is helpful for the following change of variables.

```
FullSimplify[D[FisherZFromR[r], r]]
```

The above step results in $\frac{1}{1-r^2}$ which is inserted in the following expression

```
DerivativeOfFisherZFromR[r_] := 1/(1 - r^2)
```

Now the density of R that results from the application of the Fisher-z transformation is defined by a change of variables.

```
RDensityFisher[x_, nu_, rho_] :=
    PDF[NormalDistribution[1/2Log[(1 + rho)/(1 - rho)],
        1/(Sqrt[nu - 1])],FisherZFromR[x]]
        DerivativeOfFisherZFromR[x]
```

Note, that the parameters of the normal distribution in MATHEMATICA are the expected value and the standard deviation. To compute the expected value and variance of this distribution, respectively, the following expressions are used to integrate over the interval [-0.99999, 0.99999] using the density of R as given above.

```
ExpectationOfFishersR[nu_, rho_] :=
     NIntegrate[x RDensityFisher[x, nu, rho], {x, -0.99999, 0.99999}]
```

With the following function call the expected value is computed for the values defined in the general part.

```
ExpectationOfFishersR[df, ActualRho]
```

For the given example a value of 0.19607 will be returned. It is now interesting to compare this value with the one resulting from using Hotelling's density for computation. The value for the latter distribution was 0.198047 so that a simulation procedure employing the Fisher approximation will generate r values that are too small in expected value!

Accordingly, the following two expressions can be used to compute the variance of the distribution.

```
SecondMomentOfFishersR[nu_, rho_] :=
     NIntegrate[x^2 RDensityFisher[x, nu, rho], {x, -0.99999, 0.99999}]

VarOfFishersR[nu_, rho_] :=
     SecondMomentOfFishersR[nu, rho] - (ExpectationOfFishersR[nu, rho])^2
```

The following function call returns a value of 0.0189376 for the variance of the distribution which is larger than the value for Hotelling's density which was 0.0188894.

```
VarOfFishersR[df, ActualRho]
```

The Harley approximation. The code for this and the following approximation is structurally identical to the Fisher approximation, so it will not be annotated.

```
HarleysTFromR[r_, nu_, rho_] :=
     (r Sqrt[-nu (-2 + rho^2)])/(Sqrt[2 - 2 r^2])

DerivativeOfHarleysTFromR[r_, nu_, rho_] :=
     (Sqrt[nu - (nu rho^2)/ 2])/( (1 - r^2)^(3/2))

HarleyDelta[nu_, rho_] := Sqrt[(1 + 2 nu) rho^2/(2 - rho^2)]

RDensityHarley[x_, nu_, rho_] :=
     DensityNoncentralT[HarleysTFromR[x, nu, rho], nu,
     HarleyDelta[nu, rho]]DerivativeOfHarleysTFromR[x, nu, rho]

ExpectationOfHarleysR[nu_, rho_] :=
     NIntegrate[x RDensityHarley[x, nu, rho], {x, -0.99999, 0.99999}]

ExpectationOfHarleysR[df, ActualRho]

SecondMomentOfHarleysR[nu_, rho_] :=
     NIntegrate[x^2 RDensityHarley[x, nu, rho],
```

```
    {x, -0.99999, 0.99999}]

VarOfHarleysR[nu_, rho_] :=
    SecondMomentOfHarleysR[nu, rho] -
    (ExpectationOfHarleysR[nu, rho])^2

VarOfHarleysR[df, ActualRho]
```

The Samiuddin-Kraemer approximation.

```
KraemersTFromR[r_, nu_, rho_] :=
    Sqrt[nu] (r - rho)/Sqrt[(1 - r^2) (1 - rho^2)]

DerivativeOfKraemersTFromR[r_, nu_, rho_] :=
    (Sqrt[nu] (-1 + r rho) (-1 + rho^2))/
    (((-1 + r^2) (-1 + rho^2))^(3/2))

RDensityKraemer[x_, nu_, rho_] :=
    DensityStudentT[KraemersTFromR[x, nu, rho], nu]
    DerivativeOfKraemersTFromR[x, nu, rho]

ExpectationOfKraemersR[nu_, rho_] :=
    NIntegrate[x RDensityKraemer[x, nu, rho], {x, -0.99999, 0.99999}]

ExpectationOfKraemersR[df, ActualRho]

SecondMomentOfKraemersR[nu_, rho_] :=
    NIntegrate[x^2 RDensityKraemer[x, nu, rho],
    {x, -0.99999, 0.99999}]

VarOfKraemersR[nu_, rho_] :=
    SecondMomentOfKraemersR[nu, rho] -
    (ExpectationOfKraemersR[nu, rho])^2

VarOfKraemersR[df, ActualRho]
```

C

Tables of Results

On the following pages of the appendix supplementary tables of results are presented. Some detailed tables not presented in the text are given to support the claims made and add further material for scrutiny. Of course, as was done in the text presentation, data had to partly be condensed to fit in the tables. In general, values are rounded off at the fourth digit. To obtain more (detailed) results, the reader is invited to contact the author of the book (rs@psy.uni-muenster.de).

Table C.1   Rejection Rates for Testing the Mean Effect Size in $\mathfrak{S}_1$, $\mu_\rho = 0$, $\alpha = .05$

k	n	HOr	HOT	HOd	RR	HS1	HS3	OP	OP-RE	DSL
4	8	.0503	.0366	.0702	.0655	.0695	.1291	.0853	.1266	.0385
	16	.0481	.0420	.0588	.0561	.0575	.1270	.0635	.0765	.0356
	32	.0477	.0450	.0525	.0505	.0518	.1266	.0548	.0579	.0371
	64	.0519	.0510	.0539	.0530	.0534	.1249	.0550	.0505	.0393
	128	.0508	.0504	.0522	.0517	.0520	.1264	.0526	.0476	.0388
	256	.0516	.0513	.0521	.0520	.0521	.1249	.0521	.0462	.0407
8	8	.0511	.0389	.0690	.0657	.0613	.0841	.0761	.1362	.0401
	16	.0487	.0437	.0579	.0560	.0544	.0852	.0601	.0878	.0400
	32	.0519	.0490	.0559	.0543	.0539	.0834	.0561	.0648	.0443
	64	.0502	.0491	.0532	.0522	.0516	.0850	.0536	.0520	.0395
	128	.0505	.0497	.0515	.0510	.0509	.0866	.0516	.0484	.0413
	256	.0505	.0503	.0508	.0507	.0505	.0827	.0508	.0433	.0377
16	8	.0510	.0355	.0682	.0666	.0575	.0658	.0717	.1512	.0405
	16	.0495	.0448	.0593	.0562	.0522	.0685	.0591	.1039	.0417
	32	.0491	.0459	.0527	.0512	.0501	.0641	.0522	.0662	.0400
	64	.0539	.0525	.0553	.0545	.0539	.0710	.0551	.0565	.0452
	128	.0505	.0502	.0516	.0513	.0511	.0701	.0515	.0493	.0436
	256	.0484	.0479	.0489	.0489	.0487	.0662	.0489	.0448	.0403
32	8	.0437	.0313	.0584	.0564	.0470	.0517	.0600	.1644	.0375
	16	.0519	.0467	.0587	.0562	.0525	.0607	.0580	.1178	.0448
	32	.0493	.0467	.0536	.0525	.0497	.0566	.0527	.0698	.0431
	64	.0508	.0492	.0522	.0517	.0508	.0598	.0520	.0550	.0448
	128	.0497	.0491	.0510	.0507	.0499	.0574	.0508	.0488	.0428
	256	.0502	.0500	.0506	.0504	.0501	.0565	.0505	.0465	.0426
64	8	.0530	.0368	.0671	.0663	.0551	.0580	.0674	.1923	.0473
	16	.0505	.0434	.0583	.0560	.0504	.0539	.0567	.1296	.0441
	32	.0512	.0480	.0543	.0532	.0511	.0532	.0535	.0752	.0453
	64	.0511	.0494	.0527	.0523	.0511	.0543	.0523	.0574	.0459
	128	.0547	.0535	.0556	.0554	.0544	.0574	.0555	.0557	.0494
	256	.0470	.0468	.0476	.0475	.0473	.0513	.0475	.0453	.0420
128	8	.0535	.0378	.0699	.0688	.0552	.0570	.0701	.2116	.0503
	16	.0514	.0442	.0591	.0568	.0516	.0537	.0571	.1404	.0477
	32	.0469	.0445	.0505	.0500	.0479	.0488	.0501	.0747	.0440
	64	.0488	.0471	.0504	.0497	.0486	.0516	.0497	.0577	.0452
	128	.0490	.0481	.0501	.0495	.0489	.0523	.0496	.0522	.0453
	256	.0503	.0503	.0511	.0510	.0507	.0529	.0511	.0500	.0464
256	8	.0442	.0323	.0592	.0564	.0460	.0475	.0579	.2224	.0421
	16	.0512	.0445	.0583	.0562	.0512	.0515	.0564	.1491	.0484
	32	.0481	.0445	.0520	.0509	.0481	.0500	.0510	.0769	.0447
	64	.0492	.0473	.0509	.0504	.0488	.0503	.0504	.0585	.0453
	128	.0503	.0495	.0513	.0512	.0501	.0517	.0512	.0531	.0469
	256	.0511	.0507	.0517	.0516	.0513	.0519	.0516	.0512	.0478

Note. Proportion for tests are given only at $\alpha = .05$. HS2 and HS4 have been omitted from the table simply for lack of space.

Table C.2 Rejection Rates for Testing the Mean Effect Size in $\mathfrak{S}_1$, $\mu_\rho = .10$ and $\mu_\rho = .20$, $\alpha = .05$

k	n	HO*r*	HOT	HO*d*	RR	HS1	HS3	OP	OP-RE	DSL
					$\mu_\rho = .10$					
	32	.2864	.2778	.3048	.2986	.3015	.4307	.3109	.3119	.2372
4	64	.4674	.4624	.4748	.4729	.4738	.5876	.4789	.4557	.3947
	128	.7271	.7253	.7313	.7297	.7306	.7940	.7321	.7026	.6532
	32	.4635	.4529	.4794	.4733	.4702	.5287	.4809	.4977	.4083
8	64	.7244	.7191	.7311	.7292	.7279	.7569	.7320	.7181	.6676
	128	.9404	.9396	.9416	.9413	.9411	.9445	.9417	.9297	.9155
	32	.7075	.6985	.7224	.7179	.7121	.7277	.7215	.7460	.6693
16	64	.9347	.9334	.9373	.9364	.9350	.9383	.9371	.9354	.9189
	128	.9984	.9984	.9984	.9984	.9984	.9980	.9984	.9982	.9973
	32	.9253	.9219	.9300	.9283	.9254	.9281	.9289	.9397	.9146
32	64	.9977	.9974	.9976	.9976	.9976	.9972	.9976	.9972	.9966
	128	1	1	1	1	1	1	1	1	1
	32	.9973	.9967	.9974	.9974	.9973	.9969	.9974	.9983	.9966
64	64	1	1	1	1	1	1	1	1	1
	128	1	1	1	1	1	1	1	1	1
	32	1	1	1	1	1	1	1	1	1
128	64	1	1	1	1	1	1	1	1	1
	128	1	1	1	1	1	1	1	1	1
					$\mu_\rho = .20$					
	32	.7126	.7036	.7296	.7235	.7270	.7903	.7349	.7247	.6362
4	64	.9367	.9344	.9399	.9386	.9390	.9457	.9410	.9273	.8927
	128	.9980	.9980	.9980	.9980	.9980	.9969	.9980	.9963	.9910
	32	.9371	.9350	.9409	.9397	.9393	.9389	.9413	.9407	.9109
8	64	.9981	.9980	.9983	.9983	.9982	.9977	.9983	.9977	.9960
	128	1	1	1	1	1	1	1	1	1
	32	.9976	.9976	.9981	.9980	.9978	.9974	.9981	.9982	.9959
16	64	1	1	1	1	1	1	1	1	1
	128	1	1	1	1	1	1	1	1	1
	32	1	1	1	1	1	1	1	1	1
32	64	1	1	1	1	1	1	1	1	1
	128	1	1	1	1	1	1	1	1	1
	32	1	1	1	1	1	1	1	1	1
64	64	1	1	1	1	1	1	1	1	1
	128	1	1	1	1	1	1	1	1	1
	32	1	1	1	1	1	1	1	1	1
128	64	1	1	1	1	1	1	1	1	1
	128	1	1	1	1	1	1	1	1	1

Note. Proportion for tests are given only at $\alpha = .05$. Several design level combinations are omitted from the table for lack of space. Almost all combinations with higher *n* or *k* show power rates larger than .80.

Table C.3   Rejection Rates for Testing the Mean Effect Size in $\mathfrak{S}_2$, $\mu_\rho = .05$ and $\mu_\rho = .10$, $\alpha = .05$

k	n	HOr	HOT	HOd	RR	HS1	HS3	OP	OP-RE	DSL
					$\mu_\rho = .05$					
	32	.1344	.1299	.1443	.1403	.1422	.2434	.1477	.1507	.1050
4	64	.1897	.1869	.1952	.1929	.1942	.2888	.1980	.1811	.1425
	128	.2994	.2980	.3029	.3009	.3019	.3590	.3047	.2580	.2113
	32	.1941	.1865	.2040	.1993	.1966	.2382	.2046	.2163	.1556
8	64	.2987	.2938	.3052	.3017	.3002	.3236	.3053	.2830	.2355
	128	.4784	.4759	.4813	.4797	.4786	.4473	.4816	.4128	.3664
	32	.3051	.2954	.3181	.3142	.3067	.3211	.3168	.3452	.2608
16	64	.4681	.4633	.4767	.4732	.4694	.4546	.4750	.4552	.3988
	128	.7289	.7268	.7310	.7298	.7282	.6637	.7306	.6648	.6282
	32	.4599	.4481	.4734	.4681	.4604	.4505	.4703	.5063	.4148
32	64	.7196	.7144	.7236	.7218	.7182	.6835	.7223	.7104	.6611
	128	.9382	.9377	.9393	.9389	.9386	.9045	.9389	.9127	.8966
	32	.7203	.7088	.7323	.7282	.7195	.7027	.7292	.7639	.6862
64	64	.9350	.9339	.9374	.9359	.9344	.9177	.9360	.9307	.9142
	128	.9981	.9979	.9981	.9981	.9981	.9961	.9981	.9967	.9959
	32	.9290	.9250	.9345	.9326	.9289	.9212	.9330	.9447	.9186
128	64	.9968	.9967	.9969	.9967	.9967	.9959	.9968	.9968	.9957
	128	1	1	1	1	1	1	1	1	1
					$\mu_\rho = .10$					
	32	.2958	.2859	.3076	.3011	.3049	.3556	.3112	.2885	.2076
4	64	.4900	.4845	.4929	.4885	.4902	.4386	.4944	.4003	.3119
	128	.7362	.7336	.7363	.7331	.7341	.5114	.7364	.5139	.3927
	32	.4789	.4677	.4885	.4834	.4796	.4495	.4880	.4683	.3680
8	64	.7313	.7268	.7336	.7295	.7278	.6065	.7326	.6266	.5455
	128	.9444	.9436	.9441	.9437	.9434	.7713	.9440	.7894	.7236
	32	.7171	.7085	.7254	.7213	.7152	.6517	.7236	.7112	.6202
16	64	.9395	.9379	.9404	.9395	.9386	.8617	.9399	.8827	.8476
	128	.9976	.9976	.9975	.9975	.9974	.9764	.9975	.9799	.9726
	32	.9289	.9249	.9314	.9299	.9268	.8910	.9300	.9252	.8843
32	64	.9984	.9982	.9984	.9983	.9983	.9910	.9984	.9932	.9902
	128	1	1	1	1	1	.9999	1	.9999	.9999
	32	.9975	.9973	.9979	.9977	.9974	.9947	.9979	.9976	.9946
64	64	1	1	1	1	1	1	1	1	1
	128	1	1	1	1	1	1	1	1	1
	32	.9999	.9999	.9999	.9999	.9999	.9999	.9999	.9999	.9999
128	64	1	1	1	1	1	1	1	1	1
	128	1	1	1	1	1	1	1	1	1

Note. Proportion for tests are given only at $\alpha = .05$. Several design level combinations are omitted).

Table C.4   Rejection Rates for Testing the Mean Effect Size in $\mathfrak{S}_2$, $\mu_\rho = .15$ and $\mu_\rho = .20$, $\alpha = .05$

k	n	HOr	HOT	HOd	RR	HS1	HS3	OP	OP-RE	DSL
						$\mu_\rho = .15$				
	32	.5206	.5105	.5304	.5234	.5268	.5266	.5368	.4864	.3760
4	64	.7831	.7795	.7828	.7793	.7804	.6667	.7840	.6531	.5433
	128	.9649	.9646	.9648	.9641	.9644	.7732	.9648	.7804	.6765
	32	.7647	.7561	.7721	.7672	.7640	.7044	.7727	.7288	.6369
8	64	.9637	.9628	.9638	.9629	.9625	.8749	.9636	.8918	.8439
	128	.9993	.9993	.9992	.9992	.9992	.9626	.9992	.9677	.9473
	32	.9560	.9534	.9580	.9568	.9555	.9164	.9574	.9397	.9018
16	64	.9991	.9991	.9992	.9992	.9990	.9911	.9992	.9930	.9895
	128	1	1	1	1	1	.9998	1	.9999	.9998
	32	.9989	.9988	.9990	.9990	.9989	.9959	.9990	.9984	.9955
32	64	1	1	1	1	1	1	1	1	1
	128	1	1	1	1	1	1	1	1	1
	32	1	1	1	1	1	1	1	1	1
64	64	1	1	1	1	1	1	1	1	1
	128	1	1	1	1	1	1	1	1	1
	32	1	1	1	1	1	1	1	1	1
128	64	1	1	1	1	1	1	1	1	1
	128	1	1	1	1	1	1	1	1	1
						$\mu_\rho = .20$				
	32	.7420	.7323	.7433	.7365	.7392	.6193	.7464	.6240	.4967
4	64	.9494	.9481	.9476	.9455	.9462	.7394	.9473	.7545	.6333
	128	.9983	.9983	.9981	.9981	.9981	.8301	.9981	.8373	.7240
	32	.9407	.9373	.9406	.9381	.9371	.8386	.9401	.8668	.8027
8	64	.9990	.9990	.9989	.9989	.9989	.9525	.9989	.9605	.9365
	128	1	1	1	1	1	.9918	1	.9930	.9869
	32	.9978	.9976	.9979	.9977	.9976	.9868	.9977	.9911	.9849
16	64	1	1	1	1	1	.9997	1	.9998	.9995
	128	1	1	1	1	1	1	1	1	1
	32	1	1	1	1	1	1	1	1	1
32	64	1	1	1	1	1	1	1	1	1
	128	1	1	1	1	1	1	1	1	1
	32	1	1	1	1	1	1	1	1	1
64	64	1	1	1	1	1	1	1	1	1
	128	1	1	1	1	1	1	1	1	1
	32	1	1	1	1	1	1	1	1	1
128	64	1	1	1	1	1	1	1	1	1
	128	1	1	1	1	1	1	1	1	1

Note. Proportion for tests are given only at $\alpha = .05$. Several design level combinations are omitted.

Author Index

Subject Index

Meta-Analysis

Meta-Analysis

New Developments and Applications in Medical and Social Sciences

Edited by *Ralf Schulze, Heinz Holling, & Dankmar Böhning*

Meta-analysis is a series of systematic approaches for synthesizing quantitative research. Since its introduction in the early 1980s, statistical and methodological aspects of meta-analysis have been substantially refined and advanced.

This volume brings together researchers from mathematical statistics, research methodology, medical and social sciences who present new developments and applications of meta-analysis. The unique and common problems of these different fields as well as some proposed solutions are presented. The first part of the book is devoted to statistical and methodological advances, with five chapters addressing important statistical issues that are currently under debate. The possibilities and limits of the application of meta-analysis to generalize causal relationships or to evaluate medical treatments, for example, are also discussed. In the second part, applications of meta-analysis are presented, ranging from quality control in the pharmaceutical industry to attitudinal research in social psychology, illustrating the breadth of practical and scientific problems to which meta-analysis can be applied.

> The latest developments concerning one of the most powerful tools available to researchers from many fields of medicine and social sciences.

2003, 288 pages, softcover
US $ / € 39.95
ISBN 0-88937-266-7

Table of Contents
